# Introduction

This Workbook has been designed to help you revise the skills you may need for the externally assessed units of your course. Remember that you won't necessarily be studying all the units included here – it will depend on the qualification you are taking.

| BTEC National Qualification | Externally assessed units |
| --- | --- |
| Certificate | 2 Creating Systems to Manage Information |
| Extended Certificate and Foundation Diploma | 1 Information Technology Systems<br>2 Creating Systems to Manage Information |
| Diploma | 1 Information Technology Systems<br>2 Creating Systems to Manage Information |
| | 11 Cyber Security and Incident Management* |
| Extended Diploma | 1 Information Technology Systems<br>2 Creating Systems to Manage Information |
| | 11 Cyber Security and Incident Management*<br>14 IT Service Delivery* |

*This book does not cover externally assessed Units 11 and 14 required for the Diploma and Extended Diploma.

## Your Workbook

Each unit in this Workbook contains either one or two sets of revision questions or revision tasks, to help you **revise the skills** you may need in your assessment. The selected content, outcomes, questions and answers used in each unit are provided to help you to revise content and ways of applying your skills. Ask your tutor or check the Pearson website for the most up-to-date **Sample Assessment Material** and **Mark Schemes** to get an indication of the structure of your actual assessment and what this requires of you. The detail of the actual assessment may change so always make sure you are up to date.

This Workbook will often include one or more useful features that explain or break down longer questions or tasks. Remember that these features won't appear in your actual assessment!

> Grey boxes like this contain **hints and tips** about ways that you might complete a task, interpret a brief, understand a concept or structure your responses.

 This icon will appear next to an **example partial answer** to a revision question or task. You should read the partial answer carefully, then complete it in your own words.

>  This is a revision activity. It will help you understand some of the skills needed to complete the revision task or question.

> 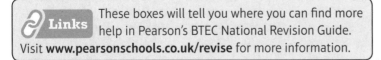 These boxes will tell you where you can find more help in Pearson's BTEC National Revision Guide. Visit **www.pearsonschools.co.uk/revise** for more information.

There is often space on the pages for you to write in. However, if you are carrying out research and making ongoing notes, you may want to use separate paper. Similarly, some units will be assessed through submission of digital files, or on screen, rather than on paper. Ask your tutor or check the Pearson website for the most up-to-date details.

2017001032

# Contents

## Unit 1: Information Technology Systems

## Unit 2: Creating Systems to Manage Information

## Answers

**A small bit of small print**

Pearson publishes Sample Assessment Material and the Specification on its website. This is the official content and this book should be used in conjunction with it. The questions in this book have been written to help you practise the knowledge and skills you will require for your assessment. Remember: the real assessment may not look like this.

endorsed for
**BTEC**

# REVISE BTEC NATIONAL
# Information Technology
## UNITS 1 AND 2

# REVISION WORKBOOK

Series Consultant: Harry Smith

Authors: Daniel Richardson and Alan Jarvis

While the publishers have made every attempt to ensure that advice on the qualification and its assessment is accurate, the official specification and associated assessment guidance materials are the only authoritative source of information and should always be referred to for definitive guidance.

This qualification is reviewed on a regular basis and may be updated in the future. Any such updates that affect the content of this Revision Workbook will be outlined at **www.pearsonfe.co.uk/BTECchanges**.

- - - - - - - - - - - - - - - - - - - - - - - - - - - - - - - - - - - - - - - - - - - - -

## A note from the publisher

In order to ensure that this resource offers high-quality support for the associated Pearson qualification, it has been through a review process by the awarding body. This process confirms that this resource fully covers the teaching and learning content of the specification or part of a specification at which it is aimed. It also confirms that it demonstrates an appropriate balance between the development of subject skills, knowledge and understanding, in addition to preparation for assessment.

Endorsement does not cover any guidance on assessment activities or processes (e.g. practice questions or advice on how to answer assessment questions), included in the resource nor does it prescribe any particular approach to the teaching or delivery of a related course.

Pearson examiners have not contributed to any sections in this resource relevant to examination papers for which they had prior responsibility.

Examiners will not use endorsed resources as a source of material for any assessment set by Pearson.

Endorsement of a resource does not mean that the resource is required to achieve this Pearson qualification, nor does it mean that it is the only suitable material available to support the qualification, and any resource lists produced by the awarding body shall include this and other appropriate resources.

**For the full range of Pearson revision titles across KS2, KS3, GCSE, Functional Skills, AS/A Level and BTEC visit:**
www.pearsonschools.co.uk/revise

**P** Pearson

Published by Pearson Education Limited, 80 Strand, London, WC2R 0RL.

www.pearsonschoolsandfecolleges.co.uk

Copies of official specifications for all Pearson qualifications may be found on the website:
qualifications.pearson.com

Text and illustrations © Pearson Education Limited 2017
Typeset and illustrated by Kamae Design, Oxford
Produced by Out of House Publishing
Cover illustration by Miriam Sturdee

The rights of Alan Jarvis and Daniel Richardson  to be identified as authors of this work have been
asserted by them in accordance with the Copyright, Designs and Patents Act 1988.

First published 2017

20 19 18 17
10 9 8 7 6 5 4 3 2 1

**British Library Cataloguing in Publication Data**
A catalogue record for this book is available from the British Library

ISBN 978 1 292 23059 7

Printed in Italy by Lego S.p.A

**Acknowledgements**
We are grateful to the following for permission to reproduce copyright material:

**Screenshots:**
Microsoft product screenshot(s) reprinted with permission from Microsoft Corporation on
pages 44–45, pages 89–91, pages 98–103, pages 105–107.

**Notes from the publisher**
1.  In order to ensure that this resource offers high-quality support for the associated Pearson
qualification, it has been through a review process by the awarding body. This process confirms that this
resource fully covers the teaching and learning content of the specification or part of a specification at
which it is aimed. It also confirms that it demonstrates an appropriate balance between the development
of subject skills, knowledge and understanding, in addition to preparation for assessment.

Endorsement does not cover any guidance on assessment activities or processes (e.g. practice
questions or advice on how to answer assessment questions), included in the resource nor does it
prescribe any particular approach to the teaching or delivery of a related course.

While the publishers have made every attempt to ensure that advice on the qualification and its
assessment is accurate, the official specification and associated assessment guidance materials are the
only authoritative source of information and should always be referred to for definitive guidance.

Pearson examiners have not contributed to any sections in this resource relevant to examination
papers for which they have responsibility.

Examiners will not use endorsed resources as a source of material for any assessment set by Pearson.

Endorsement of a resource does not mean that the resource is required to achieve this Pearson
qualification, nor does it mean that it is the only suitable material available to support the
qualification, and any resource lists produced by the awarding body shall include this and other
appropriate resources.

2.  Pearson has robust editorial processes, including answer and fact checks, to ensure the accuracy
of the content in this publication, and every effort is made to ensure this publication is free of
errors. We are, however, only human, and occasionally errors do occur. Pearson is not liable for any
misunderstandings that arise as a result of errors in this publication, but it is our priority to ensure that
the content is accurate. If you spot an error, please do contact us at resourcescorrections@pearson.
com so we can make sure it is corrected.

**Websites**

Pearson Education Limited is not responsible for the content of any external internet sites. It is
essential for tutors to preview each website before using it in class so as to ensure that the URL is still
accurate, relevant and appropriate. We suggest that tutors bookmark useful websites and consider
enabling students to access them through the school/college intranet.

# Unit 1: Information Technology Systems

## Your exam

Unit 1 will be assessed through an exam, which will be set by Pearson. You will need to use your understanding of the role of computer systems and the implications of their use in personal and professional situations. You then respond to questions that require short and long answers.

## Your Revision Workbook

This Workbook is designed to **revise skills** that might be needed in your assessed task. The details of your actual assessed task may change from year to year so always make sure you are up to date. Ask your tutor or check the **Pearson website** for the most up-to-date **Sample Assessment Material** to get an idea of the structure of your assessed task and what this requires of you.

To support your revision, this Workbook contains revision questions to help you to practise the relevant exam skills.

## Questions

Your response to the questions will help you to revise:

- digital devices in IT systems
- transmitting data
- operating online
- protecting data and information
- the impact of IT systems on individuals and organisations
- issues resulting from the use of IT systems.

Just as in your actual exam, some questions will start with a **case study** relating to an individual or organisation. For these questions, make sure you focus **your answers** on the needs of the individual or organisation described in the case study..

 This Workbook contains two sets of revision questions starting on pages 2 and 13. See the introduction on page iii for more information on features included to help you revise.

# Revision test 1

**1**

> Excelsior IT Support are a contract IT support company.
> Their employees need to travel to different offices regularly in order to complete repairs and they often do not return to Excelsior IT Support's head office all day.
> When the technicians take on a job they need to:
> - look up the location of the company they need to visit
> - look up the details of the problem
> - update the status of the job once the visit has been completed.

(a) Explain two features of mobile devices that would make them suitable for use by Excelsior IT Support's technicians for tracking their jobs.

**4 marks**

> Firstly, you need to identify each feature and then expand on each one appropriately, in this case explaining why that feature would be useful for Excelsior IT Support. The features have been given in these example answers – you need to add the expansion for each.

- Mobile devices, such as smartphones and tablets can use mobile internet connections, which .............

.........................................................................................................

.........................................................................................................

- Mobile devices are also extremely portable, which ............................................................

.........................................................................................................

.........................................................................................................

.........................................................................................................

> **Links** Revise the features of different digital devices by looking at pages 1 and 2 of Unit 1 in the Revision Guide.

(b) Excelsior IT Support has also considered investing in personal laptop computers for their technicians as an alternative to mobile devices.

Discuss the features of laptops that might make them more suitable for the technicians.

> The question asks you to 'Discuss the features of laptops…'. This discussion requires you to identify a good range of features and give appropriate reasons for their importance, in the context of the question.

**6 marks**

- Laptops are portable computing devices which ...........................................................

.........................................................................................................

.........................................................................................................

.........................................................................................................

.........................................................................................................

.........................................................................................................

.........................................................................................................

.........................................................................................................

- A laptop has a separate keyboard, as well as a large screen and a touchpad. These ....................

......................................................................................................................................

......................................................................................................................................

......................................................................................................................................

......................................................................................................................................

......................................................................................................................................

......................................................................................................................................

(c) In order for the IT technicians to access and update customer information on their mobile devices, this information needs to be transmitted over the internet.

The management at Excelsior IT Support are concerned about the legal and ethical issues of transmitting personal data, such as customers' names and addresses, and storing them on the portable devices.

> You can discuss a range of factors here. Laws such as the Data Protection Act and the Computer Misuse Act clearly apply, as do moral and ethical issues, such as customer privacy and protection of data.
>
> As this is an evaluation question, make sure you look at both the positive and negative issues and the extent of their impact on Excelsior IT Support.

Evaluate the impact on Excelsior IT Support of the legal, moral and ethical issues that relate to the use of this data in this way.

`12 marks`

The Data Protection Act is a piece of legislation that requires businesses like Excelsior to ensure that personal information is kept secure. If Excelsior is found to be not protecting the data being stored and transmitted sufficiently, then the company could potentially face penalties of hundreds of thousands of pounds. In order to comply with the Data Protection Act, Excelsior need to implement security measures, including technology, training and procedures, which could be very costly.

However, a positive impact of the Data Protection Act is that it increases consumer confidence in supplying their data to a business, which makes it a lot easier for Excelsior to carry out their work.

> Go on to evaluate the Computer Misuse Act, explaining its positive impacts on Excelsior.

......................................................................................................................................

......................................................................................................................................

......................................................................................................................................

......................................................................................................................................

......................................................................................................................................

......................................................................................................................................

......................................................................................................................................

......................................................................................................................................

......................................................................................................................................

......................................................................................................................................

......................................................................................................................................

......................................................................................................................................

Continue by covering Excelsior's moral obligations regarding the transmission and storage of customers' personal information, such as protecting customer privacy and use of personal data only for clearly defined purposes. You might also consider ethical issues, such as the environmental impact of using portable devices.

..................................................................................................................................

..................................................................................................................................

..................................................................................................................................

..................................................................................................................................

..................................................................................................................................

..................................................................................................................................

..................................................................................................................................

..................................................................................................................................

..................................................................................................................................

...............................................................................

Make sure you include a conclusion, summing up the extent of the impact of the legal, moral and ethical issues on Excelsior IT.

...............................................................................

...............................................................................

..................................................................................................................................

..................................................................................................................................

..................................................................................................................................

..................................................................................................................................

..................................................................................................................................

..................................................................................................................................

..................................................................................................................................

..................................................................................................................................

..................................................................................................................................

..................................................................................................................................

..................................................................................................................................

**Links** You can revise legal issues on pages 27 and 38 of Unit 1 in the Revision Guide. Look at pages 36 and 37 to revise moral and ethical issues.

**Total for Revision Question 1 = 22 marks**

**Guided**    2    A2B Taxis are a small taxi company based in Reading, Berkshire.

In order to expand their business, A2B Taxis are researching new ways of increasing awareness of their business and attracting customers.

They are looking at using IT systems and the internet in order to communicate with customers and raise brand awareness.

In particular, they are considering the use of online communities but are unsure about what benefits these will bring them.

They would also like to investigate how they could use technology to:

- help drivers work more efficiently, by navigating and allocating jobs
- assist dispatchers to deploy drivers in an effective manner
- be more accessible to customers.

(a)    Describe three ways that A2B Taxis could use online communities in order to communicate with their customers.    **6 marks**

> You need to identify and describe each online communication method and expand on it by commenting on how it could be used by A2B Taxis to communicate with their customers.

✎ Fill in the gaps in this example answer using these words:
blogs    forums    social media    network    up-to-date    feedback    service    advertise

- ......................................... websites allow businesses to create and share information and to

......................................... One example is the use of business pages, which would allow A2B

Taxis to ......................................... deals directly to customers.

- ......................................... are regularly updated websites that are often used by businesses

to share ......................................... news and information. A2B Taxis could use this method to

inform customers of improvements and innovations in the ......................................... they offer.

- ......................................... are online discussion sites which could be used by the business

to gain customer ......................................... on their services.

 **Links**    You can revise uses of online communities on page 23 of Unit 1 in the Revision Guide.

(b)    The management at A2B Taxis have some concerns about the potential negative impact of online communities on their business, but they are also aware of the potential benefits.

Analyse the impact that online communities might have on A2B Taxis.    **10 marks**

> Break down this question into parts. What will have a positive impact? Why will it have a positive impact? How does that relate to A2B Taxis? Then look at the negative impacts the same way.

One way that online communities might have a

positive impact on A2B Taxis is in helping them to

understand customer needs. This is achieved as

online communities allow .........................................

> Explain how online communities can help A2B Taxis understand their customers' needs. Then go on to discuss two more potentially positive implications for A2B Taxis.

.........................................................................................................................................

.........................................................................................................................................

5

....................................................................................................

....................................................................................................

....................................................................................................

....................................................................................................

....................................................................................................

....................................................................................................

....................................................................................................

> **Links** You can revise the implications of business uses of online communities on page 24 of Unit 1 in the Revision Guide.

A negative impact on A2B Taxis of using online communities could be the costs involved. Costs are incurred because

> Explain why costs are involved in the use of online communities. Then go on to cover a couple more potentially negative impacts on the business.

.............................................................................................

.............................................................................................

....................................................................................................

....................................................................................................

....................................................................................................

....................................................................................................

....................................................................................................

....................................................................................................

....................................................................................................

....................................................................................................

....................................................................................................

....................................................................................................

(c) The management at A2B Taxis have also been considering how they could use digital devices to improve the efficiency of their business.

> You need to consider a range of devices here, not just the most obvious ones (e.g. smartphones). Think about those that will be of most benefit to a taxi company.

Discuss how digital devices could improve the efficiency of A2B Taxis.

`10 marks`

In-car navigation systems have become a major part of the service provided by taxi companies

like A2B Taxis because ....................................................................................

....................................................................................................

....................................................................................................

....................................................................................................

....................................................................................................

...................................................................................................................................................

...................................................................................................................................................

...................................................................................................................................................

Mobile devices, specifically smartphones, would be useful to A2B taxis as ..................................

...................................................................................................................................................

...................................................................................................................................................

...................................................................................................................................................

...................................................................................................................................................

...................................................................................................................................................

...................................................................................................................................................

...................................................................................................................................................

Personal computers could be used in the offices of A2B Taxis to help them ..................................

...................................................................................................................................................

...................................................................................................................................................

...................................................................................................................................................

...................................................................................................................................................

...................................................................................................................................................

...................................................................................................................................................

...................................................................................................................................................

...................................................................................................................................................

Communication devices used for internet access would also be of benefit for ..................................

...................................................................................................................................................

...................................................................................................................................................

...................................................................................................................................................

...................................................................................................................................................

...................................................................................................................................................

...................................................................................................................................................

...................................................................................................................................................

...................................................................................................................................................

> **Links** You can revise a range of digital devices and their uses on pages 1–3 of Unit 1 in the Revision Guide.

Total for Revision Question 2 = 26 marks

**Guided**    **3**   Benjamin runs a small finance company that employs four members of staff, in addition to Benjamin himself.

Each member of staff has their own standalone PC, which stores the files they work on locally.

Staff members often need to share documents, which they do either by emailing them using the business's internet connection, or by transferring them using a USB memory stick.

The documents they share often contain sensitive personal and financial information about the customers who invest with them.

(a) Analyse the benefits of using cloud storage facilities for the finance company's staff to share documents.

**6 marks**

> There are a wide variety of benefits to cloud storage services to choose from. Here are some suggestions. Expand on these points by clearly explaining how these are benefits to Benjamin's finance company.

Cloud storage services would allow the finance

company to share access to folders ..........................

........................................................................................................................................................

........................................................................................................................................................

........................................................................................................................................................

........................................................................................................................................................

Employees could access the files while away from the office computers ...........................................

........................................................................................................................................................

........................................................................................................................................................

........................................................................................................................................................

........................................................................................................................................................

Cloud storage would make it easier for employees to work on the same documents ......................

........................................................................................................................................................

........................................................................................................................................................

........................................................................................................................................................

........................................................................................................................................................

> **Links**   You can revise cloud storage on pages 21 and 22 of Unit 1 in the Revision Guide.

(b) Benjamin has heard that a possible alternative to using cloud computing for sharing files would be a local area network. He has also heard that a LAN has other uses.

> Two uses have been identified in the answer (see page 9). Finish them by explaining why each use is helpful to Benjamin's business.

Explain two uses, other than sharing files, of using a LAN in Benjamin's business.

**4 marks**

> **Links**   You can revise security techniques on page 26 of Unit 1 in the Revision Guide.

A local area network can be used to share a printer ...............................................................................................

.........................................................................................................................................................

.........................................................................................................................................................

.........................................................................................................................................................

A local area network could provide security by .................................................................................................

.........................................................................................................................................................

.........................................................................................................................................................

.........................................................................................................................................................

(c) Benjamin is also considering using cloud computing software. However, he is concerned about the potential drawbacks of using these services.

Analyse whether Benjamin should start using cloud computing software in his business. **10 marks**

> Make sure you cover both the benefits and drawbacks of cloud computing software (note that you need to address cloud software, not storage). Include a range and make sure you relate each back to the finance company.

Cloud computing software could benefit Benjamin's business as it will help ...................................

.........................................................................................................................................................

.........................................................................................................................................................

.........................................................................................................................................................

.........................................................................................................................................................

.........................................................................................................................................................

.........................................................................................................................................................

Some disadvantages of cloud computing software for Benjamin could be .......................................

.........................................................................................................................................................

.........................................................................................................................................................

.........................................................................................................................................................

.........................................................................................................................................................

.........................................................................................................................................................

.........................................................................................................................................................

**Links** You can revise cloud computing software on pages 21 and 22 of Unit 1 in the Revision Guide.

Total for Revision Question 3 = 20 marks

**4** Jessica wants to start making a video series in which she will review newly released technology devices. She wants to share her videos online using well-known video-sharing websites.

Jessica would like her videos to be in high definition, even though she is aware that sharing large video files online can be difficult as they can take a long time to download.

(a) Explain how bandwidth and latency affect streaming video over the internet. **4 marks**

Complete the definitions of bandwidth and latency, and then complete the explanation of how each of these affects video streaming. Choose from these sentence endings:

**a)** the time delay for a data packet to transfer to its destination.

**b)** to transfer the large amounts of data in a high definition video file.

**c)** to avoid buffering (ensure that video reaches your computer as fast as it is playing).

**d)** the rate of data transfer over a network.

- Bandwidth is .................................................................................................................................

.................................................................................................................................................................

High bandwidth is required ................................................................................................................

.................................................................................................................................................................

.................................................................................................................................................................

- Latency is ......................................................................................................................................

.................................................................................................................................................................

Low latency, or lack of latency, is preferred ...................................................................................

.................................................................................................................................................................

.................................................................................................................................................................

🔗 **Links** To revise data transmission issues, turn to page 20 of Unit 1 in the Revision Guide.

(b) Jessica knows that the file format used for videos can affect the file size and suitability for sharing online.

Analyse the impact of different file types for streaming video content. **6 marks**

> For this question you should look at a couple of different video file formats and explain both the benefits and the drawbacks of that format for Jessica's needs.

One file format that is commonly used for videos is the .avi format. This would potentially be of use

to Jessica as ......................................................................................................................................

.................................................................................................................................................................

.................................................................................................................................................................

The drawback for Jessica of this file type is ...................................................................................

.................................................................................................................................................................

.................................................................................................................................................................

Another file format for videos is the .mp4 format. This would be of use to Jessica as .....................

......................................................................................................................................................

......................................................................................................................................................

The drawback for Jessica of using this file type is ...............................................................

......................................................................................................................................................

......................................................................................................................................................

> **Links** To revise file formats, look at page 11 of Unit 1 in the Revision Guide.

(c) To reduce the file size of her videos, Jessica is thinking of using compression. However, she is concerned with how this might affect the quality of her videos.

Assess the impact of different compression tools and techniques on the videos. **12 marks**

> The command word here is 'assess'. So for this question you should compare the pros and cons of a range of compression tools and techniques.

Compression is used to reduce the amount of data required to store a file. By compressing the

video files Jessica will .............................................................................................................................

......................................................................................................................................................

......................................................................................................................................................

......................................................................................................................................................

......................................................................................................................................................

......................................................................................................................................................

......................................................................................................................................................

......................................................................................................................................................

There are two types of compression that are used. One is lossy, the other is lossless. Lossy

compression is ..........................................................................................................................................

......................................................................................................................................................

......................................................................................................................................................

......................................................................................................................................................

......................................................................................................................................................

......................................................................................................................................................

......................................................................................................................................................

......................................................................................................................................................

......................................................................................................................................................

......................................................................................................................................................

An extremely important tool for compressing video files for transmitting over a network is a codec.

This is used to ...........................................................................................................................................

...........................................................................................................................................

...........................................................................................................................................

...........................................................................................................................................

...........................................................................................................................................

...........................................................................................................................................

...........................................................................................................................................

...........................................................................................................................................

...........................................................................................................................................

...........................................................................................................................................

...........................................................................................................................................

...........................................................................................................................................

...........................................................................................................................................

...........................................................................................................................................

...........................................................................................................................................

...........................................................................................................................................

...........................................................................................................................................

...........................................................................................................................................

...........................................................................................................................................

...........................................................................................................................................

...........................................................................................................................................

...........................................................................................................................................

...........................................................................................................................................

...........................................................................................................................................

...........................................................................................................................................

🔗 **Links** Revise compression issues by turning to pages 11 and 20 of Unit 1 of the Revision Guide.

Total for Revision Question 4 = 22 marks

# END OF REVISION TEST  **TOTAL FOR TEST = 90 MARKS**

# Revision test 2

**1** Lloyd works for a game development company as a game artist. He performs a variety of tasks including:

- creating high-quality 3D models of landscapes and player characters
- creating 2D textures for game models
- user interface design for game menus, etc.

(a) Lloyd needs to save his 2D graphic files in a format that can be used in the games.

Explain two features of the PNG format that would make it appropriate for this use.

> You need to identify two features and explain why each feature is useful for Lloyd's game art.

**4 marks**

...................................................................................................................................

...................................................................................................................................

...................................................................................................................................

...................................................................................................................................

...................................................................................................................................

...................................................................................................................................

...................................................................................................................................

> **Links** To revise file formats, turn to page 11 of Unit 1 in the Revision Guide.

(b) Lloyd wants to purchase a new PC to produce his artwork as the one he is using is quite old and it is running slowly.

The table shows the specifications of two computers Lloyd is considering.

| | Computer 1 | Computer 2 |
| --- | --- | --- |
| Processor | 2.7 GHz Quad Core | 3.5 GHz Dual Core |
| RAM | 8 GB | 4 GB |
| Storage | 1 TB Hard Disk Drive | 250 GB Solid State Drive |
| Graphics | 4 GB Dedicated Graphics | Integrated Graphics |

> You can approach this question by looking at each of the categories in turn and comparing which is more suitable. You should provide a recommendation for which system would be better for Lloyd.

Assess the suitability of these two specifications for Lloyd's needs.

**8 marks**

...................................................................................................................................

...................................................................................................................................

...................................................................................................................................

...................................................................................................................................

...................................................................................................................................

...................................................................................................................................

...................................................................................................................

...................................................................................................................

...................................................................................................................

...................................................................................................................

...................................................................................................................

...................................................................................................................

...................................................................................................................

...................................................................................................................

...................................................................................................................

...................................................................................................................

...................................................................................................................

...................................................................................................................

...................................................................................................................

> **Links** To revise choosing an IT system, turn to page 14 of Unit 1 of the Revision Guide.

(c) Lloyd is thinking of using cloud storage for saving his graphics files.

Discuss the features and implications of using cloud storage for Lloyd.

**10 marks**

> As well as exploring how cloud storage can help Lloyd, you also need to explain ways in which it might be a hindrance. Some things to consider could be sharing files and security issues.

...................................................................................................................

...................................................................................................................

...................................................................................................................

...................................................................................................................

...................................................................................................................

...................................................................................................................

...................................................................................................................

...................................................................................................................

...................................................................................................................

...................................................................................................................

...................................................................................................................

...................................................................................................................

..................................................................................................

..................................................................................................

..................................................................................................

..................................................................................................

..................................................................................................

..................................................................................................

..................................................................................................

..................................................................................................

..................................................................................................

..................................................................................................

..................................................................................................

..................................................................................................

..................................................................................................

**Links** Revise cloud storage by looking at pages 21–22 of Unit 1 of the Revision Guide.

Total for Revision Question 1 = 22 marks

**2** Harold owns a chain of four fast food restaurants.

He employs a manager as well as several till workers at each restaurant.

The manager at each restaurant is responsible for ordering stock, but Harold keeps the accounts for the business himself on his home desktop PC.

To help improve efficiency, Harold is looking into implementing new self-service food ordering EPOS systems.

(a) Describe two input devices that might be used on a self-service EPOS till.

**4 marks**

> Think of two different input devices that are commonly used at the checkout in shops. To help you, think back to when you've used a self-service check-out or food ordering point.

....................................................................................................

....................................................................................................

....................................................................................................

....................................................................................................

....................................................................................................

....................................................................................................

....................................................................................................

....................................................................................................

....................................................................................................

....................................................................................................

....................................................................................................

....................................................................................................

....................................................................................................

**Links** You can revise relevant input devices on pages 2 and 4 of Unit 1 of the Revision Guide.

(b) The new self-service EPOS till system requires a menu-based user interface. The first screen of the user interface should allow the customers to:

- choose from a range of food categories
- choose to go to payment.

Draw a suitable user interface for this first screen in the space provided.

Don't just draw a simple menu. Consider prompts to help the user enter the data, and don't forget accessibility requirements. For example, what options could you add to help people with a visual impairment use the interface?

6 marks

Links Revise user interfaces on page 9 of Unit 1 of the Revision Guide.

(c) Harold would like to gather data from customers on whether there is enough interest in adding these new self-service tills.

Discuss the benefits to Harold of using primary data collection over secondary sources.

10 marks

Discuss a range of benefits of primary data collection and compare each of them to secondary sources to show why primary sources are better for Harold's needs. Don't worry about including the benefits of secondary data collection – that's not needed here.

......................................................................................................................................................

......................................................................................................................................................

......................................................................................................................................................

......................................................................................................................................................

......................................................................................................................................................

......................................................................................................................................................

......................................................................................................................................................

......................................................................................................................................................

......................................................................................................................................................

......................................................................................................................................................

......................................................................................................................................................

......................................................................................................................................................

......................................................................................................................................................

......................................................................................................................................................

......................................................................................................................................................

......................................................................................................................................................

......................................................................................................................................................

......................................................................................................................................................

......................................................................................................................................................

......................................................................................................................................................

......................................................................................................................................................

......................................................................................................................................................

......................................................................................................................................................

**Links** You can revise primary data collection on page 32 of Unit 1 in the Revision Guide.

Total for Revision Question 2 = 20 marks

3 | Aaliyah is a sales representative for a large multinational soft drinks company.

She has a desk and computer at the company's head office, but she rarely goes there. She works mainly from home or during train journeys as she travels between stores that stock the company's drinks.

She completes the bulk of her work on her home desktop PC, using spreadsheet software and word processing software.

While travelling, she takes notes by hand which she enters on the desktop PC when she returns home.

(a) Explain two technologies that will help Aaliyah to work remotely but still have access to her desktop applications, and secure access to company documents and systems.

**4 marks**

> Think about how Aaliyah could access the files and software on the computer at the head office while working from home. Also consider how to ensure data can be transferred securely between her home and the office.

...................................................................

...................................................................

...................................................................

...................................................................

...................................................................

...................................................................

...................................................................

...................................................................

🔗 **Links** To revise technologies used in remote working, look at page 22 of Unit 1 of the Revision Guide.

(b) Aaliyah has decided that she needs a digital device for working on while she is travelling. She is considering asking the company to buy her a tablet computer.

Discuss the features of a mobile computing device, such as a tablet, that will make it suitable for Aaliyah's needs.

**6 marks**

> Always refer back to the case study. Remember that Aaliya will be using her mobile computing device to use productivity software while travelling. What makes such a device appropriate for her needs? This question asks you to 'discuss'. You need to begin by explaining a wide range of features, continuing on to consider how they will be suitable for Aaliyah and how she might use the device.

...................................................................

...................................................................

...................................................................

...................................................................

...................................................................

...................................................................

...................................................................

..............................................................................................................................

..............................................................................................................................

..............................................................................................................................

..............................................................................................................................

> **Links** To revise mobile devices, see page 1 of Unit 1 of the Revision Guide.

(c) Aaliyah's manager has told her that the company is considering setting up a fan page on social media to promote the company and encourage direct communication, in order to strengthen their brands.

Evaluate the implications that the company needs to consider before setting up a presence on social media.

**12 marks**

> You should consider how the company can be affected in both a positive and negative manner, as well as the more obvious considerations such as cost and security.

..............................................................................................................................

..............................................................................................................................

..............................................................................................................................

..............................................................................................................................

..............................................................................................................................

..............................................................................................................................

..............................................................................................................................

..............................................................................................................................

..............................................................................................................................

..............................................................................................................................

..............................................................................................................................

..............................................................................................................................

..............................................................................................................................

..............................................................................................................................

..............................................................................................................................

..............................................................................................................................

..............................................................................................................................

..............................................................................................................................

..............................................................................................................................

.......................................................................................................................................

.......................................................................................................................................

.......................................................................................................................................

.......................................................................................................................................

.......................................................................................................................................

.......................................................................................................................................

.......................................................................................................................................

.......................................................................................................................................

.......................................................................................................................................

.......................................................................................................................................

.......................................................................................................................................

.......................................................................................................................................

.......................................................................................................................................

.......................................................................................................................................

.......................................................................................................................................

.......................................................................................................................................

.......................................................................................................................................

.......................................................................................................................................

.......................................................................................................................................

.......................................................................................................................................

.......................................................................................................................................

.......................................................................................................................................

.......................................................................................................................................

.......................................................................................................................................

.......................................................................................................................................

.......................................................................................................................................

.......................................................................................................................................

.......................................................................................................................................

.......................................................................................................................................

.......................................................................................................................................

**Links** Revise cloud storage and computing by looking at pages 21 and 22 of Unit 1 of the Revision Guide.

Total for Revision Question 3 = 22 marks

4 | Haldrech Security are a security company that have been providing physical security for businesses for many years.

They are becoming increasingly aware that they need to modernise their security services.

This will include making better use of technology in the security services they already provide, as well as offering security for IT-based threats.

(a) Before they go any further in implementing new technology systems, Haldrech Security's management would like to know more about the ethical issues involved in using technology systems.

> You need to identify and describe each of these ethical implications. Make sure you relate each one to Haldrech Security.

Explain three ethical implications of using technology systems.

**6 marks**

................................................................................................................................................................

................................................................................................................................................................

................................................................................................................................................................

................................................................................................................................................................

................................................................................................................................................................

................................................................................................................................................................

................................................................................................................................................................

................................................................................................................................................................

................................................................................................................................................................

................................................................................................................................................................

**Links** You can revise the moral and ethical implications of using IT systems on pages 36 and 37 of Unit 1 of the Revision Guide. Page 37 is particularly relevant here.

(b) Haldrech Technology want to ensure they have all the processes and technologies in place to protect their clients' IT systems from threats.

> Here you need to look at relevant IT security techniques (not legislation) and explain how they protect IT systems and the data stored on them from harm.

Explain how different techniques for protecting IT systems and data work.

**8 marks**

................................................................................................................................................................

................................................................................................................................................................

................................................................................................................................................................

................................................................................................................................................................

................................................................................................................................................................

................................................................................................................................................................

................................................................................................................................................................

..........................................................................................................................
..........................................................................................................................
..........................................................................................................................
..........................................................................................................................
..........................................................................................................................
..........................................................................................................................
..........................................................................................................................
..........................................................................................................................
..........................................................................................................................
..........................................................................................................................
..........................................................................................................................
..........................................................................................................................
..........................................................................................................................
..........................................................................................................................

**Links** You can revise data protection techniques on page 26 of Unit 1 in the Revision Guide.

(c) Haldrech Security want to gain a better understanding of exactly how legislation will help them to prevent the threats that impact on IT systems.

Evaluate the impact of relevant legislation on the use of technology systems for Haldrech Security in their decision to modernise their services.

Here you should cover a range of legislation, look at what threats they protect against and how they protect against these threats (e.g. what the penalties are for people who break these laws).

**12 marks**

..........................................................................................................................
..........................................................................................................................
..........................................................................................................................
..........................................................................................................................
..........................................................................................................................
..........................................................................................................................
..........................................................................................................................
..........................................................................................................................
..........................................................................................................................
..........................................................................................................................
..........................................................................................................................
..........................................................................................................................

..........................................................................................

..........................................................................................

..........................................................................................

..........................................................................................

..........................................................................................

..........................................................................................

**Links** To revise the legislation, turn to pages 27 and 38 of Unit 1 in the Revision Guide.

Total for Revision Question 4 = 26 marks

# END OF REVISION TEST     **TOTAL FOR TEST = 90 MARKS**

# Unit 2: Creating systems to manage information

## Your set task

Unit 2 will be assessed through a task, which will be set by Pearson. You will need to use your understanding of how to design, create, test and evaluate a relational database system to manage information in response to a brief.

## Your Revision Workbook

> This Workbook is designed to **revise skills** that might be needed in your assessed task. The details of your actual assessed task may change from year to year so always make sure you are up to date. Ask your tutor or check the **Pearson website** for the most up-to-date **Sample Assessment Material** to get an idea of the structure of your assessed task and what this requires of you.

To support your revision, this Workbook contains revision tasks to help you practise the skills that might be needed in your assessed task.

## Tasks

Your response to the tasks will help you to revise:

*   reading a brief and analysing a scenario (page 27)

*   producing an entity relationship diagram (ERD) by normalising the given data to third normal form (page 30)

*   producing a data dictionary (page 32)

*   completing the design specification documents for a database and ensuring sufficient information is provided for a third party to implement the interface for a solution (page 34)

*   creating a test log in order to test a completed database (page 41)

*   developing and testing a database (page 43)

*   recording database development as annotated screenshots (page 44)

*   evaluating a solution by considering:

    *   how well it meets the requirements of a given scenario

    *   the quality, performance and usability of a database

    *   the changes made during the development and testing process (page 56).

 This Workbook contains two sets of revision questions starting on pages 2 and 13. See the introduction on page iii for more information on features included to help you revise.

# Revision task 1

## Reading the brief

Below is a brief similar in style to the one you will receive in your assessment. Read it through and answer the questions which follow in order to practise the skills you will need in your assessment.

**Scenario**

Your supervisor at Harrow Fix-IT, a small IT support company, has asked you to develop a database to record IT customer support requests. The company provides IT support for five customers, which are local small businesses. The company employs four technicians:

Wendy Simpson – Senior Technician, mobile number 07899 22222

Mohammed Ahmed – Technician, mobile number 07877 33333

David Platt – Technician, mobile number 07888 44444

Winston Jamal – Junior Technician, mobile number 07866 55555

The five customers are:

AB Supplies – 55 High Street, Wembley, HA0 9XX

Station Garage – Station Road, Neasden, NW10 8ZZ

Smith Partners – 21 The Avenue, Neasden, NW10 4OO

Western Engineering – Wembley Industrial Estate, Wembley, HA9 7BB

West London Accountants – 34 Main Road, Harrow, HA1 2YY

You need to:

- design a database structure that:
  - includes support request, customer and technician data
  - avoids unnecessary duplication of data
  - validates data input to ensure integrity
  - has a suitable user interface for technicians that enter support requests, and updates support requests with resolution of problems.

> The bullet points under 'You need to' give lots of information about what you need to include in your database.

1. The first sub-bullet point above gives clues as to which tables you will need in your database.

   - How many tables will you need?

   ........................

2. The bullet point above tells you which data entry forms you will need for your database.

   How many data entry forms will you need to create?

   ........................

- import and manipulate the given data
- provide database outputs showing:
  - all unresolved queries
  - all unresolved queries for a particular technician
  - a monthly summary report of all queries dealt with by a particular technician
  - a monthly summary report of all queries from a particular customer
  - a report showing the time a particular technician takes to resolve requests.

3. The sub-bullet points at the bottom of page 27 tell you which queries and reports you will need for your database.

   (a) How many queries will you need to create?

   ........................

   (b) How many reports will you need to create?

   ........................

- test your database, adding data to ensure that the database meets all requirements
- evaluate your database against the given requirements.

**Information**

Currently your supervisor uses a spreadsheet to record support requests and resolutions. Figure 1 shows an extract of the data.

4. Look at the table in Figure 1 and identify the two sets of repeating data, together with the fields that are associated with them. Use a different colour highlighter for each.

You can download the .csv file containing the data for the Harrow FIX-IT database by scanning this link with your smartphone or tablet. Alternatively, go to the following link: http://activetea.ch/2gNTa18.

Figure 1

| Request ID | Customer | Customer address | Reported by | Date/time reported | Problem description | Technician allocated | Technician job title | Technician mobile no. | Resolved? | Date/time resolved | Resolution description |
|---|---|---|---|---|---|---|---|---|---|---|---|
| 1 | AB Supplies | 55 High Street, Wembley, HA0 9XX | Hannah McMahon | 27/2/16 0945 | Mouse does not work | David Platt | Technician | 07888 44444 | Yes | 28/2/16 1430 | Replaced mouse |
| 2 | Station Garage | Station Road, Neasden, NW10 8ZZ | Kyle Jones | 27/2/16 1030 | Application error | Winston Jamal | Junior Technician | 07866 55555 | No | | |
| 3 | AB Supplies | 55 High Street, Wembley, HA0 9XX | Holly Williams | 27/2/16 1415 | Forgot login password | Mohammed Ahmed | Technician | 07877 33333 | Yes | 28/2/16 1015 | Password reset |
| 4 | Smith Partners | 21 The Avenue, Neasden, NW10 4OO | Aras Kudirka | 27/2/16 1610 | No internet access | Mohammed Ahmed | Technician | 07877 33333 | Yes | 1/3/16 1100 | Reset router |
| 5 | Western Engineering | Wembley Industrial Estate, Wembley, HA9 7BB | Mohsin Iqbal | 28/2/16 1020 | Shared folder not accessible | Wendy Simpson | Senior Technician | 07899 22222 | Yes | 1/3/16 1545 | Mapped shared drive |
| 6 | West London Accountants | 34 Main Road, Harrow, HA1 2YY | Sunita Shah | 28/2/16 1115 | Emails not sending | David Platt | Technician | 07888 44444 | No | | |
| 7 | Smith Partners | 21 The Avenue, Neasden, NW10 4OO | James Smith | 28/2/16 1430 | Website certificate error | David Platt | Technician | 07888 44444 | Yes | 1/3/16 0915 | Checked and all OK |
| 8 | AB Supplies | 55 High Street, Wembley, HA0 9XX | Keith Evans | 28/2/16 1545 | Cannot print | Winston Jamal | Junior Technician | 07866 55555 | Yes | 2/3/16 1030 | Reset printer |
| 9 | Western Engineering | Wembley Industrial Estate, Wembley, HA9 7BB | Jack Dyson | 1/3/16 1015 | Mapped drive error | Wendy Simpson | Senior Technician | 07899 22222 | No | | |
| 10 | Smith Partners | 21 The Avenue, Neasden, NW10 4OO | Mai Chen | 1/3/16 1100 | Files missing | Winston Jamal | Junior Technician | 07866 55555 | No | | |
| 11 | Smith Partners | 21 The Avenue, Neasden, NW10 4OO | Alice Scott | 1/3/16 1530 | Keyboard characters incorrect | Mohammed Ahmed | Technician | 07877 33333 | No | | |
| 12 | Station Garage | Station Road, Neasden, NW10 8ZZ | Olivia Hill | 1/3/16 1620 | Cannot connect to WiFi | David Platt | Technician | 07888 44444 | Yes | 2/3/16 1415 | Reset WiFi access point |
| 13 | West London Accountants | 34 Main Road, Harrow, HA1 2YY | Amy Sugar | 2/3/16 0920 | Hard disk full | Mohammed Ahmed | Technician | 07877 33333 | No | | |
| 14 | Western Engineering | Wembley Industrial Estate, Wembley, HA9 7BB | Tinashe Deka | 2/3/16 1015 | Internet very slow | Wendy Simpson | Senior Technician | 07899 22222 | No | | |
| 15 | Station Garage | 21 The Avenue, Neasden, NW10 4OO | Roger Bradley | 2/3/16 1245 | Virus alert | Winston Jamal | Junior Technician | 07866 55555 | No | | |
| 16 | West London Accountants | 34 Main Road, Harrow, HA1 2YY | Nick Lawson | 2/3/16 1500 | Accidentally deleted files | David Platt | Technician | 07888 44444 | No | | |

# Creating an entity relationship diagram

Produce an entity relationship diagram (ERD) for the database by normalising the given data to third normal form.

> Remember that normalisation avoids **data redundancy** and makes your database more efficient.

**Guided**

1. Look at the table of data on page 29. Identify two types of repeating data. The first one has been done for you.

   (a)  Customer

   (b) ...............................................

   > These will be the **tables** which will store one record for each of the repeating items in the data.

2. Write down the **attributes** (fields) which belong to each item of repeating data. The first two have been started for you. You may not need all the boxes.

   | Customer | |
   |---|---|
   | Customer address | |
   | | |

3. Check if all the fields in these two tables are atomic. List any fields which are not atomic, and list the fields they should be split into.

   ..................................................................................................................................................

   ..................................................................................................................................................

4. Identify the **primary key** for each of these tables.

   Primary key for the Customer table is ........................

   Primary key for the ................. table is .................

   > Remember a 'made up key' is often the best choice for a primary key. You will need to add a field for this.

> **Links** You can revise primary and foreign keys by looking at page 52 of Unit 2 in the Revision Guide.

5. The remaining data stores information about individual support requests. You can call the table containing this data **Support_request**.

   List the fields for this table from the sample data, and identify the primary key.

   | |
   |---|
   | |
   | |
   | |
   | |
   | |
   | |
   | |
   | |

> **Links** Revise the normalisation process by looking at pages 55 and 56 of Unit 2 in the Revision Guide.

6. What type of relationships will exist between the tables?

   (a) The **Customer** table is related to the **Support_request** table by a

      ☐ one-to-one relationship

      ☐ one-to-many relationship

      ☐ many-to-many relationship.

> Remember that you create the relationship between the tables by taking the primary key from the table at the 'one' end of a relationship and inserting it in the related records at the 'many' end, where it is referred to as a **foreign key**.

   (b) The ........................ table is related to the **Support_request** table by a

      ☐ one-to-one relationship

      ☐ one-to-many relationship

      ☐ many-to-many relationship.

> The first two table headings have been included for you. Look at your answer to the guided revision activity above to identify the third table heading.

7. The Support_request table will need two foreign keys.

What will these be?

................................. and .................................

Complete the entity relationship diagram for your database.

**Customer**

**Support_request**

**Technician**

> Add the links between the tables (one has been done for you). Then draw in the 'crow's feet' to show the 'many' end of each relationship.

 **Links** Revise ERDs by looking at pages 49 and 50 of Unit 2 in the Revision Guide.

# Creating a data dictionary

Produce a data dictionary for your database using the tables below.

You need to complete a **data dictionary** for each table (Support_request, Customer and Technician). The first one or two entries in each table have been added for you.

If completing this activity on a computer you can use an electronic template for the tables, duplicate the table, extend the box space and add as many rows as you need.

| Table Name: | Customer |
|---|---|
| **Field name** | **Attributes** |
| Customer_ID | Primary key, autonumber data type |
| | |
| | |
| | |
| | |

Add validation where required. Fields such as a person's name or description of the problem cannot be validated. But use validation for:

- fields with a fixed format – use an input mask
- fields with a limited number of valid entries – use a lookup table
- fields with a datatype of date and/or time – these are automatically validated by Access, but you can use validation to check things such as that the date is not in the future.

Remember to:
- make sure the fields are **atomic**. Ask yourself, 'Do any of the fields need to be split into several separate fields?' (look for fields containing data such as names and addresses)
- identify the **primary key** in each table, and the **foreign key** in the tables at the 'many' end of the relationships
- be consistent in your **field naming**
- make sure you include the **data type** and any **validation** necessary in the Attributes column.

 **Links** To revise validation, look at pages 67–69 of Unit 2 in the Revision Guide.

| Table Name: | Support_request |
|---|---|
| **Field name** | **Attributes** |
| Request_ID | Primary key, autonumber data type |
| Customer_ID | Foreign key linking to the Customer table. Integer data type |
| | |
| | |
| | |
| | |
| | |
| | |
| | |
| | |

| Table Name: | Technician |
| --- | --- |
| **Field name** | **Attributes** |
| Technician_ID | Primary key, autonumber data type |
| Technician_f_name | Text data type, 25 characters, no validation |
| | |
| | |
| | |

The exact length of text data type fields is not critical as long as they are long enough to contain the intended values.

 **Links** Revise data dictionaries by looking at page 57 of Unit 2 in the Revision Guide.

# Creating a design specification

Complete the 'Design specification document' given below.

Ensure sufficient information is provided for a third party to implement the interface for your solution.

> Make sure you create user interface designs for all the objects (forms, queries and reports) required for the database.
>
> If completing this activity on a computer you can use an electronic template for the tables, duplicate the table, extend the box space and add as many rows as you need.
>
> Include each design in a separate row.

> All the items you need to produce for the IT support company database are listed below. Some of the designs have been completed for you. Complete the remaining designs.

> Make sure your designs are clear enough for someone else to implement. You need to add annotations so it is clear how the form, report or query will work.

**Design specification document:**

| Name and type | |
|---|---|
| **Type:** Form<br>**Name:** Menu<br><br>This form is not linked to any specific table, it just provides a menu to all the other database facilities. Each button links to the appropriate form, query or report. | **Support request menu**<br><br>Add support request  [ Go ]<br><br>Update support request  [ Go ]<br><br>List all unresolved requests  [ Go ]<br><br>List a technician's unresolved requests  [ Go ]<br><br>Monthly report on requests by technician  [ Go ]<br><br>Monthly report on requests by customer  [ Go ]<br><br>Report on time taken to resolve requests  [ Go ] |

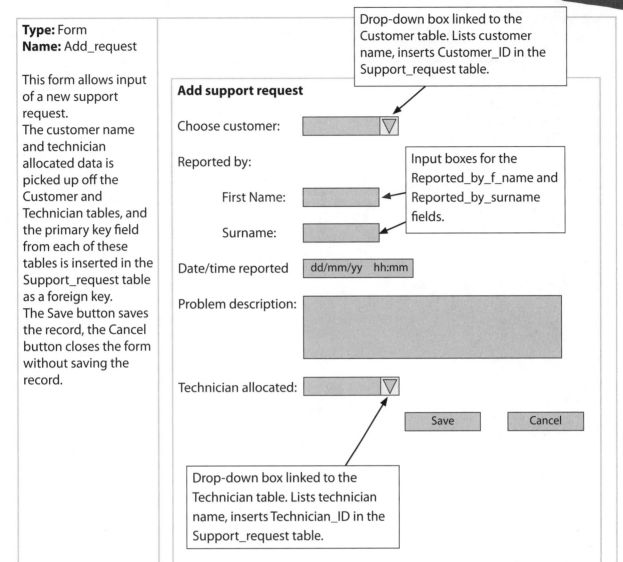

**Type:** Form
**Name:** Add_request

This form allows input of a new support request.
The customer name and technician allocated data is picked up off the Customer and Technician tables, and the primary key field from each of these tables is inserted in the Support_request table as a foreign key.
The Save button saves the record, the Cancel button closes the form without saving the record.

Drop-down box linked to the Customer table. Lists customer name, inserts Customer_ID in the Support_request table.

**Add support request**

Choose customer:

Reported by:

    First Name:

Input boxes for the Reported_by_f_name and Reported_by_surname fields.

    Surname:

Date/time reported    dd/mm/yy    hh:mm

Problem description:

Technician allocated:

Save        Cancel

Drop-down box linked to the Technician table. Lists technician name, inserts Technician_ID in the Support_request table.

---

**Links**   Revise form design by looking at page 74 of Unit 2 in the Revision Guide.
Revise adding automated features (such as Save and Cancel command buttons) to forms on page 75 of Unit 2 in the Revision Guide.

This form needs to be based on a query to allow the user to input the request ID of the request they want to update.

**Type:** Form
**Name:** Update_support_request

The fields shown on the form should be the same as those on the Add_request form, with the addition of fields allowing the user to enter that the request has been resolved, the date and time of resolution and the resolution description.

The user should not be allowed to change all the fields on the form. For example, the customer, the person who reported the query and the date and time reported should be displayed but should be locked so they cannot be changed.

 **Links** To revise how to use the Locked and Enabled properties on forms see page 74 of Unit 2 in the Revision Guide.

**Type:** Query
**Name:** List_all_unresolved_requests

This query lists all unresolved queries. It brings together the Support_request table and the Customer table so the customer name can be listed.

| Table | Support_request | Support_request | Customer | Support_request | Support_request |
|---|---|---|---|---|---|
| **Field** | Request_ID | Customer_ID | Customer_name | Problem_description | Resolved |
| **Criteria** | | | | | No |
| **Sort** | | | | | |

The criterion for this query is on the Resolved field. It is set to 'No' so only requests that have not been resolved are selected.

Make sure you add annotation explaining the criterion or criteria you use for each query.

**Type:** Query
**Name:** List_a_
technician's_
unresolved_requests

Think about what fields you need to include in your query, and which tables these will come from.

From the Support_request table you will need the Request_ID, the Customer_ID, Problem_description and Resolved fields.

From the Technician table you will need the Technician_surname field.

From the Customer table you should include the Customer_name field.

You will need to include a message box prompting the user to enter the technician's surname.

Remember to set the 'Resolved' field criterion to 'No' so only unresolved queries are listed.

**Links** Revise query design, including how to add prompt boxes to your criteria, on page 64 of Unit 2 in the Revision Guide.

**Type:** Report
**Name:** Monthly report of support requests by technician

This report is based on a query which brings together the Technican, Customer and Support_request tables. The criterion for the query is the month required.

The report groups the output by technician, listing each request allocated to that technician in the month in question.

| Support requests listed by Technician | | | |
|---|---|---|---|
| Month: | June 2016 | | |
| Technician: | Xxxxxxxxxx Xxxxxxxxx | | |
| Customer | Date/time reported | Problem | Resolved? |
| Xxxxxxxxx | dd/mm/yy hh:mm | Xxxxxxxxxxxxxxxxxxxxxxxxxx | X |
| Xxxxxxxxx | dd/mm/yy hh:mm | Xxxxxxxxxxxxxxxxxxxxxxxxxx | X |
| Xxxxxxxxx | dd/mm/yy hh:mm | Xxxxxxxxxxxxxxxxxxxxxxxxxx | X |
| Technician: | nnnnnnn nnnnnnn | | |
| Customer | Date/time reported | Problem | Resolved? |
| Xxxxxxxxx | dd/mm/yy hh:mm | Xxxxxxxxxxxxxxxxxxxxxxxxxx | X |

**Type:** Report
**Name:** Monthly report of support requests by customer

As well as drawing the design for the report, make sure you include annotation describing the query behind your report.

Which tables will be included in the query and which fields?

What will be the criterion or multiple criteria for the query?

How does the report group the output?

**Type:** Report
**Name:** Report on time taken to resolve requests

The criterion for the query will be a calculation: Date_time_reported subtracted from Date_time_resolved.
Also think about how you will sort the results.

 **Links**    Revise queries using calculated fields by looking at page 71 of Unit 2 in the Revision Guide.
Revise how to design reports by looking at page 63 of Unit 2 in the Revision Guide.

# Devising a test plan

Use the 'Test log document' given below to plan how you will test your completed database.

> The tests for the Customer table have been entered for you.

> Create the test plan using your data dictionary as a guide. Make sure you include tests for every field in the data dictionary. You do not need to add tests for autonumber fields as these are inserted automatically by Access, and you should not change them as they are used for the primary keys.

> If completing this activity on a computer you can use an electronic template for the tables, duplicate the table, extend the box space and add as many rows as you need.

**Test log document:**

| Test number | Purpose of test | Test data | Expected result | Actual result | Comments and action taken |
|---|---|---|---|---|---|
| **Tests for fields in the Customer table** | | | | | |
| 1 | Customer_name field | Joe Smith and Co | Accepted | | |
| 2 | Address field | 26 The Avenue | Accepted | | |
| 3 | Town field | Bristol | Accepted | | |
| 4 | Postcode field | a4bbx | Rejected | | |
| 5 | Postcode field | BR99 1ZZ | Accepted | | |

> Include tests of the validation in any fields which have validation applied. Remember to include, normal, extreme and erroneous data.

> Always include the expected result for each test and check carefully that you've done this correctly.

 **Links** To revise test plans, look at page 65 of Unit 2 in the Revision Guide.

> In the test plan for the Support_request table, include tests for referential integrity of foreign keys.

| Tests for fields in the Support_request table | | | | | |
|---|---|---|---|---|---|
| 6 | Customer_ID field referential integrity | 9 | Rejected (no Customer_ID 9) | | |
| 7 | Customer_ID field referential integrity | 4 | Accepted | | |
| | Technician_ID field referential integrity | | | | |
| | Technician_ID field referential integrity | | | | |
| | | | | | |
| | | | | | |
| | | | | | |
| | | | | | |
| | | | | | |
| | | | | | |
| | | | | | |
| | | | | | |
| **Tests for fields in the Technician table** | | | | | |
| | | | | | |
| | | | | | |
| | | | | | |
| | | | | | |
| | | | | | |
| | | | | | |

**Links** To revise the meaning of referential integrity, look at page 53 of Unit 2 in the Revision Guide. To revise how to enforce referential integrity, look at page 70 of Unit 2 in the Revision Guide.

# Database development and testing

Develop and test your database using the information in the documents you produced for the activities on pages 30–42

Record your database development as annotated screenshots in a single document.

Your screenshots should show:

- your tables, including the fields and attributes
- your table relationships
- your queries, including fields and criteria
- the output of your queries
- the forms you have created
- the reports you have created
- evidence of working validation.

Record your testing including test results, comments and actions taken to resolve issues in the 'Test log document' you created in the activity on page 41.

**Database development**

You can access the .csv file containing the data for the Harrow FIX-IT database by scanning this link with your smartphone or tablet. Alternatively, go to the following link: http://activetea.ch/2gNTa18. Use this file to create your database. The first task is to import the raw data from the .csv file.

 Revise how to import data from a .csv file into Access by turning to page 82 of Unit 2 in the Revision Guide.

You will need to compile your screenshots and annotations in a separate document.

Look at the next few pages for examples of screenshots you could include, and how you can annotate your screenshots. Read the hints to get more help with creating your database.

You don't have to take a screenshot of every single detail. Just make sure you provide enough annotated screenshots to document the development process.

  1. Look at the screenshots below, provided as evidence for this activity. Complete the student's commentary and annotations by filling in the blanks.

My database development screenshots.

The first task I completed was to create the (a) .........................................,

using my data (b) ......................................... as a guide.

Remember to use object names (the names you use for tables and fields as well as forms, queries and reports) which are clear and would enable anyone else looking at the database to see what they are used for.

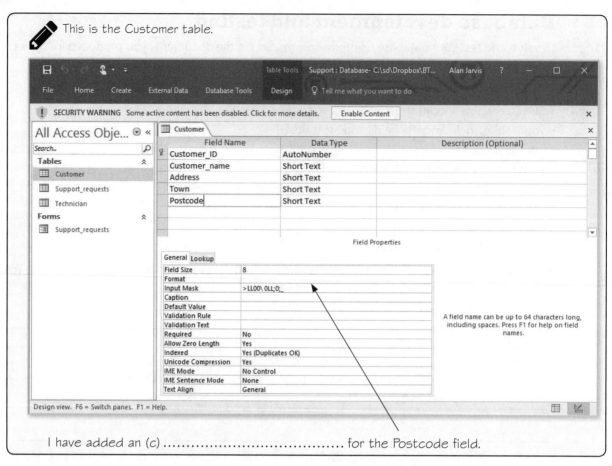

✎ This is the Customer table.

I have added an (c) ..................................... for the Postcode field.

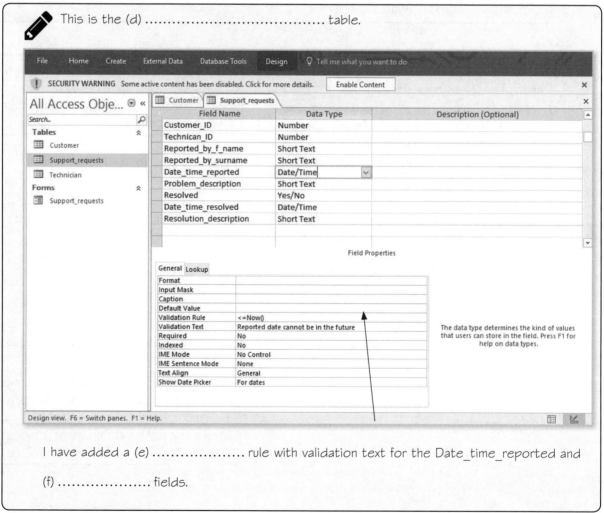

✎ This is the (d) ..................................... table.

I have added a (e) ................... rule with validation text for the Date_time_reported and

(f) ................... fields.

This is the (g) ..................... table.

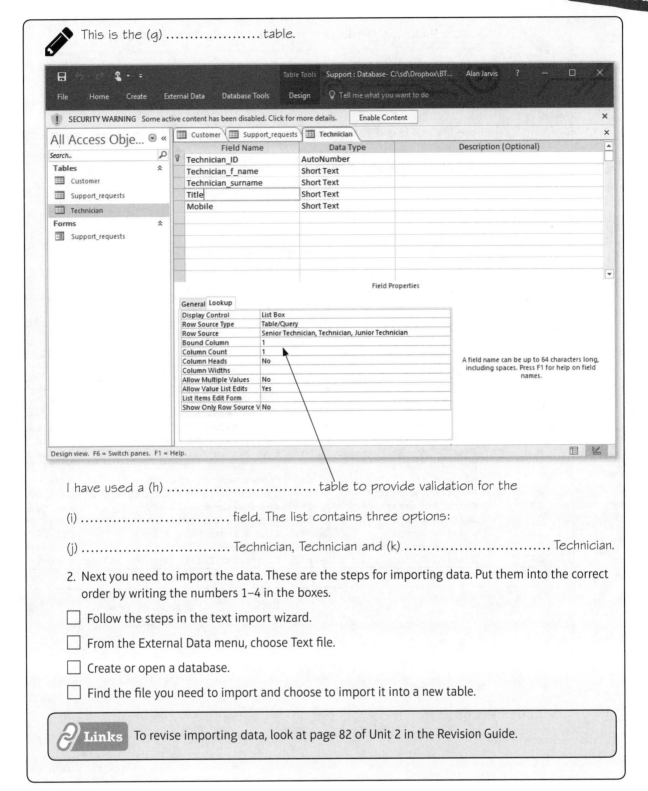

I have used a (h) ............................... table to provide validation for the

(i) ............................... field. The list contains three options:

(j) ............................... Technician, Technician and (k) ............................... Technician.

2. Next you need to import the data. These are the steps for importing data. Put them into the correct order by writing the numbers 1–4 in the boxes.

☐ Follow the steps in the text import wizard.

☐ From the External Data menu, choose Text file.

☐ Create or open a database.

☐ Find the file you need to import and choose to import it into a new table.

Links  To revise importing data, look at page 82 of Unit 2 in the Revision Guide.

✎ 3. Look at the student's screenshots of importing the data, and fill in the blanks.

Importing data

The next task I completed was importing the sample (a) ...............................

I used the Import Text (b) ...............................

This is one of the steps in the wizard.

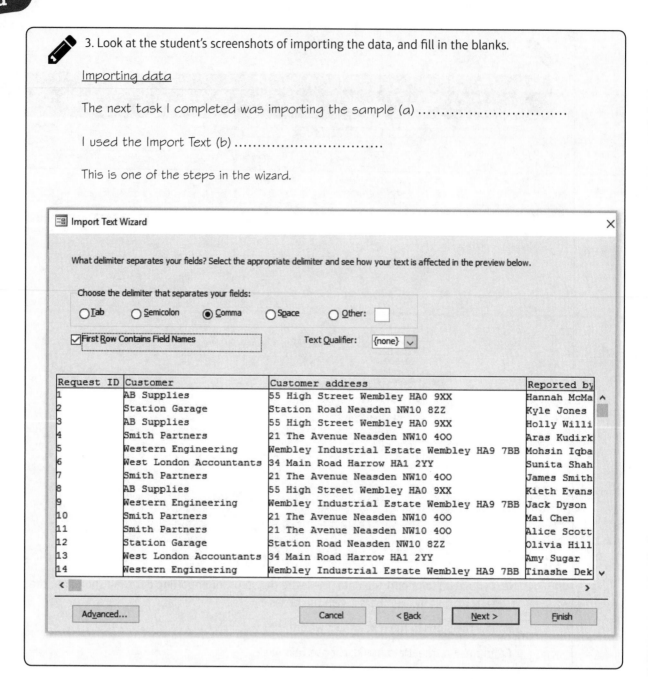

Once the data had been imported I used Append queries to split it up into the

(c) ........................................... I created before.

Append queries are similar to standard queries accept that the results of the query are inserted into a new or existing table. You can make any query an append query by selecting the Append icon in the Query Tools Design toolbar.

Here is the Append query I used to put records in the Support_requests table.

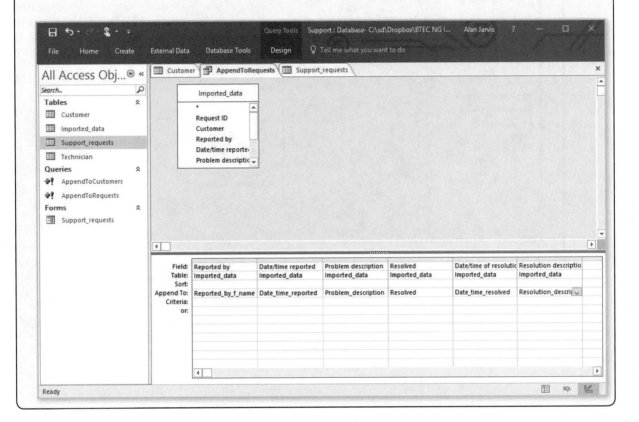

✎ Once the data was imported, I checked the (d) ................................ keys in the

Support_requests table. I was then able to create the (e) ...............................

between the tables. Here are the (f) ................................ I created.

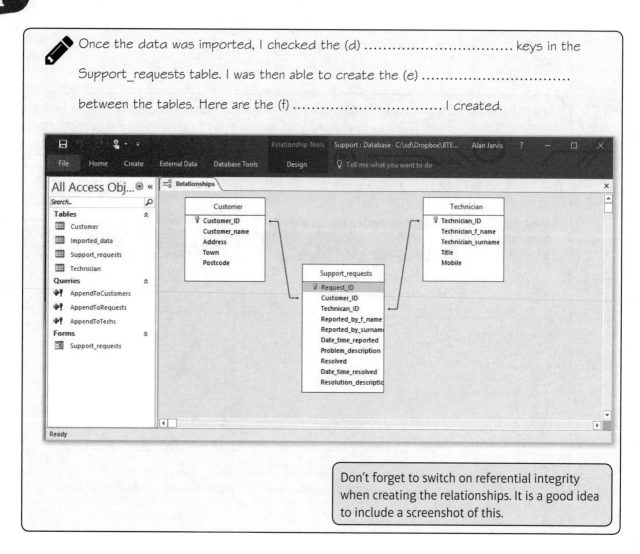

Don't forget to switch on referential integrity when creating the relationships. It is a good idea to include a screenshot of this.

✏️ 4. Look at the student's screenshots of creating the forms, queries and reports, and fill in the blanks.

<u>Creating the objects</u>

The next task was to create the forms.

This is the Add support requests (a) ................................

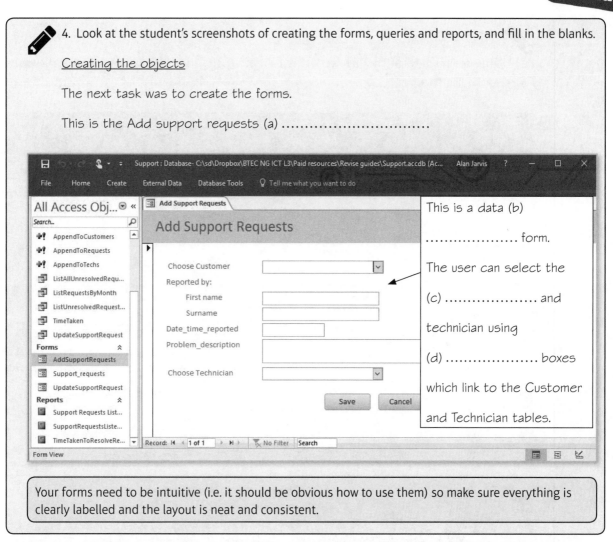

Your forms need to be intuitive (i.e. it should be obvious how to use them) so make sure everything is clearly labelled and the layout is neat and consistent.

✏️ This is the (e) ................................ form.

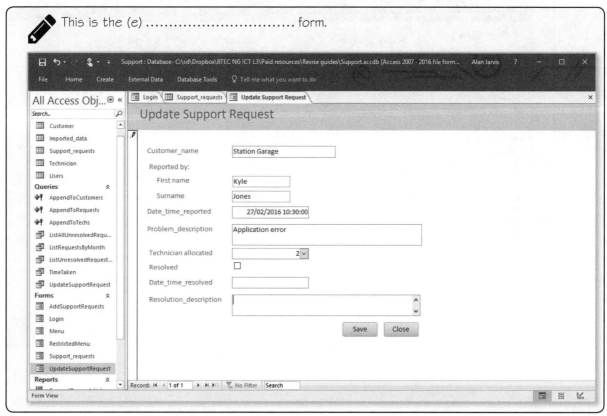

These are the (f) ................................. I created:

The design view of the (g) ................................. for listing all unresolved requests looks like this.

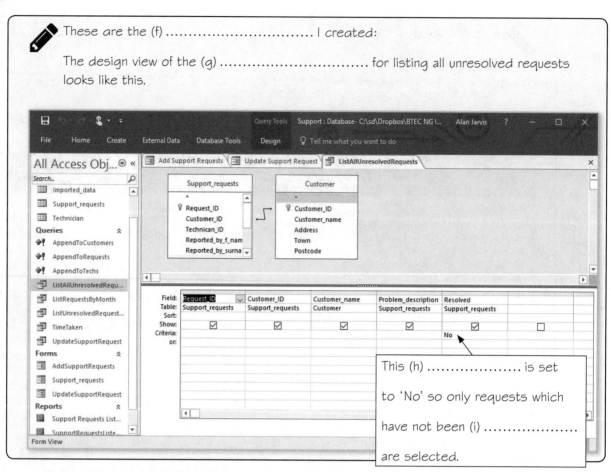

This (h) ..................... is set to 'No' so only requests which have not been (i) ..................... are selected.

The (j) ................................. of the query looks like this.

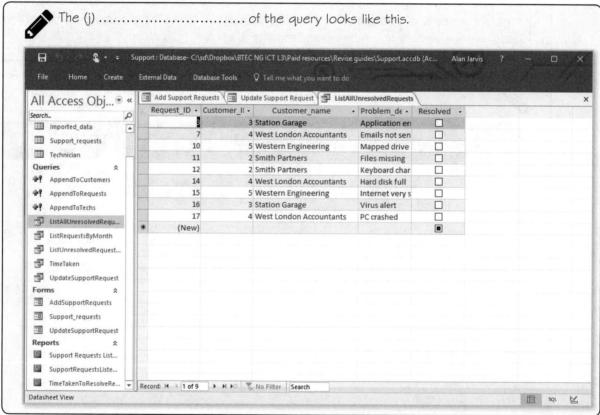

Here is the (k) .............................. view of the query for listing a technician's

unresolved support requests.

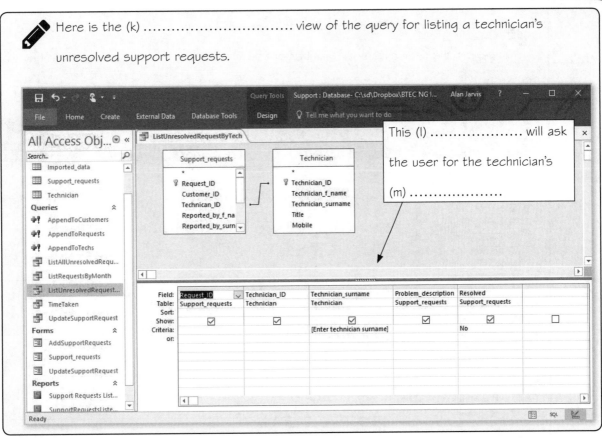

This is the result when the user enters the surname (n) ............................... and the

query is (o) ...............................

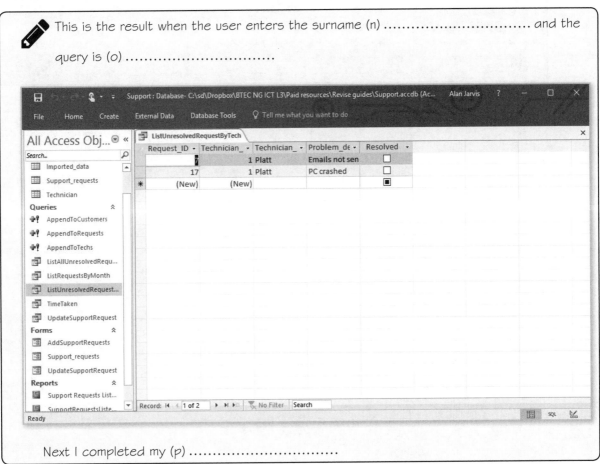

Next I completed my (p) ...............................

🖉 This is the report for listing support requests by (q) ................................ To run the report the user enters the number of the (r) ................................ that they want for the report.

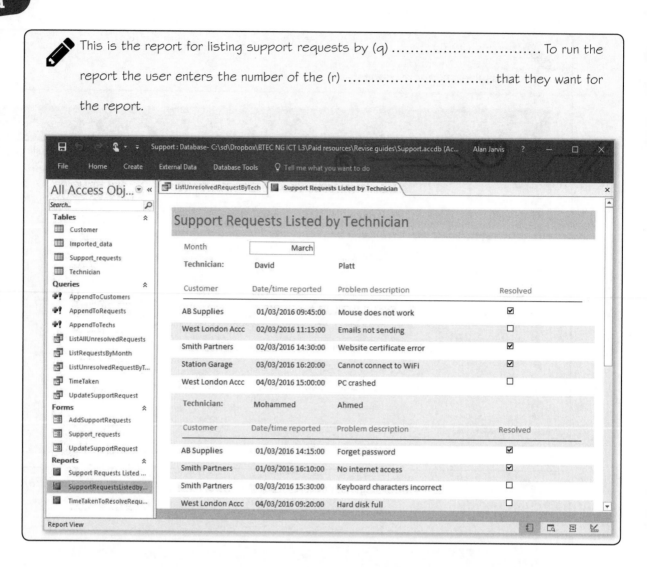

✏️ This is the report for listing support requests by (s) ...............................

The user needs to enter the month number to (t) ............................. this report.

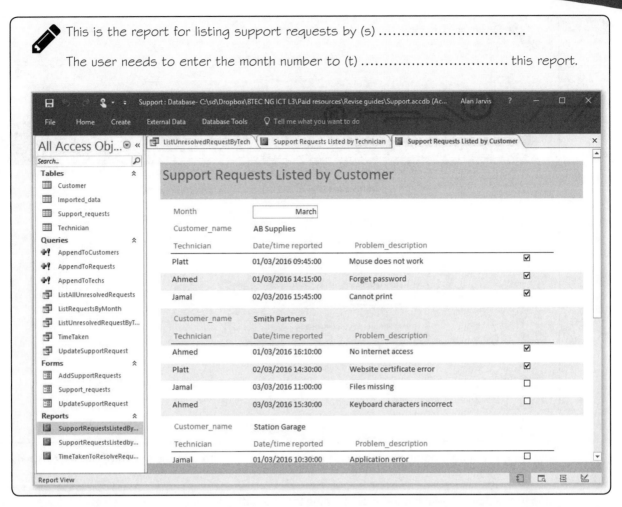

✏️ This is the report for showing the (u) ............................. taken to resolve support

requests.

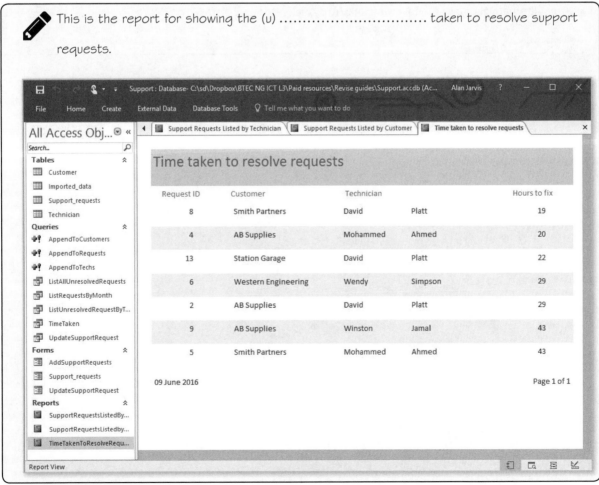

✏️ Once all the forms, reports and queries were complete, I created the

(v) ............................... form, which has (w) ................................. to access all the

objects.

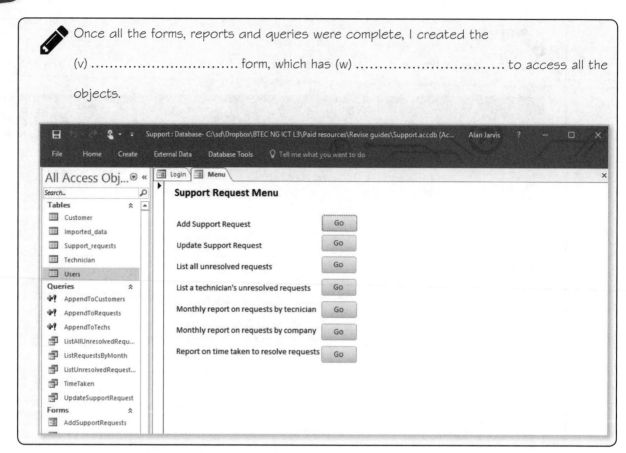

Now create your own database, following the designs you created in the activities on pages 30–42.

Import the data for your database by scanning this link with your smartphone or tablet.
Alternatively, go to the following link: http://activetea.ch/2gNTa18.

## Database testing

Record your testing including test results, comments and actions taken to resolve issues in the 'Test log document' you created in the activity on page 41.

> As well as the screenshots of your database development you also need to provide screenshots of the testing you carry out on your completed database.

> You will need to make a copy of the test plan you created on page 41 and fill in the 'Actual result' column as you carry out the tests. If you find the actual result does not match the expected result you need to explain that this happened in the comments column, and state what action you took to deal with the problem. This will provide evidence of using an **iterative** development and testing process.

> This is an example of the completed test log for the first few tests. The student has added comments explaining the validation and has included a screenshot of the validation.

| Test number | Purpose of test | Test data | Expected result | Actual result | Comments and action taken |
|---|---|---|---|---|---|
| **Tests for fields in the Customer table** | | | | | |
| 1 | Customer field | Joe Smith and Co | Accepted | Accepted | |
| 2 | Address field | 26 The Avenue | Accepted | Accepted | |
| 3 | Town field | Bristol | Accepted | Accepted | |
| 4 | Postcode field | a4bbx | Rejected | Rejected | The input mask converts the lower case characters to upper case automatically and will not allow a digit in the second character. |
| | | | | | Here you can see the input mask working. |
| | | | | | Add screenshots showing that any validation you have used works as intended. |
| 5 | Postcode field | BR99 1ZZ | Accepted | Accepted | |

Your evaluation

> You will complete an evaluation of your database solution as your final activity (see page 56).

Create a copy of the test plan you created in the activity on page 41 in a separate document. Carry out your tests on your completed database and record the results, adding comments and screenshots as necessary.

# Evaluating a database solution

Evaluate your solution.

You should consider:

- how well your solution meets the requirements of the scenario
- the quality, performance and usability of the database
- the changes made during the development and testing process.

Record your response in the evaluation section of the 'Test log document' you created in the activity on page 41.

 1. Read the sample student evaluation and insert the appropriate heading for each paragraph (a to j). Choose the paragraph headings from those below – they are currently in the wrong order.

During testing I discovered that:

Elements of my database that work well are:

Elements of my database I could improve are:

How well my database matches my designs:

I could improve the usability of my database in these ways:

In conclusion,

My database is easy to use because:

My database meets the needs of the brief in the following ways:

My database failed to meet the needs of the brief in the following ways:

Some problems I encountered during development:

**(a)** ..................................................................................................................

The database I created has all the features listed in the Task Scenario and all the main features work

as they should.

**(b)** ..................................................................................................................

Although all the features work, there are a number of things that would need improving if this

database was to be used for real.

**(c)** ..................................................................................................................

There were no errors in the tests I have done. This suggests that I have not tested the database

thoroughly enough, and if I had more time I would create a more comprehensive test plan.

**(d)** ..................................................................................................................

Everything is labelled clearly and all the forms have Save and Cancel buttons. The layout for the

forms is consistent (same colour scheme and fonts used) and fairly neat. The reports are also neat

and consistent and clearly labelled.

**(e)** ...............................................................................................................

- Some of the labels on the forms still have the underscores for the field names (e.g. date_time_reported). These should be removed and the name made clear (e.g. Date and time reported).

- When the queries are run from the main menu there is no button to return to the menu, so it would be easier to use if the results of the queries were displayed in a form.

- On the Update support request form it would be better if, when you click the resolved check box, the date and time resolved field is automatically completed with the current date and time.

- When a user wants to update a support request, they need to know the request ID. To improve usability, it would be better if there were other ways to search for a support request, such as by company or person who reported it.

**(f)** ...............................................................................................................

The table structure and relationship links all work fine and the referential integrity options ensure, for example, that a support request record must relate to a record on the Customer table. The use of drop-down combo boxes on the form makes the user select a valid customer for each request.

I think the reports also work fine and do not need any improvement.

**(g)** ...............................................................................................................

There is not really enough information on the database about the customer. For example, the name of the person at the company who reported the fault is recorded but not their contact details (email address, phone number, etc).

When reporting a new fault, the date and time reported should have the current date/time inserted automatically.

On the Update support request form the technician allocated is only shown by their ID number.

It would be better if their name was shown.

The database should really have another table linked to the Support_request table that allows each update to an individual request to be recorded on a separate record. This would require a complete redesign of how supported requests are updated.

**(h)** ...............................................................................................................

My design mostly matched the database I developed, although I had to change some minor layout features of the forms and reports as I went along. The designs of the ERD and data dictionary were correct and I did not need to modify them.

**(i)** ...............................................................................................................

I had a lot of difficulty getting the query behind the Time taken to resolve requests report to work.

At first I just had the date of resolving the request subtracted from the date of reporting it.

This gave me the number of days, when it would make much more sense to give the result as the hours. I spent some time trying to remember how to use a function to display just the hours, and eventually I got it to work.

(j) ...............................................................................................................................................

I think my database does have all the required functions and they work fine. There is a lot more refinement I could do (as described above) if I had more time. I think the database might be OK as a prototype to get user opinions as to what else needs adding, but I don't think it would be very effective for use in real life because of the missing features I have listed. I think the database needs a lot more testing as I didn't really have time to test the forms and queries properly.

> Always back up the statements you make with evidence. For example, a poor statement would be 'My forms are easy to use'. But a good example of evidence is 'My forms are easy to use because they all have a consistent layout, are clearly labelled so the user knows what to do and what each input box and button is for, and they all have OK and Cancel buttons to allow the user to confirm or back out of an action'.

 **Links** To revise evaluating your database design, development and testing, look at pages 78, 79 and 91 of Unit 2 in the Revision Guide.

Write an evaluation of your database in the space below.

> You will need to enter your evaluation of the whole database design, development and testing process in the box at the bottom of your completed test log.
>
> The guidelines below give one way of structuring your evaluation. You can structure your evaluation as you like, but do make sure it is clear and logical and covers all the points listed in the activity

My database meets the needs of the brief in the following ways:

.............................................................................................................................................

.............................................................................................................................................

.............................................................................................................................................

.............................................................................................................................................

.............................................................................................................................................

.............................................................................................................................................

It failed to meet the needs of the brief in the following ways:

.............................................................................................................................................

.............................................................................................................................................

.............................................................................................................................................

.............................................................................................................................................

.............................................................................................................................................

> In the first two sections, include how well the database you developed meets the requirements of the scenario.
> • Does it do all the things that are listed in the Task Scenario, particularly those listed in the bullet points underneath 'You need to:'?
> • You may not have managed to get everything working fully. Explain which features you could not get to work and why this happened, for example, lack of time or problems you encountered.
> • Even if you did manage to get all the features to work, there are almost certainly things that could be improved to make the database better suited to the application.

During testing I discovered that

.............................................................................................................................................

.............................................................................................................................................

.............................................................................................................................................

.............................................................................................................................................

.............................................................................................................................................

.............................................................................................................................................

> Your testing should help you ensure the quality of the database, but it is unlikely that you will have had time to do very through testing of every aspect of the database, including the forms, queries and reports. It is a good idea to mention this here.

My database is easy to use because

..............................................................................................................................

..............................................................................................................................

..............................................................................................................................

..............................................................................................................................

..............................................................................................................................

..............................................................................................................................

I could improve the usability of my database by ...............................................................

..............................................................................................................................

..............................................................................................................................

..............................................................................................................................

..............................................................................................................................

..............................................................................................................................

..............................................................................................................................

You should consider the usability of the system you created.
- Is it intuitive and easy to use?
- What aspects of the menus, forms, queries and reports could be made easier for a novice user to understand and use?
- Are there aspects of the user interface that could be improved? For example, could the forms or reports be laid out better, in a neater and more consistent way?

Elements of my database that worked well are ...............................................................

..............................................................................................................................

..............................................................................................................................

..............................................................................................................................

..............................................................................................................................

..............................................................................................................................

..............................................................................................................................

Elements of my database I could improve are ...............................................................

..............................................................................................................................

..............................................................................................................................

..............................................................................................................................

..............................................................................................................................

..............................................................................................................................

..............................................................................................................................

Some issues you might cover in these two sections are:
- Did your testing reveal any problems with the database? If so how did you deal with them?
- Imagine a user actually using your database. What might you need to change or add to make it fully functioning?

How well my database matches my design: ...................................................................

........................................................................................................

........................................................................................................

........................................................................................................

........................................................................................................

........................................................................................................

........................................................................................................

Did your design prove to be correct or did you need to modify it when you came to develop the database?

Some problems I encountered during development: ...............................................

........................................................................................................

........................................................................................................

........................................................................................................

........................................................................................................

........................................................................................................

........................................................................................................

Were there some parts of the database you could not get working properly?

In conclusion, .............................................................................................

........................................................................................................

........................................................................................................

........................................................................................................

........................................................................................................

........................................................................................................

........................................................................................................

# Revision task 2

## Reading the brief

Below is a brief similar in style to the one you will receive in your assessment. Read it through and answer the questions that follow in order to practise the skills you will need in your assessment.

### Scenario

Your friend is running a dog show in the local town of Byford and has asked you to create a database to track the dogs being entered in the various competitions in the show.

The competitions are:

- the best behaved dog, which is at 2 pm on the day of the show
- the best groomed dog which is at 3 pm
- the most agile dog which is at 3:30 pm
- the best dog overall which is at 4 pm.

A number of dogs have already been entered. Each owner can only enter one dog, but they can enter the dog into as many competitions as they like.

You need to:

- design a database structure that:
  - includes dog, competition and competition entry data
  - avoids unnecessary duplication of data
  - validates data input to ensure integrity.
- create a robust database with a suitable user interface for your friend to enter new dogs and competition entries and to enter the winning dog for a competition
- import and manipulate the given data
- provide database outputs showing:
  - all dogs entered for a given competition
  - all the competitions that a given dog has been entered for
  - all the dogs of a given breed entered for a given competition
  - all the dogs born after 1/1/2013, sorted by name
  - a report showing the details of the winning dog for a given competition
  - a report showing all the details (including dogs, entered) for a given competition sorted by owner name
  - a report for an individual dog, showing in which competitions a dog has been entered, with the times of these competitions
- test your database, adding data to ensure that the database meets all requirements
- evaluate your database against the given requirements.

> This first sub-bullet point gives a strong clue as to the tables you will need in your dog show database

> The second bullet point lists the two data entry forms you will need to produce.
>
> You will also need to provide a menu form for accessing all the features of your database.

> The sub-bullets under the fourth bullet point list all the queries and reports you will need to produce.

### Information

The raw data that has been provided contains the entries that have been made so far for the various competitions in the dog show. Figure 1 on page 63 shows an extract of the data (you will download the .csv file that includes this data as part of the activity on page 76 when you develop and test your database).

**Figure 1**

| Dog name | Dog breed | Date of birth | Owner first name | Owner surname | Competition category | Time of competition | Competition judge | Competition winner |
|---|---|---|---|---|---|---|---|---|
| Shep | German Shepherd | 01/10/2010 | Kelly | Birch | Best dog | 16:00 | Alice Wilson | |
| Shep | German Shepherd | 01/10/2010 | Kelly | Birch | Best behaved dog | 14:00 | Simon Jones | |
| Shep | German Shepherd | 01/10/2010 | Kelly | Birch | Most agile dog | 15:30 | Eric Smith | |
| Lilly | Jack Russell | 10/05/2009 | Liz | Cartmell | Best groomed dog | 15:00 | Anita Patel | |
| Lilly | Jack Russell | 10/05/2009 | Liz | Cartmell | Best behaved dog | 14:00 | Simon Jones | |
| Winston | Pug | 20/02/2011 | Smita | Shah | Best groomed dog | 15:00 | Anita Patel | |
| Winston | Pug | 20/02/2011 | Smita | Shah | Best behaved dog | 14:00 | Simon Jones | |
| Spot | Dalmatian | 05/04/2014 | Rita | Evans | Most agile dog | 15:30 | Eric Smith | |
| Spot | Dalmatian | 05/04/2014 | Rita | Evans | Best dog | 16:00 | Alice Wilson | |
| Holly | German Shepherd | 03/09/2012 | Sara | Lloyd | Most agile dog | 15:30 | Eric Smith | |
| Holly | German Shepherd | 03/09/2012 | Sara | Lloyd | Best dog | 16:00 | Alice Wilson | |
| Holly | German Shepherd | 03/09/2012 | Sara | Lloyd | Best groomed dog | 15:00 | Anita Patel | |
| Buster | Bulldog | 16/07/2011 | Phil | Myers | Best dog | 16:00 | Alice Wilson | |
| Buster | Bulldog | 16/07/2011 | Phil | Myers | Best behaved dog | 14:00 | Simon Jones | |
| Buster | Bulldog | 16/07/2011 | Phil | Myers | Most agile dog | 15:30 | Eric Smith | |
| Honey | Beagle | 12/04/2012 | Ruth | Hamilton | Best dog | 16:00 | Alice Wilson | |
| Honey | Beagle | 12/04/2012 | Ruth | Hamilton | Most agile dog | 15:30 | Eric Smith | |
| Honey | Beagle | 12/04/2012 | Ruth | Hamilton | Best behaved dog | 14:00 | Simon Jones | |
| Milly | Yorkshire Terrier | 05/03/2014 | Piotr | Janowski | Most agile dog | 15.30 | Eric Smith | |
| Milly | Yorkshire Terrier | 05/03/2014 | Piotr | Janowski | Best groomed dog | 15:00 | Anita Patel | |
| Milly | Yorkshire Terrier | 05/03/2014 | Piotr | Janowski | Best behaved dog | 14:00 | Simon Jones | |
| Frisky | Collie | 15/02/2011 | Nicki | Spencer | Best behaved dog | 14:00 | Simon Jones | |
| Frisky | Collie | 15/02/2011 | Nicki | Spencer | Most agile dog | 15:30 | Eric Smith | |
| Scruff | Springer Spaniel | 21/03/2013 | Rashpal | Kaur | Best dog | 16:00 | Alice Wilson | |
| Scruff | Springer Spaniel | 21/03/2013 | Rashpal | Kaur | Best groomed dog | 15:00 | Anita Patel | |
| Sandy | Whippet | 23/12/2010 | Kieran | Hales | Best behaved dog | 14:00 | Simon Jones | |
| Sandy | Whippet | 23/12/2010 | Kieran | Hales | Most agile dog | 15:30 | Eric Smith | |

# Creating an entity relationship diagram

Produce an entity relationship diagram (ERD) for the database by normalising the given data to third normal form.

Draw your ERD in the space below. In your actual set task you will create your ERD in software of your choice and save it as a PDF file.

Look at the first bullet point under 'You need to:' in the brief above. The first sub-bullet point gives a very strong clue as to the tables needed.

Then look at the example data provided in Figure 1 on page 63, and identify the repeating groups.

Always check carefully for the types of relationship that exist between the entities.

Here, there is a many-to-many relationship between the Dog and Competition tables, as one dog can enter many competitions, and one competition can have many dogs entered into it.

Many-to-many relationships are always resolved in the same way. You need to create a link entity (table) between the two tables, which, in this case, you can call Competition_entries. This table takes the primary key from both the tables it links and uses them as foreign keys. It has a one-to-many relationship with each table (with the 'many' end of the relationship in the link table).

 To revise how to deal with many-to-many relationships, see page 51 of Unit 2 in the Revision Guide.

Revise the normalisation process by looking at pages 55 and 56 of Unit 2 in the Revision Guide.

Remember to identify the primary key in each table. Which table will require foreign keys, and what should these be?

 You can revise primary and foreign keys on page 52 of Unit 2 in the Revision Guide.

# Creating a data dictionary

Produce a data dictionary for your database using the tables below.

> You need to complete a data dictionary for each table you identified on page 64. You may not need to use all the rows in each table.

> Remember that the 'Attributes' column needs to specify the **data type** of each field and any **validation** you will apply.
>
> Text fields, such as dog's name, cannot be validated but other fields can be. What meaningful validation is it appropriate to apply?

> **Links** You can revise data dictionaries by looking at page 57 of Unit 2 in the Revision Guide.

| Table Name: | |
|---|---|
| **Field name** | **Attributes** |
| | |
| | |
| | |

> **Links** To revise validation, look at pages 67–69 of Unit 2 in the Revision Guide.

| Table Name: | |
|---|---|
| **Field name** | **Attributes** |
| | |
| | |
| | |
| | |
| | |
| | |

> Remember to use consistent **field names** with no spacing between words.

| Table Name: | |
|---|---|
| **Field name** | **Attributes** |
| | |
| | |
| | |
| | |
| | |

# Creating a design specification

Complete the 'Design specification document' given below.

Ensure sufficient information is provided for a third party to implement the interface for your solution.

> If completing this activity on a computer you can use an electronic template for the tables, duplicate the table, extend the box space and add as many rows as you need.

> Include each design in a separate row.

> Remember to add annotations to your designs, either in the first column of the template or as labels on your sketches.
>
> Read the brief on page 62. The hints on that page will help you to identify all the forms, queries and reports you need to design.

**Design specification document**

> Start with your designs for the forms. The brief on page 62 specifies three different forms that are needed.
>
> Also remember to include a menu form, so users can access all the facilities from one place

> **Links** Revise form design by looking at page 74 of Unit 2 in the Revision Guide.
> Revise adding automated features (such as Save and Cancel command buttons) to forms on page 75 of Unit 2 in the Revision Guide.

| Name and type (form, query or report) | Fields used, including relevant details of data entry, calculations, presentation of data and navigation required. |
|---|---|
| Type:.......................................<br><br>Name:.......................................<br><br>................................................. | |

Your annotation should state which table the form/fields link to (where relevant), and describe how the boxes on the form support data validation and help the user to enter the required data.

| Name and type (form, query or report) | Fields used, including relevant details of data entry, calculations, presentation of data and navigation required. |
|---|---|
| Type:....................................<br><br>Name:....................................<br><br>.................................................... | |
| **Name and type (form, query or report)** | **Fields used, including relevant details of data entry, calculations, presentation of data and navigation required.** |
| Type:....................................<br><br>Name:....................................<br><br>.................................................... | |

Remember to include accessibility features on your forms, where possible.

| Name and type (form, query or report) | Fields used, including relevant details of data entry, calculations, presentation of data and navigation required. |
|---|---|
| Type:.......................................<br><br>Name:.....................................<br><br>........................................... | |

Now design the queries. The brief on page 62 specifies four different queries that are needed.

Choose carefully the fields that you want to be displayed when you run your queries. Only include those that will be useful for the user to see. Make sure you list the correct table for each field.

 **Links** Revise query design, including how to add prompt boxes to your criteria, on page 64 of Unit 2 in the Revision Guide.

The criterion for the first query will need to prompt the user to select the competition they want to view.

Remember to put your prompt in the Criteria row under the required field, and to put it inside square brackets.

| Name and type (form, query or report) | Fields and tables used, including relevant details of criteria included, user input of criteria, calculations, presentation of data and sorting required. |
|---|---|
| Type:................................<br><br>Name:...............................<br><br>.............................. | |

The second query will also need to have a user prompt in the Criteria row. Which field will this link to?

| Name and type (form, query or report) | Fields and tables used, including relevant details of criteria included, user input of criteria, calculations, presentation of data and sorting required. |
|---|---|
| Type: .................<br>Name: .................<br>    .................... | |

The third query requires two user prompts as criteria, to select the dog breed and competition.

| Name and type (form, query or report | Fields and tables used, including relevant details of criteria included, user input of criteria, calculations, presentation of data and sorting required. |
|---|---|
| Type:..............<br>Name:..............<br>..............| |

For the final query you will need to use a comparison symbol in your criterion for the Date_of_birth field. Don't forget the sort.

| Name and type (form, query or report | Fields and tables used, including relevant details of criteria included, user input of criteria, calculations, presentation of data and sorting required. |
|---|---|
| Type: ............. Name: ............. ............. | |

Now design your reports. The brief on page 62 specifies three different reports that are needed.

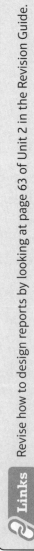

**Links** Revise how to design reports by looking at page 63 of Unit 2 in the Revision Guide.

The first report needs to select the winning dog for a given competition. First create a query which will ask the user to enter the competition (you do not need to show the design for the query, but you can if you wish). Then create a report to format and display the results of the query.

You can design this report as a certificate to give to the winning dog's owner.

| Name and type (form, query or report) | Fields used, including relevant details of data entry, calculations, presentation of data and navigation required. |
|---|---|
| Type:...................................<br><br>Name:....................................<br><br>............................................. | |

The second report will be a list for the judges so they know which dogs are in the competition they are judging.

| Name and type (form, query or report) | Fields used, including relevant details of data entry, calculations, presentation of data and navigation required. |
|---|---|
| Type:...................................<br><br>Name:....................................<br><br>............................................. | |

Design the final report as an information sheet for owners.

| Name and type (form, query or report) | Fields used, including relevant details of data entry, calculations, presentation of data and navigation required. |
|---|---|
| Type:.....................................<br><br>Name:....................................<br><br>............................................ | |

# Devising a test plan

Use the 'Test log document' given below to plan how you will test your completed database.

If completing this activity on a computer you can use an electronic template for the tables, duplicate the table, extend the box space and add as many rows as you need.

You need to include a range of data to test any validation for the fields listed in your data dictionary. Where fields have no validation, you can test that data can actually be input to the field – you do not need to include a range of different test data for these fields.

**Test log document**

| Test number | Purpose of test | Test data | Expected result | Actual result | Comments and action taken |
|---|---|---|---|---|---|
| **Tests for fields in the ........................................ table** | | | | | |
| | | | | | |
| | | | | | |
| | | | | | |
| | | | | | |
| | | | | | |
| | | | | | |
| | | | | | |
| | | | | | |
| | | | | | |
| | | | | | |
| **Tests for fields in the ........................................ table** | | | | | |
| | | | | | |
| | | | | | |
| | | | | | |
| | | | | | |
| | | | | | |
| | | | | | |
| | | | | | |
| | | | | | |
| | | | | | |
| | | | | | |
| | | | | | |
| | | | | | |
| **Tests for fields in the ........................................ table** | | | | | |
| | | | | | |
| | | | | | |
| | | | | | |
| | | | | | |
| | | | | | |
| | | | | | |

**Links** To revise test plans, look at page 65 of Unit 2 in the Revision Guide.

# Database development and testing

Develop and test your database using the information in the documents you produced for the activities on pages 64–75. Record your database development as annotated screenshots in a single document.

Your screenshots should show:

- your tables, including the fields and attributes
- your table relationships
- your queries, including fields and criteria
- the output of your queries
- the forms you have created
- the reports you have created
- evidence of working validation.

> Work through the bullet points one by one as you create your database to make sure you include all the screenshots needed.

> Annotate the screenshots clearly to explain what they show. The document you produce for this activity should provide a clear 'story' of your database development.

> You will need to use database software to create your database. The first task is to import the raw data from the .csv file.

> You can download the .csv file containing the data for the dog show database by scanning this link with your smartphone or tablet. Alternatively, go to the following link: http://activetea.ch/2fSK0vG.

>  **Links** To revise developing your database, refer to pages 66–76 of Unit 2 in the Revision Guide.

> **Links** To revise importing data, look at page 82 of Unit 2 in the Revision Guide.

Record your testing, including test results, comments and actions taken to resolve issues in the 'Test log document' you created in in the activity on page 75.

> Fill in the 'Actual result' column as you carry out the tests. Add comments in the final column where necessary, recording the action you take to resolve unexpected results.

> Remember to take notes throughout the development and testing stage to use when you write your evaluation.

> **Links** To revise testing your database, refer to page 77 of Unit 2 in the Revision Guide.

# Evaluating a database solution

Evaluate your solution.

You should consider:

- how well your solution meets the requirements of the scenario
- the quality, performance and usability of the database
- the changes made during the development and testing process.

Record your response in the evaluation box below.

> You need to enter your evaluation in the 'Your evaluation' box on the 'Test log document' that you created for the activity on page 76.

> Remember to use the 'point and explain' method in your evaluation: make a point, then explain it.

> You could use the bullet points from the instructions for this activity (see page 77) as headings to help you structure your evaluation. For example:
> - How well does my solution meet the requirements of the scenario?
> - Evaluation of the quality, performance and usability of the database
> - Evaluation of the changes made during the development and testing process
> - Conclusion
>
> Alternatively, you could use the paragraph beginnings used in the sample evaluation for Revision task 1 (see page 56) or choose your own way of setting out the evaluation – as long as it covers all the points required.

**Your evaluation**

..................................................................................................................................

..................................................................................................................................

..................................................................................................................................

..................................................................................................................................

..................................................................................................................................

..................................................................................................................................

..................................................................................................................................

..................................................................................................................................

..................................................................................................................................

..................................................................................................................................

..................................................................................................................................

..................................................................................................................................

..................................................................................................................................

..................................................................................................................................

..................................................................................................................................

..................................................................................................................................

..................................................................................................................................

..................................................................................................................................

..................................................................................................................................

..................................................................................................................................

..................................................................................................................................

..................................................................................................................................

..................................................................................................................................

..................................................................................................................................

..................................................................................................................................

 **Links** To revise evaluating your database design, development and testing, look at pages 78, 79 and 90 of Unit 2 in the Revision Guide.

# Answers

## Unit 1: Revision test 1

(Other answers will be possible if they cover similar points. The suggestions that follow are not prescriptive. Answers may cover some/all of the indicative content but you can reward other relevant answers.)

**1** (a) (1 mark for each identification and 1 additional mark for each appropriate expansion, up to a maximum of 2 marks each.)
- Mobile devices such as smartphones and tablets can use mobile internet connections (1), which allow the technicians to look up problems, combine with GPS and software to use online maps to navigate to jobs, or update the job card while out of the office. (1)
- Mobile devices are also extremely portable (1), which makes it easier for the technicians to carry and use these devices while travelling to repair jobs. (1) **(4)**

(b) (Marks are allocated based on the depth and quality of answers. To ensure maximum marks, you should make appropriate use of technical language and have reasoning that is technically accurate.)
- Laptops are portable computing devices (1) which are able to run diagnostic software (1) and potentially connect to problematic hardware more easily than a mobile device. (1)
- A laptop has a separate keyboard, as well as a large screen and a touchpad. (1) These will make it easier to input and gain output from the device (1), so the technicians can provide more detailed updates and feedback on problems. (1) **(6)**

(c) Provide an evaluation of the impact on Excelsior IT Support of the legal, moral and ethical issues, stating if you think the impacts will be largely positive or negative. Your evaluation should be supported by relevant points which may include:

**Legislation**
- The Data Protection Act requires that organisations keep personal data secure. If the business was found to be in breach of the Data Protection Act by the Information Commissioner then they could be subject to a large fine, potentially hundreds of thousands of pounds.
- In order to comply with the Data Protection Act, the business will need to implement the necessary security measures, including technology, training and procedures, which could be very costly.
- However, the Data Protection Act can make consumers more confident about supplying their data to a business, which makes it easier for the business to perform their activities.
- The Computer Misuse Act provides a mechanism to prosecute offenders that attempt to gain unauthorised access to a computer system and who wish to steal or damage the data stored on those systems.
- Such offences can be punished with up to ten years in jail and a large fine.
- This act benefits the business by deterring individuals from attempting to harm the business's systems.

**Moral and ethical issues**
- Privacy of individuals should be maintained. An individual's data could be misused for many reasons (e.g. identity fraud) which would seriously negatively affect their life.
- The business has a moral (as well as legal) duty to define and enforce the acceptable use of the data stored on their computer systems to avoid misuse by an employee, such as being shared with someone who should not have access. The business is morally (as well as legally) obliged to protect data being transmitted over the internet, by taking measures such as using appropriate encryption.
- The use of portable storage devices can lead to negative environmental impacts in the form of techno trash due to the regular replacing of hard drives, as these devices are prone to damage. **(12)**

**2** (a) (1 mark for each identification and 1 additional mark for each appropriate expansion, up to a maximum of 2 marks each.)
- **Social media** websites allow businesses to create and share information and to **network**. One example is the use of business pages (1) which would allow A2B Taxis to **advertise** deals directly to customers. (1)
- **Blogs** are regularly updated websites that are often used by businesses to share **up-to-date** news and information. (1) A2B Taxis could use this method to inform customers of improvements and innovations in the **services** they offer. (1)
- **Forums** are online discussion sites (1) which could be used by the business to gain customer **feedback** on their services. (1) **(6)**

(b) Provide an analysis of the potential impact of online communities on A2B Taxis, supported by relevant points which may include the following.

**Positive impacts**
- Better communication with customers – online communities allow direct communication between a business and its customers, such as to gain feedback on services.
- Advertising – online communities provide excellent marketing opportunities, allowing businesses to target customers based on their specific interests.
- Understanding customer needs – strong communication links allow businesses to find out about customer needs more effectively and release new services/products to meet those needs.

**Negative impacts**
- Cost – setting up online communities, such as a blog or forum, requires an investment in order to develop the systems and maintain them correctly, for example, hiring staff to run the online community.
- Timescales – setting up a new online community takes a long time in terms of development and implementation, and it may take some time before users start taking part in the community.
- Security – online communities can be infiltrated by hackers who try to gain access to the personal data kept on users, so protection is needed against this. **(10)**

(c) In-car navigation systems have become a major part of the service provided by taxi companies like A2B Taxis because they can be used by taxi drivers to ensure they find the destinations, take the quickest route and avoid roadworks and traffic jams, thus providing a better service.
- Mobile devices, specifically smartphones, would be useful to A2B taxis as they can be used by drivers to keep in touch with head office regarding new pickups required or emergencies. The built-in GPS can be used for satellite navigation.
- Personal computers could be used in the offices of A2B Taxis to help them keep track of fares, maintain company finances, contact suppliers, etc.
- Communication devices used for internet access would also be of benefit for allowing the use of email and web

services in the head office. Can maintain a website to advertise the business online.

*Additional guidance*
- Any reasonable response that relates to the use of digital devices to the efficient running of a taxi business is also acceptable.
- Generic answers about business uses of digital devices are not acceptable. **(10)**

3  (a)  You should consider how using cloud storage services will be beneficial when sharing documents.
- Cloud storage services would allow the finance company to share access to folder and facilitate collaborative working, allowing employees in different locations to work simultaneously on the same project. Employees could be more effective by not having to wait until they return to the office to update or access important documents.
- Employees could access the files while away from the office computers allowing them to continue to work remotely without the same security implications of using email attachments or portable media, such as USB sticks.
- Cloud storage would make it easier for employees to work on the same documents eliminating potential issues presented by different users working on their own copies and then trying to combine them at a later date. Users could simultaneously access the same document.

(b)  (1 mark for each identification and 1 additional mark for each appropriate expansion, up to a maximum of 2 marks each.)
- A local area network can be used to share a printer (1) so several employees can all make use of the same device. (1)
- A local area network could provide security (1) by having a server and logins rather than standalone machines. (1) **(4)**

(c)  Provide an analysis of whether Benjamin's business would benefit from using cloud computing software, supported by relevant points which may include the following.

**Advantages**
- Software management – the software is not installed on the business's computers so less time and money is needed for managing the software, such as running updates, therefore all employees would be working with the latest/same version of software to prevent any potential conflicts.
- Hardware requirements – cloud computing software runs on the service provider's servers and not the individual workstations, so a business can use cheaper, less powerful computers.
- Flexibility – businesses can adapt to their needs, whether in growth or shrinking in size, by easily increasing or reducing access to cloud computing services.

**Disadvantages**
- Access to software – if the business's internet connection is down then the software will not be accessible to be used, which leads to loss of productivity.
- Security – the business has no control over the updating of software and security practices for the data stored, which could lead to security issues.
- Ongoing costs – cloud computing software is usually a subscription service, which means increased ongoing costs for running the business.
- Features – *sometimes* cloud-based software has reduced feature sets, when compared with their desktop equivalents. **(10)**

4  (a)  (1 mark for each identification and 1 additional mark for each appropriate expansion, up to a maximum of 2 marks each.)
- Bandwidth is the rate of data transfer over a network. (1) High bandwidth is required to transfer the large amounts of data in a high-definition video file. (1)
- Latency is the time delay for a data packet to transfer to its destination. (1) Low latency or lack of latency, is preferred to avoid buffering (ensure that video reaches your computer as fast as it is playing). (1) **(4)**

(b)  The response may look like the following, but other answers are also acceptable if they cover similar points.

You should consider how using different file types will affect the suitability for streaming video content.
- One file format that is commonly used for videos is the .avi format. This would potentially be of use to Jessica as it would provide very high-quality video. The drawback for Jessica of this file type is that it has a large file size that would take a long time to download.
- Another file format for videos is the .mp4 format. This would be of use to Jessica as it is very good for streaming video over the internet. The drawback for Jessica of using this file type is that its file sizes are still quite large when compared to many other compressed file formats.

Other acceptable formats are:
- MOV is a compressed or uncompressed format designed for use with Apple QuickTime.
- MKV supports high-quality video playback, but is not well supported by some devices, e.g. iPads cannot play .mkv files (any other suitable formats could be included, such as FLV; this list is not exhaustive). **(6)**

(c)  Compression is used to reduce the amount of data required to store a file. By compressing the video files Jessica will use less bandwidth when uploading the videos and users will not have to worry about downloading large video files. Her videos should still have the same impact and detail but ultimately take up less space and place less demand on network connections. It may place some load on Jessica's machine as she compresses the files though.
There are two types of compression that are used. One is lossy, the other is lossless. Lossy compression is where the file size is reduced but also some actual video content is lost in the process. It may not be immediately visible but sometimes colours can appear blocky or some fine detail may be lost. Even when uncompressed the original video file cannot be retrieved.
An extremely important tool for compressing video files for transmitting over a network is a codec. This is used to decipher the compressed video on a user's machine so they can watch the video. Codecs are available for a wide range of compression formats and machines, although some may be more efficient than others – some may allow streaming (watching the video before it has all downloaded) and some may not. **(12)** (Marks are awarded based on the content and quality of the whole answer. You can maximise your potential for achieving all available marks by fully answering the question posed, using appropriate technical language and considering viewpoints with confidence and detail.)

# Unit 1: Revision test 2

1  (a)  (1 mark for each identification and 1 additional mark for each appropriate expansion, up to a maximum of 2 marks each.)
- PNG files can store transparent colours (1), allowing Lloyd to create 2D graphics that are partially visible or completely transparent so they match the rest of the interface. (1)

- PNG files use lossless compression (1), so if Lloyd wants to increase the quality of the image back to an uncompressed form, he can do so. (1) **(4)**
  (b) Analyse the features of the two computers to assess their suitability for use in creating and editing computer graphics.

  **Processor**
  - Computer 1 has a quad-core processor which means it can simultaneously perform more operations albeit at a slower speed than the dual-core processor in computer 2, despite computer 2's faster clock speed.
  - Graphics editing tasks are often very processor intensive and so the more powerful quad-core processor would help with these tasks.

  **RAM**
  - Computer 1 has twice the amount of RAM as computer 2, which means it can store more instructions ready for processing and more data while it is being worked on.
  - Graphics editing tasks often require a lot of RAM, as the software requires a lot of RAM to run and graphics files that are in use take up a lot of RAM.

  **Storage**
  - Computer 1 has 1 TB of storage compared to 250 GB in computer 2. Graphics files require a large hard disk for storage as files are often very large.
  - Computer 2 uses a solid state drive which will make loading and saving the files quicker than computer 1's hard disk drive.

  **Graphics**
  - Computer 1 has a 4 GB dedicated graphics card, which is important for graphics editing tasks, particularly 3D modelling, which is very graphics-processing intensive.
  - Computer 2 has an integrated graphics card, which uses main memory for storing instructions for graphics processing. The main memory will struggle with the kinds of tasks that Lloyd needs to complete. **(8)**

  (c) Features
  - Accessibility – files are available to be accessed on any internet connected device with appropriate capabilities, from digital photo frames for display to desktop devices for editing.
  - Scalability – easy to increase or decrease storage available by changing subscription to cloud storage service.
  - Reduced upgrade costs – smaller local hard disk storage required as fewer files are stored locally.
  - Security – improved security due to files being stored offsite, which keeps them safe from fire, flood, etc.
  - Teleworking – makes it easier to work remotely as files can be saved to the cloud at an office and then accessed and worked on from home.
  - Collaboration – cloud storage files can be shared with multiple users so that co-workers (e.g. Lloyd and his colleagues) can work together on the same files.

  **Limitations**
  - Downtime – if Lloyd's internet connection goes down he will not be able to access the files that are stored on the cloud.
  - Heavy bandwidth use – constant saving and loading of large files (such as graphics) will make heavy use of network bandwidth, which could reduce network speeds and use up data allowances. Large data files may take long periods to sync before they can be worked on.
  - Privacy – cloud storage files could potentially be accessed by a hacker and distributed without Lloyd's consent, or used for fraud.

*Additional guidance*
- Any reasonable response that relates the features and implications of cloud storage in the context of a games graphics artist is acceptable.
- Generic answers about cloud storage are not acceptable. **(10)**

2 (a) (1 mark for each identification and 1 additional mark for each appropriate expansion, up to a maximum of 2 marks each.)
- A touch screen (1) will allow users to choose menu options to pick their meal. (1)
- A barcode scanner (1) could be used to scan vouchers for discounts or loyalty cards; or to scan items chosen from a chiller cabinet. (1) **(4)**

(b) Provide a diagram of a user interface for a data entry screen, for a given data set.
(1 mark for inclusion of each of the following in the design, up to a maximum of 5 marks.)
- menu options for food choices
- menu option to go to payment screen
- at least one accessibility feature included (e.g. option to increase/decrease font size, 'listen to this page' feature)
- onscreen instructions/prompts/example data entry to help users
- button/navigation to move to next screen.

There is 1 additional mark for suitable layout/design showing all of the following: good use of layout and screen space. **(6)**

(c) Primary research will allow Harold to directly address what he wants to find out as he can target the exact audience that uses his fast food restaurants and ask them the exact questions he wants answered, whereas secondary sources would provide information about someone else's priorities.
- Primary data is likely to be far more recent and up-to-date than secondary sources, as he will carry out his data collection at the time he needs it.
- Harold will be able to gain more in-depth understanding of his customers as he can follow up answers by asking respondents further questions.
- The data collected may be more reliable than secondary sources as Harold can be sure of the methodology used to gather the information and put his own steps in place to prevent bias, etc.
- Harold can choose his own method of collecting data depending on the type of data he wants. For example, he can decide whether a questionnaire or one-to-one interviews will provide him with the most relevant and useful data, whereas he would have no control over the type of data available in secondary sources.

*Additional guidance*
- Any reasonable response that relates the benefits of primary data collection to the customer research that Harold wants to carry out is acceptable.
- Generic answers about primary data collection are not acceptable. **(10)**

3 (a) (1 mark for each identification and 1 additional mark for each appropriate expansion, up to a maximum of 2 marks each.)
- Virtual private networks (VPNs) create a secure connection over a public network such as the internet. (1) This will allow Aaliyah to connect to the drinks company's systems securely. (1)
- Remote desktop technologies allow users to access their computer from a different computer (1), so Aaliyah will be able to connect to her computer at the head office while she is at home. (1) **(4)**

(b) (1 mark for each identification and up to 2 additional marks for each appropriate expansion, up to a maximum of 3 marks each.)

- Mobile computing devices often have a mobile broadband connection (1), which allow users to access internet services wherever they are (1), so Aaliyah can use email, the web and even VoIP to keep in touch with the business while travelling. (1)
- Mobile computing devices have long battery life (1), which means they can be used for long periods of time without needing to be plugged in (1), so Aaliyah can continue to use the device even while travelling long distances without access to a plug socket. (1) **(6)**

(c) Provide an evaluation of the implications on Aaliyah's company when embarking on the launch of a social media presence. You should ensure you comment on which of these would be the most important. Your evaluation should be supported by relevant points which may include:

### Employee and customer experience
- ease of use
- performance
- availability
- accessibility

### Customer needs
- Is it what users want?
- Is it going to provide the 'right' information and experience?

### Cost
- Is there a cost? One-off or subscription?
- Enhancement costs for building a presence (e.g. advertising, post promotion)?

### Replacement or integration with current systems
- Does the social media presence integrate into an existing customer management system?
- How does the company robustly identify existing customers?

### Productivity
- Is there a social media policy in place?
- How do you manage the personal use of social media?

### Working practices
- Do employees have a policy to adhere to?
- How do you maintain a consistent and appropriate company image?

### Security
- Is there any protection from attack by competitors/enemies, and procedures in place to detect and manage?
- How do you ensure your presence isn't impacted by (or used to distribute) malware? (12)

**4** (a) (1 mark for each identification and 1 additional mark for each appropriate expansion, up to a maximum of 2 marks each.)
- Privacy of users and their data is an ethical issue (1). If they permit data to be used (e.g. to target advertising) without their users consent, this could breach their privacy. (1)
- Health and safety is an ethical issue when employees use IT systems in the workplace. (1) Organisations have an ethical duty to help prevent employees developing health problems such as repetitive strain injury (RSI). (1)
- The accessibility of an organisation's IT systems is an ethical issue. (1) If appropriate assistive technologies are not in place, the IT systems may be inaccessible to employees with disabilities and therefore discriminatory. (1) **(6)**

(b) **File permissions and access levels**
- Users can be assigned different access levels to files, such as read-only, read/write and full control.
- These measures ensure a user cannot damage all data within the system as their access is limited.

### Backup and recovery procedures
- These put in place clear steps for backing up data and recovering the data if it is damaged.
- These procedures ensure a business can recover quickly if a malicious user damages the IT system.

### Passwords
- Using passwords to gain access to systems helps ensure that only authorised users who know the password can access them.
- Setting good complexity rules to passwords adds greater security by ensuring that passwords cannot be easily guessed.

### Physical access control
- Techniques like locks and keys or biometrics to gain access to IT systems can prevent unauthorised users from physically gaining access to the systems.
- This helps prevent theft of and damage to systems.

### Digital certificates
- These allow companies to transfer data securely over the internet using public key encryption.
- This means that they can use the HTTPS protocol for secure communication.
- Any data intercepted by a malicious user would not be readable. **(8)**

### Firewall and Digital Security
- A firewall helps to prevent unauthorised access to the company network from the wider internet.
- It protects against hacking attempts and viruses.
- It can also protect devices inside the company from using unathorised services (for example BitTorrent).

(c) Provide an evaluation of the relevant legislation, stating if you think the decision is appropriate or not. Your evaluation should be supported by relevant points which may include some of the points below. You should ensure that your evaluation relates the legislation directly to the impact it may have on Haldrech Security.

### Computer Misuse Act
- Protects against attacks on computer systems to gain unauthorised access and cause damage or theft to data, for example, hacking, viruses.
- Anyone found in breach of this act is subject to unlimited fines and up to five years in jail.
- This helps deter any potential malicious users from attacking a business's systems.

### Data Protection Act
- Protects the privacy of an individual's data being processed by anyone.
- Anyone found in breach of this act is liable to fines of up to £500 000 as well as compensation to any individuals harmed by the breach.
- This act imposes significant costs on a business to ensure they have the right level of security to comply with legislation.
- However, it does improve consumer confidence in providing personal data for a business to use in their IT systems. **(12)**

**For example, an answer might begin:**
When considering the options available to Haldrech security to modernise their systems, they need to look at what protection is afforded them by current legislation, as well as what demands that legislation places upon them. Whilst the Computer Misuse Act provides a deterrent for hackers and a means for punishment, the Data Protection Act places the onus on the provider of the computer system to ensure sufficient steps are taken in the first place to prevent intrusions.
*You might then go on to discuss the specific requirements of the legislation in relation to security.*

# Unit 2: Revision task 1

## Reading the brief

### Guided activities

1 Three tables (Support_request, Customer, Technician) create a robust database with a suitable user interface for technicians to enter support requests and to update support requests with resolutions of problems. Although 'Resolved' does repeat, this is connected to the Support_request table identified.

2 Two data entry forms (Enter a support request, Update a support request).

3 (a) Two queries (All unresolved queries, All unresolved queries for a particular technician) plus three more queries behind the reports listed in part (b) – so five queries altogether.

   (b) Three reports (Monthly summary report of requests dealt with by a particular technician, Monthly summary report of requests from a particular customer, Report of times taken by a particular technician to resolve queries).

4 You should highlight two items of repeating data:
- Customer, Customer address
- Technician allocated, Technician job title, Technician mobile no.

## Creating an entity relationship diagram

### Guided activities

1 (a) Customer
   (b) Technician allocated

2

| Customer | Technician allocated |
|---|---|
| Customer address | Technician job title |
| | Technician mobile no. |

3 • Customer address: Address, Town, Postcode
- Technician allocated: Technician first name, Technician surname

4 • Primary key for the Customer table is: Customer_ID (autonumber).
- Primary key for the Technician table is: Technician_ID (autonumber).

5

| Request ID (primary key) |
|---|
| Reported by |
| Date/time reported |
| Problem description |
| Resolved? |
| Date/time resolved |
| Resolution description |

6 (a) The **Customer** table is related to the **Support_request** table by a one-to-many relationship.
   (b) The **Technican** table is related to the **Support_request** table by a one-to-many relationship.

7 Customer_ID and Technician_ID

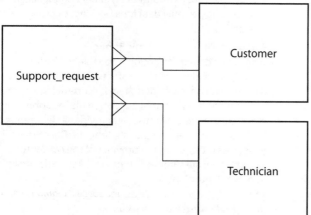

## Creating a data dictionary

| Table Name: | Customer |
|---|---|
| **Field name** | **Attributes** |
| Customer_ID | Primary key, autonumber data type |
| Customer_name | Text data type, 25 characters, no validation |
| Address | Text data type, 25 characters, no validation |
| Town | Text data type, 25 characters, no validation |
| Postcode | Text data type, 8 characters, input mask to validate |

| Table Name: | Support_request |
|---|---|
| **Field name** | **Attributes** |
| Request_ID | Primary key, autonumber data type |
| Customer_ID | Foreign key linking to the Customer table. Integer data type |
| Technician_ID | Foreign key linking to the Technician table. Integer data type |
| Reported_by_first_name | Text data type, 25 characters, no validation |
| Reported_by_surname | Text data type, 25 characters, no validation |
| Date_time_reported | Date data type, default value of the current date/time, cannot be in the future. |
| Problem_description | Text data type, 150 characters, no validation |
| Resolved | Yes/No data type, default value of No |
| Date_time_resolved | Date data type, cannot be in the future |
| Resolution_description | Text data type, 150 characters, no validation |

Note that you can set a default value for a field in the field properties. When used appropriately, default values help make the database easier to use as the user does not have to enter the data unless they want to change it.

| Table Name: | Technician |
|---|---|
| **Field name** | **Attributes** |
| Technician_ID | Primary key, autonumber data type |
| Technician_f_name | Text data type, 25 characters, no validation |
| Technician_surname | Text data type, 25 characters, no validation |
| Title | Text data type, 20 characters, can only be Senior technician, Technician or Junior Technician |
| Mobile | Text data type, 12 characters, number only, no text characters |

# Creating a design specification

| Name and type | |
|---|---|
| **Type:** Form<br>**Name:** Menu<br><br>This form is not linked to any specific table, it just provides a menu to all the other database facilities.<br>Each button links to the appropriate form, query or report. | **Support request menu**<br><br>Add support request     ( Go )<br><br>Update support request     ( Go )<br><br>List all unresolved requests     ( Go )<br><br>List a technician's unresolved requests     ( Go )<br><br>Monthly report on requests by technician     ( Go )<br><br>Monthly report on requests by customer     ( Go )<br><br>Report on time taken to resolve requests     ( Go ) |
| **Type:** Form<br>**Name:** Add_request<br><br>This form allows input of a new support request. It is a data entry form. The customer name and technician allocated data is picked up off the Customer and Technician tables, and the primary key field for each is inserted in the Support_request table as a foreign key.<br>The Save button saves the record, the Cancel button closes the form without saving the record. | **Add support request**<br><br>Choose customer: [ ▽ ] ← Drop-down box linked to the Customer table. Lists customer name, inserts Customer_ID in the Support_request table.<br><br>Reported by:<br><br>    First Name: [ ] ← Input boxes for the Reported_by_f_name and Reported_by_surname fields.<br><br>    Surname: [ ]<br><br>Date/time reported   [ dd/mm/yy   hh:mm ]<br><br>Problem description: [              ]<br><br>Technician allocated: [ ▽ ] ← Drop-down box linked to the Technician table. Lists technician name, inserts Technician_ID in the Support_request table.<br><br>( Save )     ( Cancel ) |
| **Type:** Form<br>**Name:** Update_ support_request<br><br>This form allows an update to be made on an existing support request. It is based on a query which uses the Request_ID (which the user enters as a parameter for the query) as a criterion and brings together the Customer, Technician and Support_request tables. | **Update support request**<br><br>Customer:     Xxxxxxxxxxxx ← These fields are displayed but are locked and cannot be changed.<br><br>Reported by:<br><br>    First Name:    Xxxxxxxxxxxx<br><br>    Surname:    Xxxxxxxxxxxx<br><br>Date/time reported   dd/mm/yy hh:mm<br><br>Problem description: [            ]<br><br>Technician allocated: [ ▽ ]<br><br>Resolved:     *<br><br>Date/time reported    dd/mm/yy hh:mm ← These fields in the lower half of the form can be updated.<br><br>Problem description: ( Save )    ( Cancel ) |

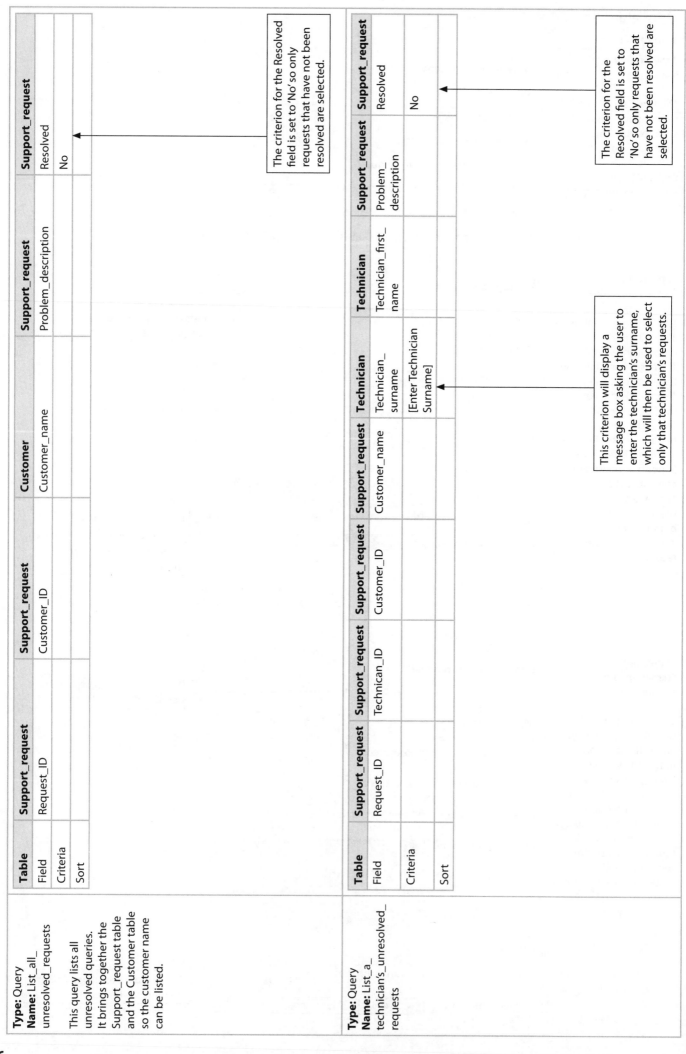

**Type:** Query
**Name:** List_all_unresolved_requests

This query lists all unresolved queries. It brings together the Support_request table and the Customer table so the customer name can be listed.

| Table | Support_request | Support_request | Customer | Support_request | Support_request |
|---|---|---|---|---|---|
| Field | Request_ID | Customer_ID | Customer_name | Problem_description | Resolved |
| Criteria | | | | | No |
| Sort | | | | | |

The criterion for the Resolved field is set to 'No' so only requests that have not been resolved are selected.

**Type:** Query
**Name:** List_a_technician's_unresolved_requests

| Table | Support_request | Support_request | Support_request | Support_request | Technician | Technician | Support_request | Support_request |
|---|---|---|---|---|---|---|---|---|
| Field | Request_ID | Technican_ID | Customer_ID | Customer_name | Technician_surname | Technician_first_name | Problem_description | Resolved |
| Criteria | | | | | [Enter Technician Surname] | | | No |
| Sort | | | | | | | | |

This criterion will display a message box asking the user to enter the technician's surname, which will then be used to select only that technician's requests.

The criterion for the Resolved field is set to 'No' so only requests that have not been resolved are selected.

**Type:** Report
**Name:** Monthly report of support requests by technician

This report is based on a query which brings together the Technican, Customer and Support_request tables. The criterion for the query is the month required.
The report groups the output by technician, listing each request allocated to that technician in the month in question.

**Support requests listed by Technician**

Month:      June 2016

Technician:      Xxxxxxxxx Xxxxxxxxx

| Customer | Date/time reported | Problem | Resolved? |
|---|---|---|---|
| Xxxxxxxxx | dd/mm/yy hh:mm | Xxxxxxxxxxxxxxxxxxxxxxxxx | X |
| Xxxxxxxxx | dd/mm/yy hh:mm | Xxxxxxxxxxxxxxxxxxxxxx | X |
| Xxxxxxxxx | dd/mm/yy hh:mm | Xxxxxxxxxxxxxxxxxxxxxx | X |

Technician:      nnnnnnn nnnnnnn

| Customer | Date/time reported | Problem | Resolved? |
|---|---|---|---|
| Xxxxxxxxx | dd/mm/yy hh:mm | Xxxxxxxxxxxxxxxxxxxxxxxxx | X |

---

**Type:** Report
**Name:** Monthly report of support requests by customer

This report is based on a query which brings together the Technican, Customer and Support_request tables. The criterion for the query is the month required.
The report groups the output by customer, listing all the requests from the customer in the month in question.

**Support requests listed by Customer**

Month:      June 2016

Customer:      Xxxxxxxxxxx

| Technician | Date/time reported | Problem | Resolved? |
|---|---|---|---|
| Xxxxxxxxx | dd/mm/yy hh:mm | Xxxxxxxxxxxxxxxxxxxxxxxxx | X |
| Xxxxxxxxx | dd/mm/yy hh:mm | Xxxxxxxxxxxxxxxxxxxxxx | X |
| Xxxxxxxxx | dd/mm/yy hh:mm | Xxxxxxxxxxxxxxxxxxxxxx | X |

Customer:      Xxxxxxxxxxx

| Technician | Date/time reported | Problem | Resolved? |
|---|---|---|---|
| Xxxxxxxxx | dd/mm/yy hh:mm | Xxxxxxxxxxxxxxxxxxxxxxxxx | X |

---

**Type:** Report
**Name:** Report on time taken to resolve requests

This report is based on a query which brings together the Technican, Customer and Support_request tables. The time to resolve the request is calculated in the query by subtracting the Date_time_reported field from the Date_time_resolved field.

**Time taken to resolve requests**

| Request ID | Customer | Technician | Hours to resolve |
|---|---|---|---|
| nnnnnnn | Xxxxxxxxxxx | Xxxxxxxxxxxxx | hh |
| nnnnnnn | Xxxxxxxxxxx | Xxxxxxxxxxxxx | hh |
| nnnnnnn | Xxxxxxxxxxx | Xxxxxxxxxxxxx | hh |
| nnnnnnn | Xxxxxxxxxxx | Xxxxxxxxxxxxx | hh |

Note that when you carry out a calculation using fields with Date/Time data type, the answer will look a little odd as it is in days, so 19 hours would show as 0.78 days. You can use the DateDiff function in Access to display the result in hours.

## Devising a test plan

| Test Number | Purpose of test | Test data | Expected result | Actual result | Comments and action taken |
|---|---|---|---|---|---|
| **Tests for fields in the Customer table** | | | | | |
| 1 | Customer_name field | Joe Smith and Co | Accepted | | |
| 2 | Address field | 26 The Avenue | Accepted | | |
| 3 | Town field | Bristol | Accepted | | |
| 4 | Postcode field | a4bbx | Rejected | | |
| 5 | Postcode field | BR99 1ZZ | Accepted | | |
| **Tests for fields in the Support_request table** | | | | | |
| 6 | Customer_ID field referential integrity | 9 | Rejected (no Customer_ID 9) | | |
| 7 | Customer_ID field referential integrity | 4 | Accepted | | |
| 8 | Technician_ID field referential integrity | 8 | Rejected (no Technician_ID 8) | | |
| 9 | Technician_ID field referential integrity | 1 | Accepted | | |
| 10 | Reported_by_first_name | Alice | Accepted | | |
| 11 | Reported_by_surname | Scott | Accepted | | |
| 12 | Date_time_reported | 30/12/2052 09:30:00 | Rejected (in the future) | | |
| 13 | Date_time_reported | 32/13/16 28:30:00 | Rejected (not a valid date) | | |
| 14 | Date_time_reported | 6/6/16 09:30:00 | Accepted | | |
| 15 | Problem_description | Mouse does not work | Accepted | | |
| 16 | Resolved | Yes | Accepted | | |
| 17 | Date_time_resolved | 24/11/2032 10:30:00 | Rejected (in the future) | | |
| 18 | Date_time_resolved | 9/14/16 08:45:00 | Rejected (not a valid date) | | |
| 19 | Date_time_resolved | 5/6/16 10:30:00 | Accepted | | |
| 20 | Resolution_description | Replaced mouse | Accepted | | |
| **Tests for fields in the Technician table** | | | | | |
| 21 | Technician_first_name | Winston | Accepted | | |
| 22 | Technician_surname | Jamal | Accepted | | |
| 23 | Title | Head Technician | Rejected | | |
| 24 | Title | Junior Technican | Accepted | | |
| 25 | Mobile | ABC123 | Rejected | | |
| 26 | Mobile | 07222 33333 | Accepted | | |

# Database development and testing

## Guided activities

### 1 My database development screenshots

The first task I completed was to create the **(a) tables**, using my data **(b) dictionary** as a guide.

I have added an **(c) input mask** for the Postcode field.

This is the **(d) Support_requests** table.

I have added a **(e) validation** rule with validation text for the Date_time_reported and **(f) Date_time_resolved** fields.

This is the **(g) Technician** table.

I have used a **(h) lookup** table to provide validation for the **(i) Title** field. The list contains three options: **(j) Senior** Technician, Technician and **(k) Junior** Technician.

### 2
4 Follow the steps in the text import wizard.

2 From the External Data menu, choose Text file.

1 Create or open a database.

3 Find the file you need to import and choose to import it into a new table.

### 3 Importing data

The next task I completed was importing the sample **(a) data**. I used the Import Text **(b) Wizard**.

Once the data had been imported I used Append queries to split it up into the **(c) tables** I created before.

Once the data was imported, I checked the **(d) foreign** keys in the Support_requests table. I was then able to create the **(e) relationships** between the tables. Here are the **(f) relationships** I created.

### 4 Creating the objects

This is the Add support requests **(a) form**.

This is a data **entry (b)** form. The user can select, the **(c) customer** and technician using **(d) drop-down** boxes which link to the Customer and Technician tables.

This is the **(e) Update support request** form.

These are the **(f) queries** I created.

The design view of the **(g) query** for listing all unresolved requests looks like this.

This **(h) criterion** is set to 'No' so only requests which have not been **(i) resolved** are selected.

The **(j) output/result** of the query looks like this.

Here is the **(k) design** view of the query for listing a technician's unresolved support requests.

This **(l) criterion** will ask the user for the technician's **(m) surname**.

This is the result when the user enters the surname **(n) Platt** and the query is **(o) run**.

Next I completed my **(p) reports**.

This is the report for listing support requests by **(q) technician**. To run the report the user enters the number of the **(r) month** that they want for the report.

This is the report for listing support requests by **(s) customer**. The user needs to enter the month number to **(t) run** this report.

This is the report for showing the **(u) time** taken to resolve support requests.

Once all the forms, reports and queries were complete, I created the **(v) menu** form, which has **(w) buttons** to access all the objects.

## Database testing

| Test Number | Purpose of test | Test data | Expected result | Actual result | Comments and action taken |
|---|---|---|---|---|---|
| **Test for fields in the Customer table** | | | | | |
| 1 | Customer_name field | Joe Smith and Co | Accepted | Accepted | |
| 2 | Address field | 26 The Avenue | Accepted | Accepted | |
| 3 | Town field | Bristol | Accepted | Accepted | |
| 4 | Postcode field | a4bbx | Rejected | Rejected | The input mask converts the lower case characters to upper case automatically and will not allow a digit in the second character. |
| | | | | | Here you can see the input mask working. |
| | | | | | |
| 5 | Postcode field | BR99 1ZZ | Accepted | Accepted | |

89

| Test for fields in the Support_request table | | | | | |
|---|---|---|---|---|---|
| 6 | Customer_ID field referential integrity | 9 | Rejected (no customer_ID 9) | Rejected | |
| | 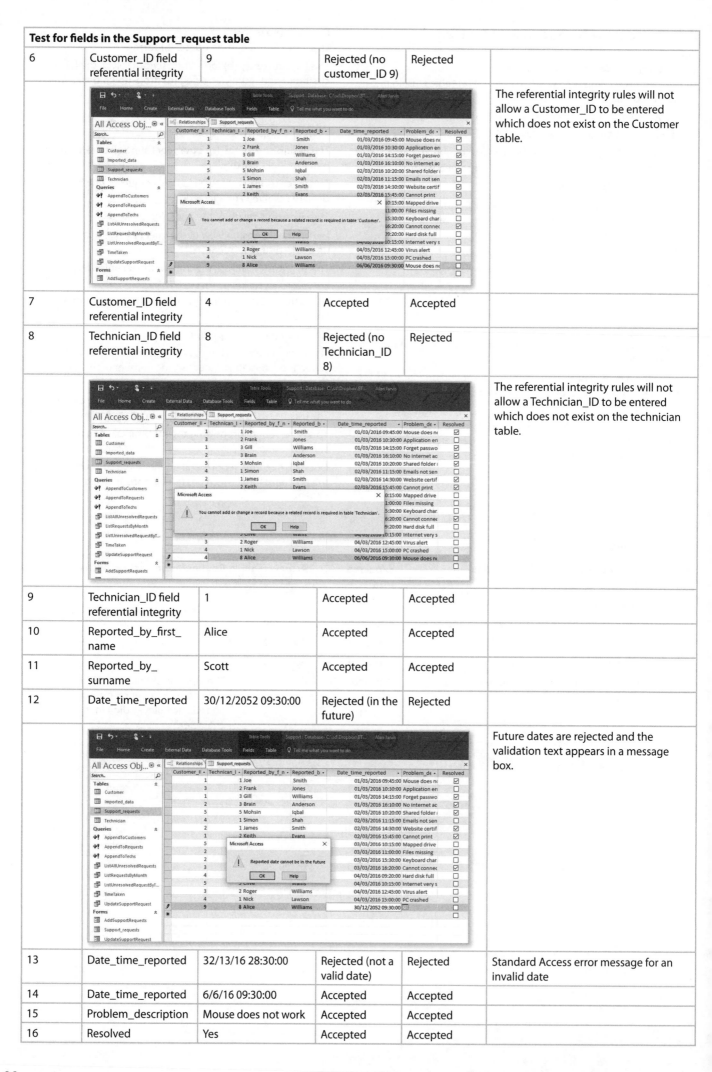 | | | | The referential integrity rules will not allow a Customer_ID to be entered which does not exist on the Customer table. |
| 7 | Customer_ID field referential integrity | 4 | Accepted | Accepted | |
| 8 | Technician_ID field referential integrity | 8 | Rejected (no Technician_ID 8) | Rejected | |
| | | | | | The referential integrity rules will not allow a Technician_ID to be entered which does not exist on the technician table. |
| 9 | Technician_ID field referential integrity | 1 | Accepted | Accepted | |
| 10 | Reported_by_first_name | Alice | Accepted | Accepted | |
| 11 | Reported_by_surname | Scott | Accepted | Accepted | |
| 12 | Date_time_reported | 30/12/2052 09:30:00 | Rejected (in the future) | Rejected | |
| | | | | | Future dates are rejected and the validation text appears in a message box. |
| 13 | Date_time_reported | 32/13/16 28:30:00 | Rejected (not a valid date) | Rejected | Standard Access error message for an invalid date |
| 14 | Date_time_reported | 6/6/16 09:30:00 | Accepted | Accepted | |
| 15 | Problem_description | Mouse does not work | Accepted | Accepted | |
| 16 | Resolved | Yes | Accepted | Accepted | |

| 17 | Date_time_resolved | 24/11/2032 10:30:00 | Rejected (in the future) | Rejected | |
|---|---|---|---|---|---|
| | 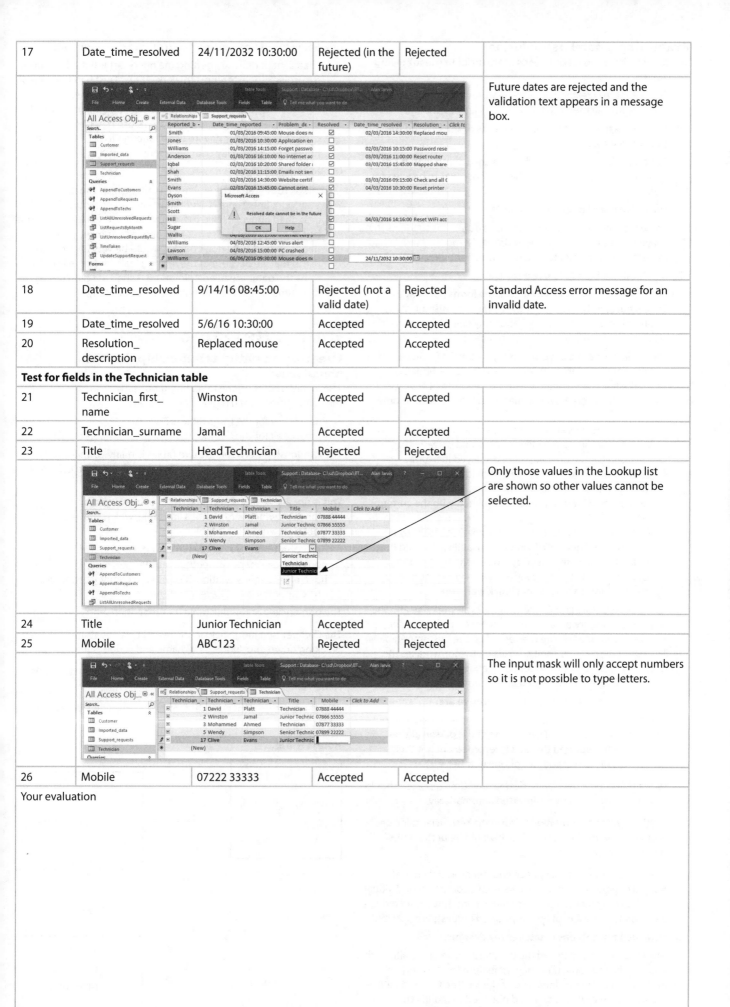 | | | | Future dates are rejected and the validation text appears in a message box. |
| 18 | Date_time_resolved | 9/14/16 08:45:00 | Rejected (not a valid date) | Rejected | Standard Access error message for an invalid date. |
| 19 | Date_time_resolved | 5/6/16 10:30:00 | Accepted | Accepted | |
| 20 | Resolution_description | Replaced mouse | Accepted | Accepted | |

**Test for fields in the Technician table**

| 21 | Technician_first_name | Winston | Accepted | Accepted | |
|---|---|---|---|---|---|
| 22 | Technician_surname | Jamal | Accepted | Accepted | |
| 23 | Title | Head Technician | Rejected | Rejected | |
| | | | | | Only those values in the Lookup list are shown so other values cannot be selected. |
| 24 | Title | Junior Technician | Accepted | Accepted | |
| 25 | Mobile | ABC123 | Rejected | Rejected | |
| | | | | | The input mask will only accept numbers so it is not possible to type letters. |
| 26 | Mobile | 07222 33333 | Accepted | Accepted | |

Your evaluation

## Evaluating a database solution

**(a) My database meets the needs of the brief in the following ways:**

The database I created has all the features listed in the Task Scenario and all the main features work as they should.

**(b) My database failed to meet the needs of the brief in the following ways:**

Although all the features work, there are a number of things that would need improving if this database was to be used for real.

**(c) During testing I discovered that:**

There were no errors in the tests I have done. This suggests that I have not tested the database thoroughly enough, and if I had more time I would create a more comprehensive test plan.

**(d) My database is easy to use because:**

Everything is labelled clearly and all the forms have Save and Cancel buttons. The layout for the forms is consistent (same colour scheme and fonts used) and fairly neat. The reports are also neat and consistent and clearly labelled.

**(e) I could improve the usability of my database in these ways:**

- Some of the labels on the forms still have the underscores for the field names (e.g. date_time_reported). These should be removed and the name made clear (e.g. Date and time reported).
- When the queries are run from the main menu there is no button to return to the menu, so it would be easier to use if the results of the queries where displayed in a form.
- On the Update support request form it would be better if, when you click the resolved check box, the date and time resolved field is automatically completed with the current date and time.
- When a user wants to update a support request, they need to know the request ID. To improve usability, it would be better if there were other ways to search for a support request, such as by company or person who reported it.

**(f) Elements of my database that work well are:**

The table structure and relationship links all work fine and the referential integrity options ensure, for example, that a support request record must relate to a record on the Customer table. The use of drop-down combo boxes on the form makes the user select a valid customer for each request. I think the reports also work fine and do not need any improvement.

**(g) Elements of my database I could improve are:**

There is not really enough information on the database about the customer. For example, the name of the person at the company who reported the fault is recorded but not their contact details (email address, phone number, etc).

When reporting a new fault, the date and time reported should have the current date/time inserted automatically.

On the Update support request form the technician allocated is only shown by their ID number. It would be better if their name was shown.

The database should really have another table linked to the Support_request table that allows each update to an individual request to be recorded on a separate record. This would require a complete re-design of how supported requests are updated.

**(h) How well my database matches my designs:**

My design mostly matched the database I developed, although I had to change some minor layout features of the forms and reports as I went along. The designs of the ERD and data dictionary were correct and I did not need to modify them.

**(i) Some problems I encountered during development:**

I had a lot of difficulty getting the query behind the Time taken to resolve requests report to work. At first I just had the date of resolving the request subtracted from the date of reporting it. This gave me the number of days, when it would make much more sense to give the result as the hours. I spent some time trying to remember how to use a function to display just the hours, and eventually I got it to work.

**(j) In conclusion,**

I think my database does have all the required functions and they work fine. There is a lot more refinement I could do (as described above) if I had more time. I think the database might be OK as a prototype to get user opinions as to what else needs adding, but I don't think it would be very effective for use in real life because of the missing features I have listed. I think the database needs a lot more testing as I didn't really have time to test the forms and queries properly.

# Unit 2: Revision task 2

## Creating an entity relationship diagram

**Normalisation:**

1NF involves splitting the repeating groups. These are the dogs and the competitions. Each needs a primary key:

- Primary key for the Dogs table is Dog_ID
- Primary key for the Competitions table is Competiton_ID.

The relationship between the two tables is many-to-many as one dog can be in many competitions and one competition can have many dogs entered.

This is not allowed, so I apply the rules of many-to-many relationships which is to create a link table, which I have called Competition_entries. This table:

- has a one-to-many relationship with the Dogs table, since one dog can have many competition entries
- has a one-to-many relationship with the competition table, since one competition can have many entries.

The primary key of this link table is Competition_entry_ID.

The Competition judge field in the raw data is not atomic – it needs breaking down into Judge_first_name and Judge_surname.

2NF: a composite key is not used so there is nothing to do at this stage.

3NF: there are no dependences for the non-key fields in any of the tables.

**Here is the ERD**

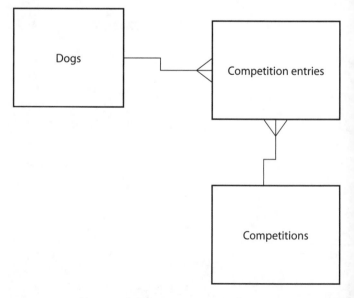

# Creating a data dictionary

| Table Name: | Dogs |
|---|---|
| **Field name** | **Attributes** |
| Dog_ID | Primary key, autonumber data type |
| Dog_name | Text, 25 characters, no validation |
| Dog_breed | Text, 25 characters, no validation |
| Date_of_birth | Date, cannot be in the future |
| Owner_first_name | Text, 25 characters, no validation |
| Owner_surname | Text, 25 characters, no validation |

| Table Name: | Competitions |
|---|---|
| **Field name** | **Attributes** |
| Competition_ID | Primary key, autonumber data type |
| Competition_name | Text, 25 characters, no validation |
| Competition_time | Time, must be a valid time |
| Judge_first_name | Text, 25 characters, no validation |
| Judge_surname | Text, 25 characters, no validation |
| Winner | Text, 25 characters, must be a dog's name entered for this competition |

| Table Name: | Competition_entries |
|---|---|
| **Field name** | **Attributes** |
| Entry_ID | Primary key, autonumber data type |
| Dog_ID | Foreign key linking to the dogs table, integer data type |
| Competition_ID | Foreign key linking to the competition table, integer data type |

# Creating a design specification

| Name and type | |
|---|---|
| **Type:** Form<br>**Name:** Menu<br><br>This form is not linked to any specific table, it just provides a menu to all the other database facilities | **Byford dog show**<br><br>Add new dog    [ Go ]<br><br>Add new competition entry    [ Go ]<br><br>Enter winning dog details    [ Go ]<br><br>List all dogs for a competition    [ Go ]<br><br>List competitions for a dog    [ Go ]<br><br>Breed entered for a competition    [ Go ]<br><br>All dogs born after 1/1/2013    [ Go ]<br><br>Winning dog report    [ Go ]<br><br>Competition report    [ Go ]<br><br>Competition entries for a dog report    [ Go ] |

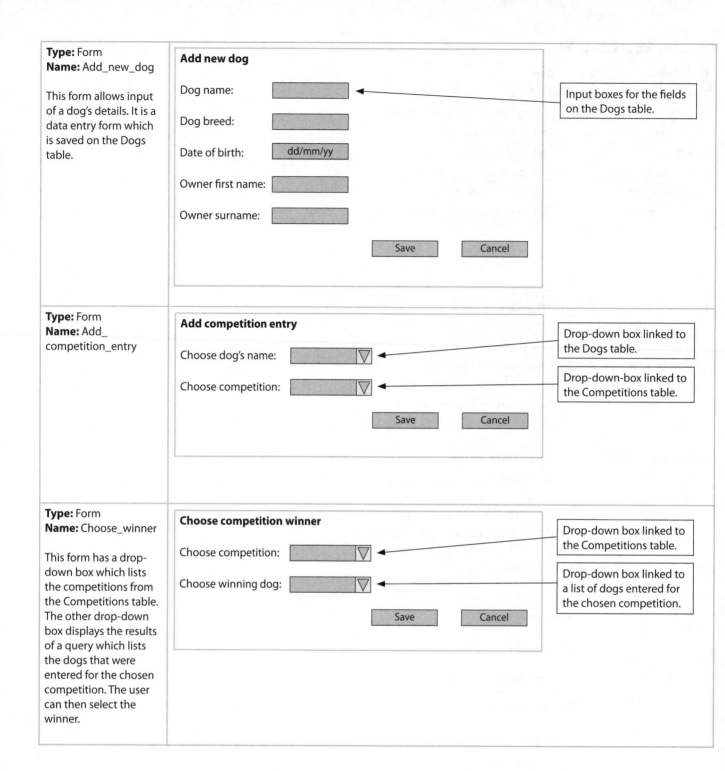

**Type:** Form
**Name:** Add_new_dog

This form allows input of a dog's details. It is a data entry form which is saved on the Dogs table.

**Add new dog**

Dog name:

Dog breed:

Date of birth: dd/mm/yy

Owner first name:

Owner surname:

Save     Cancel

Input boxes for the fields on the Dogs table.

**Type:** Form
**Name:** Add_competition_entry

**Add competition entry**

Choose dog's name:

Choose competition:

Save     Cancel

Drop-down box linked to the Dogs table.

Drop-down-box linked to the Competitions table.

**Type:** Form
**Name:** Choose_winner

This form has a drop-down box which lists the competitions from the Competitions table. The other drop-down box displays the results of a query which lists the dogs that were entered for the chosen competition. The user can then select the winner.

**Choose competition winner**

Choose competition:

Choose winning dog:

Save     Cancel

Drop-down box linked to the Competitions table.

Drop-down box linked to a list of dogs entered for the chosen competition.

**Type:** Query
**Name:** Dogs_entered_in_competition

| Table | Competitions | Competitions | Competitions | Dogs |
|---|---|---|---|---|
| **Field** | Competition_ID | Competition_name | Competition_time | Dog_name |
| **Criteria** | [Enter competition ID] | | | |
| **Sort** | | | | |

Criteria here asks the user for the competition ID to use as a criterion to select the competition.

**Type:** Query
**Name:** Competitions_by_dog

| Table | Dogs | Dogs | Dogs | Dogs | Competitions |
|---|---|---|---|---|---|
| **Field** | Dog_ID | Dog_name | Owner_first_name | Owner_surname | Competition_name |
| **Criteria** | | [Enter dog name] | | | |
| **Sort** | | | | | |

Criteria here asks the user for the dog name to use as a criterion to select the dog.

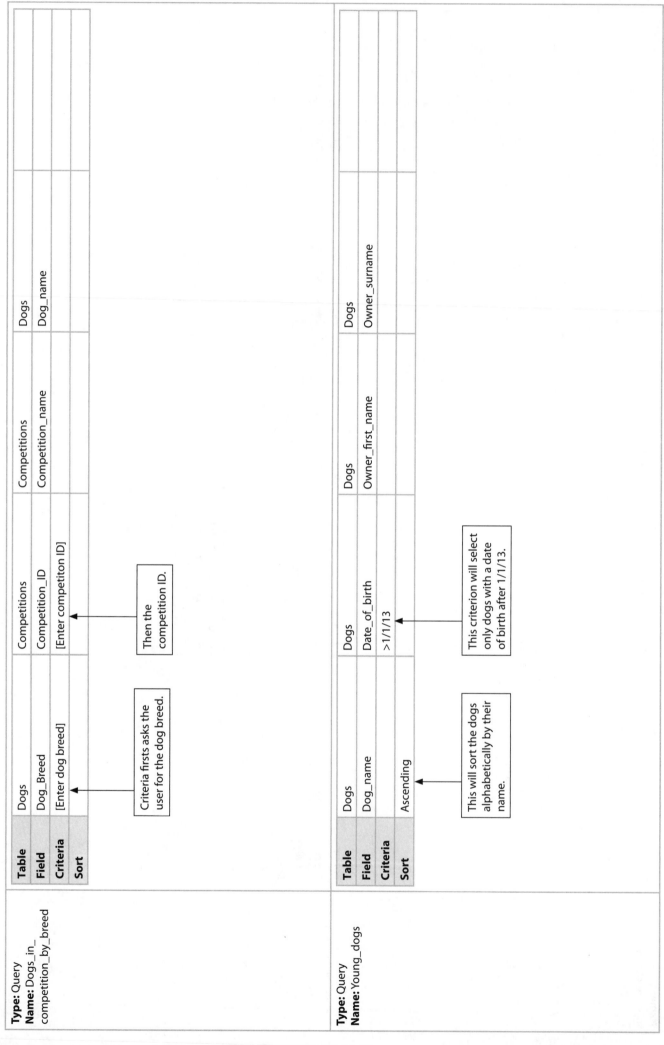

**Type:** Query
**Name:** Dogs_in_competition_by_breed

| Table | Dogs | Competitions | Competitions | Dogs |
|---|---|---|---|---|
| **Field** | Dog_Breed | Competition_ID | Competition_name | Dog_name |
| **Criteria** | [Enter dog breed] | [Enter competiton ID] | | |
| **Sort** | | | | |

Criteria firsts asks the user for the dog breed.

Then the competition ID.

**Type:** Query
**Name:** Young_dogs

| Table | Dogs | Dogs | Dogs | Dogs |
|---|---|---|---|---|
| **Field** | Dog_name | Date_of_birth | Owner_first_name | Owner_surname |
| **Criteria** | | >1/1/13 | | |
| **Sort** | Ascending | | | |

This will sort the dogs alphabetically by their name.

This criterion will select only dogs with a date of birth after 1/1/13.

**Type:** Report
**Name:** Certificate

This shows the winning dog for a given competition in the format of a certificate.

---

### Certificate

Congratulations to

Nnnnnnnn

Owned by: Xxxxxxxxxxx

For winning the

Xxxxxxxxxxxx

category

At Byford Dog Show 2016

---

**Type:** Report
**Name:** Entries_report

This lists the details (including dogs entered) of a given competition.
It uses a query to bring together the data from the Competition_entries table which identifies which dogs are entered in a competition. Other details are selected from the Dogs and Competitions tables. The query sorts the data by owner.

**Entries report**
**Competition:** Xxxxxxxxxxxx       **Time:HH:MM**

| Dog name | Breed | Owner |
|---|---|---|
| Xxxxxxxxxxx Xxxxxxxxxxx | Xxxxxxxxx | Xxxxxxxxxx |
| Xxxxxxxxxxx Xxxxxxxxxxx | Xxxxxxxxx | Xxxxxxxxxx |
| Xxxxxxxxxxx Xxxxxxxxxxx | Xxxxxxxxx | Xxxxxxxxxx |
| Xxxxxxxxxxx Xxxxxxxxxxx | Xxxxxxxxx | Xxxxxxxxxx |

---

**Type:** Report
**Name:** Competitions_for_your_dog

**Competitions for your dog**
**Dog:** Xxxxxxxxxxx
**Owner:** Xxxxxxxxxxx Xxxxxxxxxxx

| Competition | Time | Judge |
|---|---|---|
| Xxxxxxxxxxx Xxxxxxxxxxx | Xxxxxxxxx | Xxxxxxxxxx |
| Xxxxxxxxxxx Xxxxxxxxxxx | Xxxxxxxxx | Xxxxxxxxxx |
| Xxxxxxxxxxx Xxxxxxxxxxx | Xxxxxxxxx | Xxxxxxxxxx |

## Devising a test plan
**Examples of possible tests**

| Test Number | Purpose of Test | Test Data | Expected result | Actual result | Comments and action taken |
|---|---|---|---|---|---|
| **Tests for fields in the Dogs table** | | | | | |
| 1 | Dog_name | Alfie | Accepted | | |
| 2 | Dog_breed | Poodle | Accepted | Accepted | |
| 3 | Date_of_birth | 10/9/2022 | Rejected (in the future) | Rejected | |
| 4 | Date_of_birth | 13/6/2012 | Accepted | Accepted | |
| 5 | Owner_first_name | Shafina | Accepted | Accepted | |
| 6 | Owner_surname | Ahmed | Accepted | Accepted | |
| **Tests for fields in the Competitions table** | | | | | |
| 7 | Competition_name | Best looking dog | Accepted | Accepted | |
| 8 | Competition_time | 56:97 | Rejected (invalid time) | Rejected | |
| 9 | Competition_time | 16:30 | Accepted | | |
| 10 | Judge_first_name | Bernard | Accepted | | |
| 11 | Judge_surname | Irons | Accepted | | |
| 12 | Winner | Shep | Rejected | | Need to ensure this dog **is not** entered for this competition |
| 13 | Winner | Alfie | Accepted | | Need to ensure this dog **is** entered for this competition |
| **Tests for fields in Competitions_entries table** | | | | | |
| 14 | Dog_ID | 99 | Rejected (no Dog_ID on the Dogs table) | | |
| 15 | Dog_ID | 1 | Accepted | | |
| 16 | Competition_ID | 50 | Rejected (no Competition_ID on the Competition table) | | |
| 17 | Competition_ID | 3 | Accepted | | |

## Database development and testing – an example solution (any working solution is valid and may differ from that given here)
**My database screenshots**

The first task I completed was to create the tables, using my data dictionary as a guide.

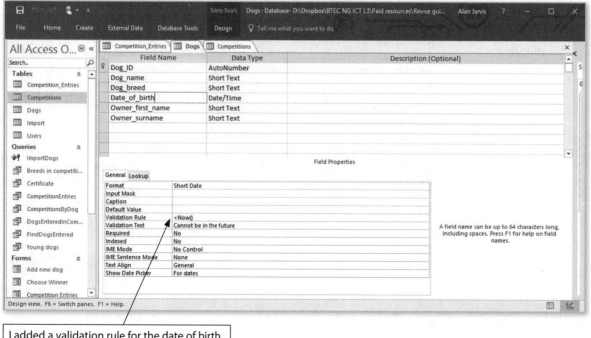

I added a validation rule for the date of birth.

This is the table design for the Competitions table.

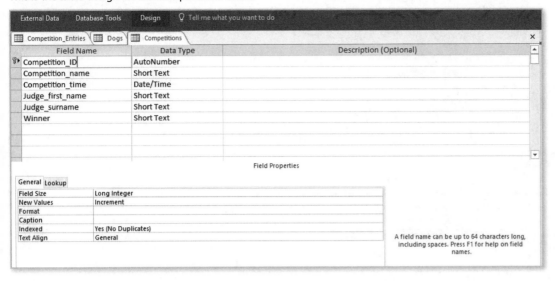

And this is the table design for the Competition_Entries table.

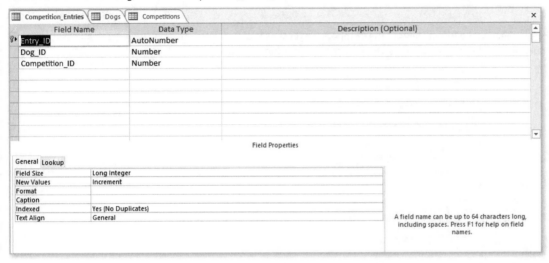

Then I imported the sample data using the Import Text Wizard:

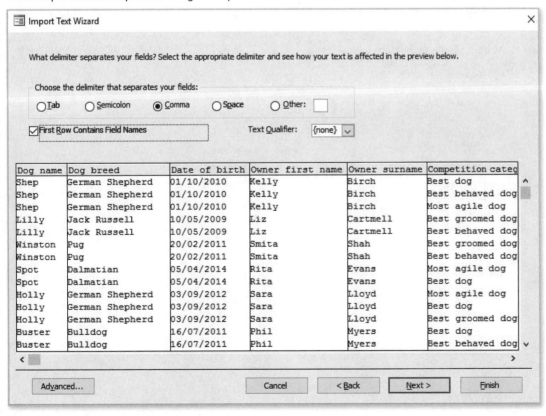

This is one of the steps of the Import Text Wizard. Once the data had been imported I used Append queries to split it up into the tables I created before.

Here is the Append query I used to put records in the Dogs table:

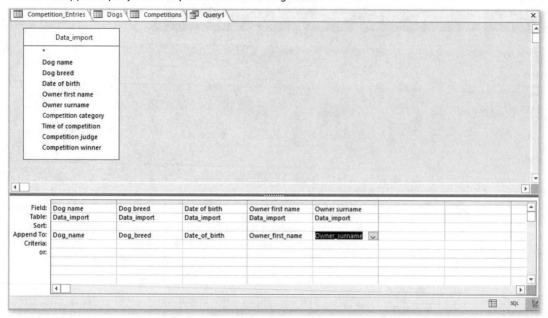

Once the data was imported and I checked the foreign keys in the Competition_Entries table, I was then able to create the relationships between the tables. Here are the relationships I created.

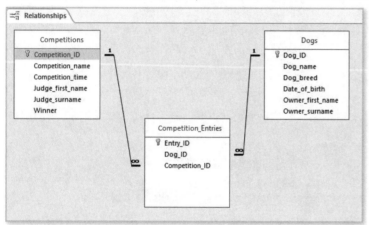

The next task was to create the forms.

This is the form I created to enter a new dog's details to the dogs table:

This form is used to add a dog to a competition. It inserts a record on the competition entries table:

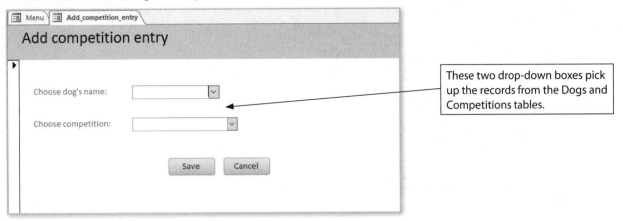

These two drop-down boxes pick up the records from the Dogs and Competitions tables.

Finally, this form is used to select the winner for a competition:

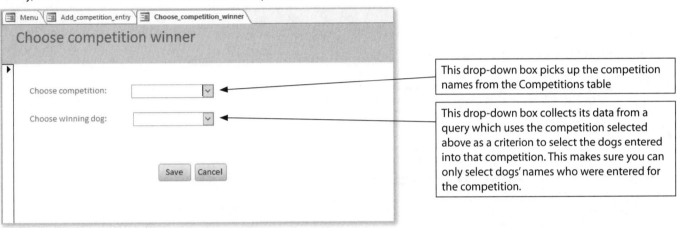

This drop-down box picks up the competition names from the Competitions table

This drop-down box collects its data from a query which uses the competition selected above as a criterion to select the dogs entered into that competition. This makes sure you can only select dogs' names who were entered for the competition.

Here are the queries I created. The first one selects all the dogs entered for a particular competition. This is the design view:

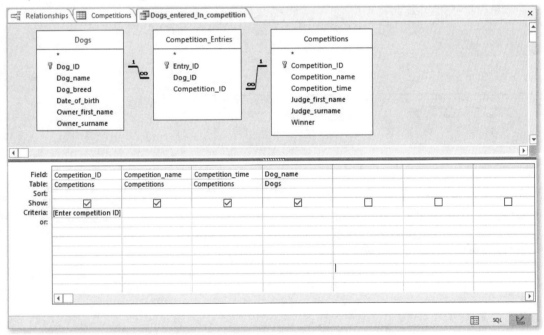

This is the output if competition number 1 is entered:

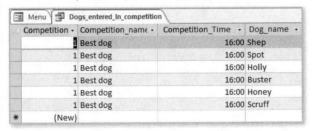

The second one selects all the competitions a particular dog is entered for:

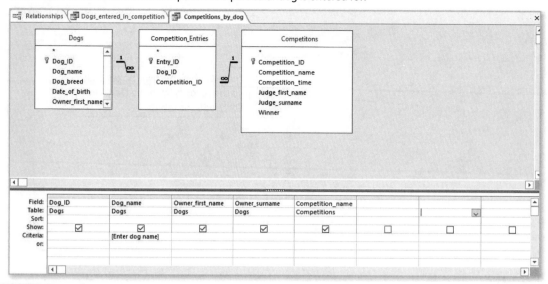

This is the output when the dog name 'Shep' is entered:

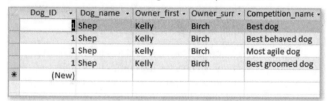

This is the design view of the query that shows all the dogs of a given breed entered for a competition:

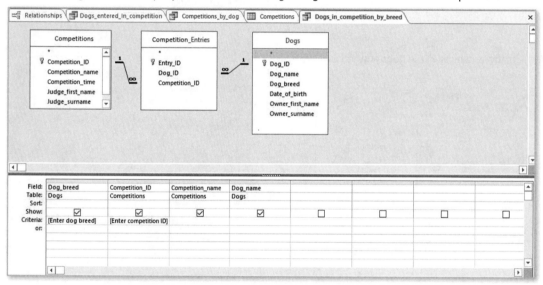

This is the query run with the breed 'Pug' and Competition_ID 1 entered:

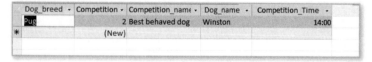

The final query lists all dogs born after 1/1/2013. This is the design view:

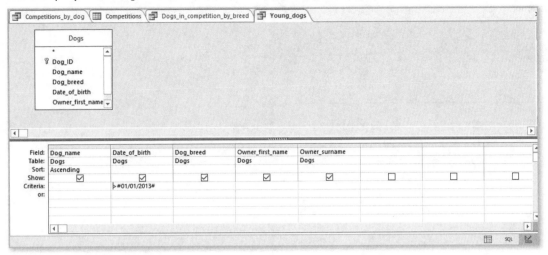

And this is the query running:

These are the reports that I created:

Here is the certificate for the winning dog. The query that provides the data for this report asks you for the competition number. This is the certificate for competition 1:

## Certificate

Congratulations to:

**Shep**

Owned by :

Kelly    Birch

For winning the:

**Best dog**

category

at the Byford Dog Show 2016

This is the report of all the dogs entered for the competition number entered by the user, sorted by owner surname:

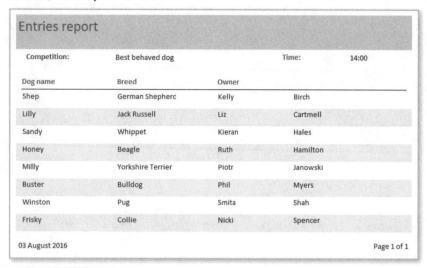

**Entries report**

| Competition: | Best behaved dog | | Time: | 14:00 |
|---|---|---|---|---|
| **Dog name** | **Breed** | **Owner** | | |
| Shep | German Shepherd | Kelly | Birch | |
| Lilly | Jack Russell | Liz | Cartmell | |
| Sandy | Whippet | Kieran | Hales | |
| Honey | Beagle | Ruth | Hamilton | |
| Milly | Yorkshire Terrier | Piotr | Janowski | |
| Buster | Bulldog | Phil | Myers | |
| Winston | Pug | Smita | Shah | |
| Frisky | Collie | Nicki | Spencer | |

| 03 August 2016 | Page 1 of 1 |
|---|---|

This is the report which lists all the competitions for a given dog (whose name is entered by the user):

**Competitions for your dog**

| Dog's name | Shep | | | |
|---|---|---|---|---|
| Owner: | Kelly | Birch | | |
| **Competition** | **Time** | *Judge* | | |
| Best behaved dog | 14:00 | Simon | Jones | |
| Best groomed dog | 15:00 | Anita | Patel | |
| Most agile dog | 15:30 | Eric | Smith | |
| Best dog | 16:00 | Alice | Wilson | |

| 03 August 2016 | Page 1 of 1 |
|---|---|

Once I had developed all the forms, queries and reports, I created the main menu:

**Byford Dog Show**

| | |
|---|---|
| Add new dog | Go |
| Add new competition entry | Go |
| Enter winning dog details | Go |
| List all dogs for a competition | Go |
| List competitions for a dog | Go |
| Winning dog report | Go |
| Breed entered for a competition | Go |
| All dogs born after 1/1/2013 | Go |
| Competition report | Go |
| Competition entries for a dog report | Go |

## Byford Dog Show

Winning dog report      [ Go ]

Competition report      [ Go ]

Competition entries for a dog report      [ Go ]

**Testing results**

| Test Number | Purpose of Test | Test Data | Expected result | Actual result | Comments and action taken |
|---|---|---|---|---|---|
| 1 | Dog_name in Dogs table | Alfie | Accepted | Accepted | |
| 2 | Dog_breed in Dogs table | Poodle | Accepted | Accepted | |
| 3 | Date_of_birth in Dogs table | 10/9/2022 | Rejected (in the future) | Rejected | |

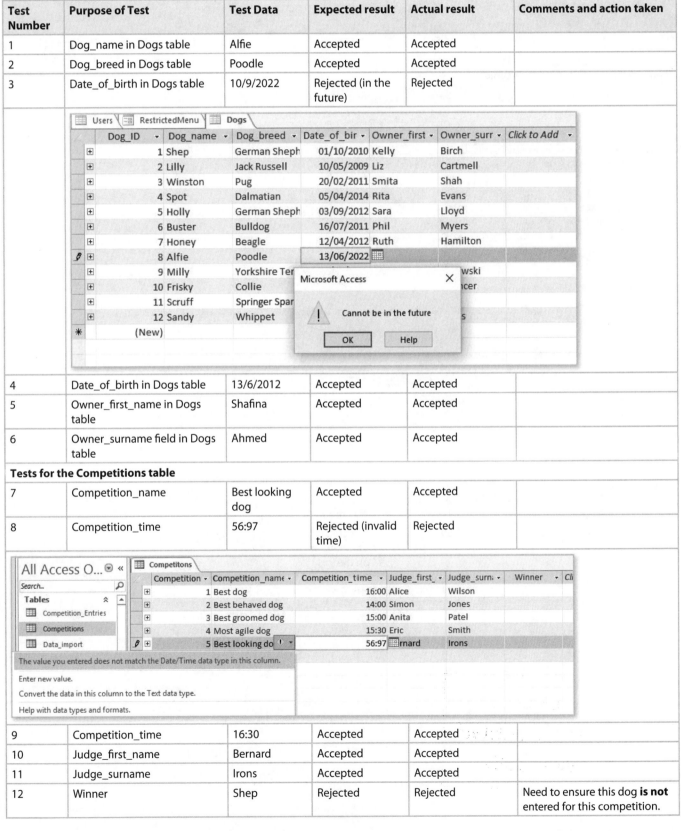

| | | | | | |
|---|---|---|---|---|---|
| 4 | Date_of_birth in Dogs table | 13/6/2012 | Accepted | Accepted | |
| 5 | Owner_first_name in Dogs table | Shafina | Accepted | Accepted | |
| 6 | Owner_surname field in Dogs table | Ahmed | Accepted | Accepted | |

**Tests for the Competitions table**

| 7 | Competition_name | Best looking dog | Accepted | Accepted | |
|---|---|---|---|---|---|
| 8 | Competition_time | 56:97 | Rejected (invalid time) | Rejected | |

| 9 | Competition_time | 16:30 | Accepted | Accepted | |
|---|---|---|---|---|---|
| 10 | Judge_first_name | Bernard | Accepted | Accepted | |
| 11 | Judge_surname | Irons | Accepted | Accepted | |
| 12 | Winner | Shep | Rejected | Rejected | Need to ensure this dog **is not** entered for this competition. |

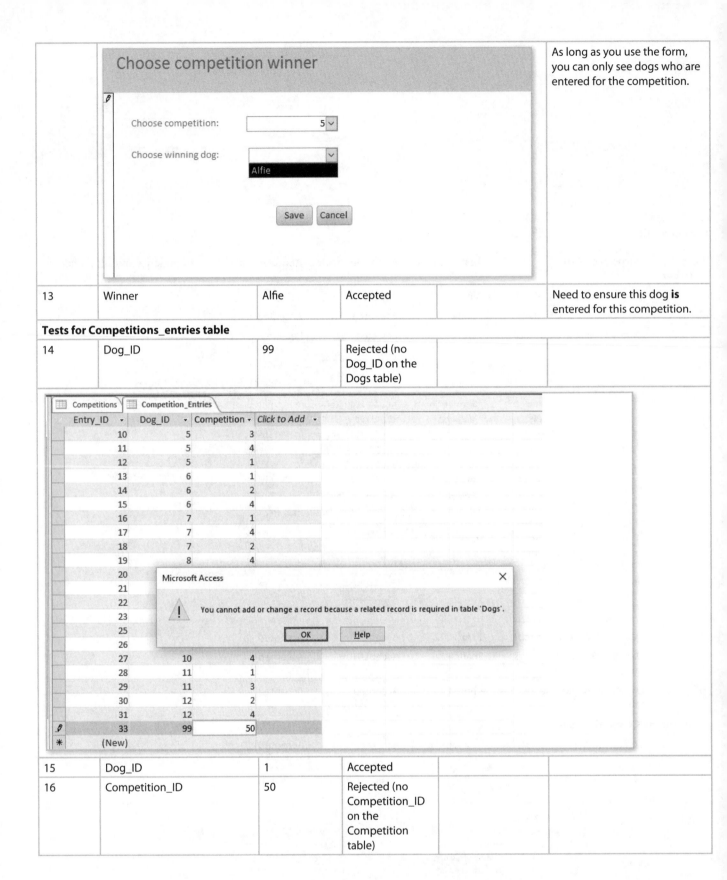

As long as you use the form, you can only see dogs who are entered for the competition.

| 13 | Winner | Alfie | Accepted | | Need to ensure this dog **is** entered for this competition. |

**Tests for Competitions_entries table**

| 14 | Dog_ID | 99 | Rejected (no Dog_ID on the Dogs table) | | |

| 15 | Dog_ID | 1 | Accepted | | |
| 16 | Competition_ID | 50 | Rejected (no Competition_ID on the Competition table) | | |

| Entry_ID | Dog_ID | Competition | Click to Add |
|---|---|---|---|
| 10 | 5 | 3 | |
| 11 | 5 | 4 | |
| 12 | 5 | 1 | |
| 13 | 6 | 1 | |
| 14 | 6 | 2 | |
| 15 | 6 | 4 | |
| 16 | 7 | 1 | |
| 17 | 7 | 4 | |
| 18 | 7 | 2 | |
| 19 | 8 | 4 | |

**Microsoft Access** ✕

⚠ You cannot add or change a record because a related record is required in table 'Competitions'.

[ OK ]  [ Help ]

| 27 | 10 | 4 | |
| 28 | 11 | 1 | |
| 29 | 11 | 3 | |
| 30 | 12 | 2 | |
| 31 | 12 | 4 | |
| 34 | 1 | 50 | |
| (New) | | | |

| 17 | Competition_ID | 3 | Accepted | Accepted | |

## Evaluating a database solution

### How well does my solution meet the requirements of the scenario?

I think my database does a reasonable job of meeting the requirements but there are some areas that need improvement.

My database has consistent menus and forms that are clear and have buttons to save or cancel the action. However, there are some areas where the interface could be made easier to use:

- When making a selection from the drop-down boxes, although the full text of the item being selected is shown when the box drops down, once the selection is made only the ID number is shown. It would be better if the full name remained in the drop-down box.
- Entering dogs into competitions is tedious because for each entry you have to go back to the main menu and choose the option again. It would be better if there was an 'Add another competition' button to make it easy to select another competition for the currently selected dog.

### Evaluation of the quality, performance and usability of the database

I have carried out some testing of the database tables for my database and the field validation and referential integrity all works correctly. However, the way the database is set up allows a user to edit the tables directly rather than using the forms. This means that they could create problems, like entering the same dog for a competition twice or selecting a dog who was not entered into a competition as the winner. The database really needs a separate user interface (perhaps web-based) where the user cannot directly edit the data in the tables. This type of user interface would also need to provide a complete range of options, including the ability to edit and update existing dog and competition entries.

There are some usability issues, as mentioned previously.

### Evaluation of the changes made during the development and testing process

The design I created was correct so I didn't need to make many changes during development, just add a few things I forgot. The testing revealed a few limitations of the system, such as those mentioned above. For example, in the table validation there is no way to prevent users entering the same dog twice into a competition, and the form does not prevent doing this either. The way to correct the form would be to use a query to select dogs which were not already in the selected competition. This query would then provide the list for the dog name drop-down box. I did not have time to implement this.

### Conclusion

I think the database I have designed and created meets some of the requirements of the user, but there is quite a lot which would need to be added or improved to make the database really useful and overcome some of the problems I have described. The designs I created for the tables, ERD and data dictionary were correct. The testing plan was adequate for the tables but the forms, queries and report also need testing.

# A

This boo

# Travel&Tourism

Philip Allan Updates, part of the Hodder Education Group, an Hachette Livre UK company, Market Place, Deddington, Oxfordshire OX15 0SE

*Orders*
Bookpoint Ltd, 130 Milton Park, Abingdon, Oxfordshire, OX14 4SB
tel: 01235 827720
fax: 01235 400454
e-mail: uk.orders@bookpoint.co.uk
Lines are open 9.00 a.m.–5.00 p.m., Monday to Saturday, with a 24-hour message answering service. You can also order through the Philip Allan Updates website:
www.philipallan.co.uk

© Philip Allan Updates 2006

ISBN 978-1-84489-433-8

*Author's acknowledgements*
Thanks as always to Debbie and Katie for inexhaustible patience and support, to Philip Cross and all at Philip Allan Updates. I would also like to thank Julia Warrilow of GNER and all those people in the world of travel and tourism whose professionalism has provided me with inspiration on which to draw, and in particular my friends in Jamaica – McGuiver, Willie and Leon.

Printed in Singapore.

Philip Allan Updates' policy is to use papers that are natural, renewable and recyclable products and made from wood grown in sustainable forests. The logging and manufacturing processes are expected to conform to the environmental regulations of the country of origin.

P01063

# Contents

# Introduction

This textbook has been written to support your learning of A2 Travel and Tourism. It covers the content of the single award units laid down by the AQA, Edexcel and OCR specifications, and some of the double award work. The matrix in the Appendix maps the coverage for all three major awarding bodies' specifications. The *A2 Travel and Tourism Student Workbook*, also published by Philip Allan Updates, accompanies this textbook.

## Course structure

A2 Travel and Tourism is made up of externally assessed (exam) and internally assessed (portfolio) units. For the latter, you have to produce a body of work, which is the evidence of your achievement.

This textbook:
- provides the key knowledge and understanding needed for the examination units
- helps build examination skills, including analysis and evaluation
- builds the knowledge, understanding and skills you need to complete your A2 portfolio work

## Assessment Objectives

Throughout the course you will acquire knowledge, understanding and skills (including research, analysis and evaluation). You will be assessed against four Assessment Objectives (AOs):
- demonstration of knowledge, understanding and skills (AO1)
- application of knowledge, understanding and skills (AO2)
- research and analysis (AO3)
- evaluation (AO4)

## Special features of this book

### Starters

Each topic in this book opens with a short Starter chapter.

- The Starter for Topic 1 lays out a range of issues faced by those who manage travel and tourism.
- In Topic 2, the Starter introduces the management of the human resource which is vital to the success of any travel and tourism organisation.
- Topic 3's Starter presents the range of travel and tourism project and event ideas.
- The Starter for Topic 4 explains what tourism development is and the impacts it has.
- Topic 5 includes chapters on adventure tourism and cultural tourism. The Starter chapter presents a range of special interest travel opportunities provided by the travel and tourism industry.

### Case studies

Real travel and tourism organisations and real destinations are the subjects of case studies that help build your knowledge and understanding of the travel and tourism industry. The case studies in this book are up-to-date at the time of publication.

Case studies are essential learning for examinations and provide a base from which you can launch your own investigations for the portfolio units. It is important that you have a good grasp of a topic before you begin to investigate and assemble your own portfolios.

The range of case studies in this book is wide. They include travel and tourism organisations from across the industry. Destinations and holidays in the UK and overseas, in both the less and more economically developed countries, are also discussed.

### Discussion points

The constantly changing travel and tourism industry and the issues it faces are flagged throughout the book by discussion points suitable for small groups.

### Support your learning

Support your learning is a collection of practical support tips and tasks that closes each chapter of this textbook, under the following headings:

- **Information sources**: this book is a key information source, but the world of travel and tourism is fast moving, and the study of the travel and

tourism industry requires you to exploit a range of other information sources. Each chapter suggests some key information sources for you or your teacher to access.

■ **Skills builder**: each chapter supports skills building and identifies a key skill-building opportunity arising from your learning of that topic. Skills of research, analysis and evaluation are developed in all the units and build up as your study proceeds. Information selection, editing and written communication are further building blocks. Key skills, including communication, ICT and number, are supported.

■ **Activities menu**: at the end of each chapter there is a menu of four activities from which you and your teacher can make selections. Each item on the menu is an activity to support a particular Assessment Objective — one activity per Assessment Objective, in numerical order. Activity 1 is for AO1, Activity 2 is for AO2 and so on. A2 Travel and Tourism is a course with a vocational emphasis. It is about an industry in which people apply the knowledge, understanding and skills that you are learning. The activities menus therefore feature vocational scenarios — settings from the world of the travel and tourism industry from which activities emerge as tasks with real-world application.

### Practical scenarios

Practical scenarios are extended practical activities, which guide you to research real travel and tourism industry organisations, products and places. They aim to help you build knowledge, understanding and skills before you embark on your own independent research for your portfolio units.

## Course advice

### General advice

■ Keep up to date. There are two dimensions to this:

– **Your own work**: the A2 course, like the AS course, does not take long. Starting in the summer or autumn, you will complete the qualification by the next May or June. There is a lot to learn and do in that time, so it is important from the start to stay on schedule with tasks you are set, with your own reading and with your portfolio work. Make yourself a written or electronic schedule and monitor yourself. If minor deviations occur, you can reschedule, but try not to fall a long way behind. If there is a problem, ask your teacher for advice.

– **The changing world of travel and tourism**: this book is as up to date as possible. However, the travel and tourism industry and the real world in which it operates are constantly changing. Use the print and broadcast media, including the specialist travel press such as *Travel Weekly* and the *Travel Trade Gazette*, to keep up to date. Other information sources, including websites like *TravelMole*, are suggested in each chapter as tools to help you.

- Read this book selectively and in bite-size chunks to support your learning in tandem with the teaching you receive. Be aware of the teaching programme and try to read a little ahead of it, reviewing each topic after you have been taught it and coming back to it as part of your revision.

- Know and understand the case studies. These provide valuable knowledge you can use to help you score more marks in the examination. For the portfolio units, the case studies provide you with important insights you can apply to your investigations.

- Practise and develop your skills, including analysis and evaluation. In the activities menu at the end of each chapter, Activities 3 and 4 provide you with analysis and evaluation opportunities. Higher-level skills score higher marks, even more so than at AS, and analysis of research and evaluation are two specific skills that are assessed in all the units of A2 Travel and Tourism.

## Examination advice

- Read each question carefully. Every word in the question will have been chosen intentionally by the examiner, so make sure you read and consider its meaning. Focus on the key words.

- Obey the command words. Each command word requires a specific type of response. Some of the common commands are:
  - **Analyse**: show you understand some statistics or interrelationships in depth by using sentences to break down a subject into its essential elements and explain their links and causes. Come to a conclusion.
  - **Assess**: say how much or how little – for example, how much effect you expect something to have.
  - **Compare and contrast**: compare means to describe the similarities and differences; contrast means to emphasise what the differences are.
  - **Define**: use a sentence to give an exact and concise meaning.
  - **Describe**: write an account of the main features of something in a little more detail using adjectives. There is no need to explain.
  - **Evaluate**: weigh up the point, giving strengths and weaknesses. Write sentences to assess extent (how much?), likelihood (what are the chances of?) or significance (how important?)

- **Explain**: use sentences to clarify why something is at it is, using linking words like 'because' and 'so'.
- **Justify**: use sentences to make clear the reasons behind a decision you have reached or a recommendation you have made.
- **Name**: write what something, someone or somewhere is called. Often, a single word or two is all that is needed. 'Identify', 'give' and 'state' are similar command words.
- **Outline**: use sentences to give just the main points that are needed to make clear that you know and understand something.
- **Suggest reasons for**: this is similar to 'explain', except that there may not be an accepted correct answer. Marks are awarded for thinking out why something might be as it is and coming up with rational ideas.

■ Practise examination-type questions from the specimen paper and past papers published by your exam board, as well as those in the activities menu at the end of each chapter and in the *A2 Travel and Tourism Student Workbook*.

■ Stick to the point with your answers to the questions. Refer back to the question wording to ensure you both satisfy its instruction and avoid irrelevance. Make use of appropriate case-study knowledge to illustrate your points.

■ Revise thoroughly.

## Coursework advice

■ Remember your portfolios are assessments of what you know, understand and are able to do.

■ Learn and understand underpinning theoretical knowledge first. This includes learning and practising the application of your knowledge and understanding to case-study examples of the real travel and tourism industry.

■ Make use of this book and the *A2 Travel and Tourism Student Workbook* that accompanies it, as well as the activities menu at the end of each chapter.

■ You should have acquired the knowledge, understanding and skills needed for at least the first assessment task you are set before embarking upon it.

■ Build each portfolio by completing one assessment task at a time.

■ Give proof of your research by quoting the sources you have used. Good practice is to identify each source within any text you produce and cross-reference it with a list of sources. For example, if you have used some figures from the Statistics on Tourism and Research UK website (**www.staruk.org**), you should name the source next to the figures and quote it again in a 'References' section at the end of your portfolio. If you quote from this book, you could refer to the book in brackets after the quotation in the format '(Rickerby, 2006)' and then give fuller details in the References section as 'Rickerby, S. (2006) *A2 Travel and Tourism*, Philip Allan Updates'.

- Meet deadlines you have agreed or have been set. Consider breaking down an assessment task into several parts and plan mini-deadlines for each part.
- Carefully follow the wording for each assessment task and ensure you do exactly what it says. Make sure you understand what the wording requires at different levels of achievement.
- Aim high.
- Act on feedback to ensure success at your target level of achievement.

# 1

# Current issues
# in travel and tourism

# Starter:
# the issues we face

The travel and tourism industry is a dynamic industry undergoing constant change. **Change** is driven by the need for travel and tourism organisations to respond to issues that are constantly arising. **Issues** are changes or problems about which different people and different organisations hold different views. If everyone agrees that a particular change is acceptable, such as building a new hotel next to a previously undeveloped ('unspoilt') sandy beach, then there is not a problem. People holding views about an issue are called **stakeholders** and they are the subjects of Chapter 1.2.

## Classifying issues

Issues faced by the travel and tourism industry can be grouped under six main headings:
1 technological issues
2 socioeconomic issues
3 consumer-demand issues
4 product development issues
5 political and security issues
6 environmental issues

As Chapter 1.1 shows, these sets of issues arise from changes in the world in which the travel and tourism industry operates, or from changes within the industry itself. For example, technological issues for the travel and tourism industry arise from technological changes that include:
■ new forms of transport — such as super-sized cruise ships (see Figure 1.4) and double-decker super-jumbo airliners such as the Airbus A380 (see Figure 1.6)
■ developing forms of telecommunication — such as the continued growth of the internet and mobile handset technology

These developments happen in the world in which the travel and tourism industry operates. Travel and tourism organisations are then faced with decisions. For example, cruise lines and airlines have to decide if they want to embrace the new technology. Here are some of the questions they need to answer.

- Will ever bigger ships and aeroplanes be economically viable?
- Will they attract sufficient customers?
- Will ports and airports be able to accommodate them?
- Will other stakeholders object to the pollution and noise they create?
- Will they be attractive terrorist targets?

Other organisations, including port and airport authorities, governments, environmental pressure groups, and local communities around cruise destinations and airports will also have views. In this way, issues develop.

Changes in information technology continue to affect the travel and tourism industry. The development of the internet is ongoing and its use by both consumer and business customers of the travel and tourism industry is growing all the time. Organisations such as travel agents, tour operators, accommodation providers, transport providers and visitor attractions are faced with the following questions:

- What changes need to be made to best attract customers?
- Does the internet spell doom to high street travel agents?
- More and more people book online but some customers still prefer face-to-face contact. So, a travel agency chain needs to decide where the balance lies — how many branches does it need and how many staff?

Hand-held mobile technology (not always literally 'hand-held') is bringing new opportunities to the industry. Tour guides (including, in the UK, qualified Blue Badge guides) have traditionally been employed to show groups of tourists around destinations such as the historic cities of Chester, Durham and Cambridge. i-Pod and MP3 mobile technologies make it possible for tourists to listen to a tour on a headset as they explore a destination. Tourist information service organisations in cities have an issue here. Should the TIC (tourist information centre) provide i-Pod/MP3 guides? Different stakeholders will have different views. In April 2006 *TravelMole*, the online news and resource centre for the UK travel and tourism industry, ran an opinion poll to test the views of readers of its online newsletter (Figure 1.1).

**Discussion point** 

How would you vote in the *TravelMole* poll in Figure 1.1? Why?

**Figure 1.1**
*The* TravelMole *poll*

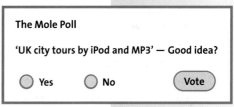

The Mole Poll

'UK city tours by iPod and MP3' — Good idea?

Yes     No     Vote

Other categories of issues that face the travel and tourism industry are summarised in Figure 1.2. One category is that of political issues. Changes of political leadership in a tourist receiving area can have impacts on the travel and tourism industry. Figure 1.3 shows the swearing into office of Jamaica's first woman prime minister, Portia Simpson Miller, in March 2006. The article suggests that her election may affect tourism, but will it do so, and how? This issue, like those summarised in Figure 1.2, is current and because it is still unresolved, has potential future impacts on the travel and tourism industry.

**Figure 1.2** *Other issues facing travel and tourism*

### Political issues
*Examples*
- Do political changes (such as a change of government) encourage more or less tourist development?
- How will terrorist attacks in a destination affect future tourist numbers?

### Product development issues
*Examples*
- Will budget airlines continue to grow?
- Will the distinction between budget and flag-carrier airlines continue to blur until they are the same?

## The travel and tourism industry

### Socioeconomic change issues
*Examples*
- How will Britain's ageing population affect the future products of the UK travel and tourism industry?
- How should tour operators adjust to a declining proportion of family groups among their customers?

### Environmental issues
*Examples*
- How will air travel be affected by developing concerns over global warming?
- Will sustainable and ecotourism development continue? Will they allow MEDW tourists to travel to LEDW destinations with a clear conscience?

**Figure 1.3**

Rudolph Brown/epa/Corbis

## 'Sista P' breaks male monopoly

Portia Simpson Miller is sworn in as Jamaica's new prime minister. Known to many as 'Sista P', she has criticised some aspects of Jamaica's tourist industry, saying the behaviour of some visitors clashes with the island's traditional morals.

## Scale of issues

Issues for the travel and tourism industry may arise at any scale:
- global — for example climatic effects of air travel
- national — how should UK travel agents respond to the internet — as a threat or an opportunity?
- local — for example should the Sands development in Scarborough go ahead (see the Starter chapter in Topic 4)?

## Researching current issues

**Current issues** are those that are alive now. This book was published in 2006 and the issues discussed in this unit seem likely to remain current for some time, but you may need to research your own topical issues. Using up to date information is the key to investigating current issues. Figure 1.4 is another 2006 newspaper extract, this time about the US cruise line Royal Caribbean commissioning a cruise ship that would be the largest in the world. Both the mass media (television and newspapers, for example) and the travel trade's own media (such as *Travel Weekly*, the *Travel Trade Gazette* and the online *TravelMole*) carry articles and features about current issues in travel and tourism.

**Discussion point** ●

What issues for travel and tourism are current in the news now?

**Figure 1.4** *These plans would make the new Project Genesis liner the largest in world in 2006*

**Discussion point** ●

What issues does Figure 1.4 raise?

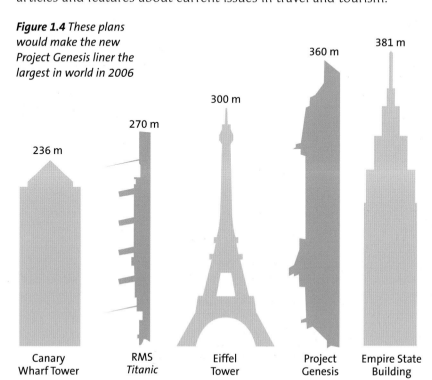

| Canary Wharf Tower | RMS *Titanic* | Eiffel Tower | Project Genesis | Empire State Building |
| 236 m | 270 m | 300 m | 360 m | 381 m |

Project Genesis
- 73 metres high
- 360 metres long
- Cost $900m
- Can take 5,400 guests
- 47% bigger than the current largest cruise liner
- 220,000 tonnes (five times as heavy as the *Titanic*)

## Support your learning

### Information sources

1 The mass media and travel press are sources of information about current issues. Some useful websites are **www.travelweekly.co.uk**, **www.ttglive.com** and **www.travelmole.com**.

2 Pressure groups such as Tourism Concern (**www.tourismconcern.org.uk**) have updates on tourism impact issues on their websites.

### Skills builder

Synthesise outline information about a current travel and tourism issue by browsing several information sources.

### Activities menu

1 Make a poster to illustrate five types of issue facing the travel and tourism industry.

2 a How would you have voted in the *TravelMole* i-Pod/MP3 poll (see Figure 1.1)?
  b Why?
  c Who from the travel and tourism industry might have voted in the same way as you? Who might have voted differently?

3 Research and analyse two differing views about any one current issue reported recently in the travel industry press.

4 *Vocational scenario*
  a As a Blue Badge Guide, evaluate the effect you think downloaded guide commentaries might have on you.
  b As a tour guide in a historic city, suggest how you could use new technology to enhance the experience of your customers.

# Change and travel and tourism

The five types of issue facing the travel and tourism industry that were identified in the Starter chapter all arise because of change. There are changes in the travel and tourism industry itself and changes in the world in which it operates. Both are likely to provoke differing views among stakeholders (people and organisations with an interest, or 'stake', in the industry) and therefore become issues.

## Technological changes

Technological changes include changes in information and communications technology (ICT) and developments in transport systems.

### ICT

The internet has had considerable impacts on the travel and tourism industry. Customers are able to research destinations and make their own bookings online, either through online bookers such as Expedia and Travelocity, or directly with providers of accommodation, transport and support services in the destination. Travel and tourism providers have responded to this technological development so that even small- and medium-sized enterprises have their own websites, e-mail addresses and online booking capabilities, including accepting online debit and credit card payments from around the world.

Tour operators have responded with their own websites (Figure 1.5) and by moving into dynamic packaging. This is an interactive process between the tour operator and the customer. Rather than just selling ready-made

**Figure 1.5**
*An example of a tour operator website*
**www.thomson.co.uk**

packages of transport, transfer and accommodation to customers, the tour operator allows the customer to build the final package from menus of transport, transfer options and accommodation types. This is a move towards tailor-made packages. A true tailor-made package is put together according to the customer's specifications from a choice of all the elements of the market that the tour operator can access. In the case of dynamic packaging, the menus are likely to be more restricted than this but they allow more flexibility than the traditional package holiday.

Dynamism is also introduced into the process by making it possible for the customer to add on extras and include these in a revised package price. An online consumer may prefer to arrange a sightseeing trip after securing the initial transport and accommodation deal. Online bookers would much rather that their customers pay them for such products than that they buy them from local suppliers in the resort and therefore allow these add-ons to the package.

Vertical integration within the industry makes dynamic packaging more available to the high street travel agent customer too. This is because tour operators such as Thomson Tui integrate online travel agency services and trading on the high street.

### Transport system developments

Figure 1.4 describes a new-generation cruise ship. Such ships are one of a range of current transport system developments. Another example is the super-jumbo Airbus A380 (Figure 1.6), an aircraft

*Figure 1.6*
*The Airbus A380*

TopFoto

designed to cope with the rising demand for air travel. It uses technology which became available early in the twenty-first century. The A380 is a double-decker aircraft capable of carrying up to 840 passengers (compared to the maximum 524-seat capacity of the jumbo jet) on busy intercontinental routes such as London to New York.

How is the size of aircraft an issue? Apart from environmental and noise concerns, not least from people who live near the airports such large planes would use, super-jumbos are not the only vision of future air travel. Another option is the air taxi. More aeroplanes, rather than bigger ones, might be the way of dealing with the increased demand for air travel.

Other transport system developments that bring issues for the travel and tourism industry include:

- city tramway systems, such as that in Geneva
- high-speed international rail links such as the French TGV system (Train à Grande Vitesse) that links Paris to Geneva — the journey time is just 3 hours

The new rail link between London's restored St Pancras Station and mainland Europe via the Channel Tunnel, due to be operational from 2007, is a technological transport development with far-reaching consequences for inbound and outbound tourism. This new link means that travel and tourism organisations in all sectors of the industry face issues about what products and services to provide.

## Socioeconomic change

Social change in the UK poses issues for the travel and tourism industry. Household trends include:

- more people living alone
- more families led by one parent
- increased numbers of empty-nester households (mature adults whose children have grown up and left home)

Such trends create issues of product and service provision for the travel and tourism industry. Organisations respond in different ways. Figure 1.7 is an extract from a newsletter sent by a travel company to customers registered on its website. The extract shows how, as a tour operator, the company is tapping into the market opportunity provided by a socioeconomic change.

**Discussion point**

What are air taxis? Why might they be a better option than bigger aircraft?

*Figure 1.7* Adventure holidays for single-parent families

## Single parent departures

The thought of an overseas holiday can be daunting if you are a single parent, yet we know that our Family Adventures provide the perfect solution! All of our departures are great for single parents but if you would like to travel with other single parents then look out for departures marked with an 'S' in the dates and prices section of our website or brochure

Ingram

Changes in lifestyle and income levels present other issues for the travel and tourism industry. Greater disposable income to spend on holidays is one trend, although it could be reversed by an economic downturn. Increased health consciousness and an appetite for adventure experiences are market-changing social trends that may continue into the future. Issues for the travel and tourism industry are about how much and in what way to invest in new developments to exploit these apparent trends.

## Changes in consumer demand

Changes in consumer demand are of two main types:
- changes to the nature of consumers
- changes to what those consumers want

The market in travel and tourism products offered to non-family groups has been growing. At one end of the age spectrum holiday-makers are more likely to be young people in groups than families and at the other end is a growing number of fit and affluent members of the grey market. Not only does this create the issue of how to provide products and services that attract these very different but expanding market segments, it also raises issues of redundant family accommodation and what should be done with it. Organisations with hotel rooms and self-catering accommodation designed for nuclear family groups may have an issue of how to convert these facilities to satisfy the demands of growing 'non-family' market segments.

| Change | Issue | Type of provider |
|---|---|---|
| A demand for a greater variety of destinations | Which new destinations will appeal to the market? | Airlines<br>Cruise lines<br>Tour operators<br>Hotel chains |
| More people wanting more holidays per year | What out-of-season products to offer | Tour operators<br>Hotel chains |
| Demand for higher quality standards but with value for money | How to deliver both together | Hotel chains<br>Airlines |
| More demand for independent travel | What will happen to the package holiday? | Tour operators |

*Table 1.1*
*Some changes in consumer demand*

Other changes in consumer demand and the issues they pose for the industry are summarised in Table 1.1.

## Product developments

Two examples of new products that have created ongoing issues for the travel and tourism industry are:

- budget (no-frills) airlines
- hotels for particular customer types

Budget airlines such as easyJet and Ryan Air have prospered in recent years. They have tapped into a variety of changes, such as increased internet booking and the consequent growth in self-packaging, the related trend of more independent travel and the demand for more holidays in a year — city breaks and ski breaks in addition to summer holidays, for example.

Some of the issues this raises are:

- Can budget airlines keep expanding or will the bubble burst? Some budget-model airlines have not survived. Air Wales ceased trading in 2006, for example.
- Will flag-carrier airlines continue to offer their own budget flights to compete? What will happen to them?
- Will the distinction between budget and flag-carrier airlines blur and disappear?

Some hotels cater for specific customer types. Not only are they aimed at a particular market segment, but they do not allow people who do not belong to that customer type to stay. The most common type are couple-only hotels. The 'Couples' hotel chain is an obvious example (**www.couples.com**), with a brand name that is clear about who these all-inclusive hotels are for. The 'Sandals' chain is another example (**www.sandals.co.uk**). Sandals has diversified from couples-only to more family-orientated hotels (the 'Beaches' brand). This illustrates an issue for hotel companies which invest heavily in the couples-only market — is it putting 'too many eggs in one basket'? Figure 1.7 shows the location of Sandals hotels in Jamaica. Both Couples and Sandals have hotels on the 7-mile beach at Negril, while Beaches has two hotels there.

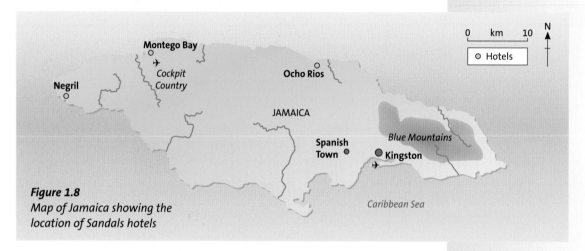

**Figure 1.8**
*Map of Jamaica showing the location of Sandals hotels*

## Political and security changes

The political stability of tourist destinations changes. Before the 1990s Yugoslavia (as it then was) was a major tourist receiving area for package holidaymakers from the UK. During the 1990s there was conflict and civil war in some parts of the country as it broke up into different nations. Tourism to Croatia and Serbia from the UK has shown signs of recovery as the political situation, especially in Croatia, has restabilised. Will this continue? Which other destinations previously off-limits or perceived as risky might now be developed? These are issues for tour operators and airlines. They are also potential ethical issues for tourists. Is it morally right to holiday in a country with a repressive government? For the industry, ethical issues also matter; they affect the market apart from being matters of conscience for travel and tourism managers themselves.

Terrorist activity around the world affects travel and tourism. Tourists can be frightened away by attacks so that visitor numbers fall. After the 11 September 2001 terrorist attacks on New York, fewer tourists

**Discussion point**

Is it ethically acceptable to holiday anywhere at any time?

visited the city, including travellers from the UK. However, tourist arrival levels did recover. Clearly, falling trade presents issues for any business — travel and tourism organisations included.

## Environmental changes

Rising concern about the effects of increased air travel on the earth's atmosphere and therefore on its climate is an issue the travel and tourism industry has to respond to. Figure 1.9 is a news headline about this issue.

# Pollution threat as flights hit 500m a year

*Observer* 2 April 2006

*Figure 1.9* Newspaper headline about the air travel and pollution issue

Awareness of the potential negative impacts of tourism (see Chapters 4.2 and 4.3) among consumers and in the industry has contributed to the development of ecotourism and sustainable tourism (see Chapter 4.4). Neither is without their issues. How sustainable are ecotourist holidays that involve long-haul flights? Do all stakeholders in a destination welcome an ecotourism approach or do people without work wish for big mass tourism hotels and the jobs and wages they perceive these bringing?

Natural disasters create issues for travel and tourism organisations similar to those of political instability and terrorism. Notable examples are the Asian tsunami that affected Indian Ocean destinations in 2004/05 and Hurricane Katrina's devastation of New Orleans in 2005, as well as human hazards such as transmittable diseases in destinations with a recent well-publicised outbreak (AIDS, bird flu or malaria, for example).

## Support your learning

### Information sources

1 The mass and travel media are major information sources. The UK government's Foreign and Commonwealth Office website (**www.fco.gov.uk**), advising travellers about precautions to take in some destinations and which destinations to avoid, is useful for investigating political and environmental change issues.

2 The Climate Care website (**www.climatecare.org/ responsibletravel/responsibletravel.cfm**) calculates the carbon dioxide emissions of flights.

### Skills builder

Brainstorm the issues stemming from one current change in travel and tourism.

**Activities menu**

1 Explain why the development of dynamic packaging is linked to technological and socioeconomic changes.

2 *Vocational scenario*
   As a tour operator, compose a letter to customers giving them the UK government's current advice for travellers to their planned destination.

3 Research and analyse the effects on the travel and tourism industry of one recent natural disaster.

4 Evaluate the extent to which any one ecotourism holiday may impact negatively on the environment.

# Stakeholders in change

Current issues in travel and tourism arise because of change. The six main types of change are:

- technological
- socioeconomic
- consumer demand
- product development
- political
- environmental

All of these types of change were considered in Chapter 1.1. Change creates issues because different people may have a range of views about whether the change is to be encouraged or about how to respond to a change that has happened.

Tourism development is change that is planned with the intention of improvement. However, most developments attract a range of different views. Very rarely, if ever, does everyone benefit from a change. A new hotel development may bring jobs, for instance, but have a negative impact on the environment.

## Stakeholders

People and organisations who are affected by or have an interest in change are **stakeholders**. Broad groups of stakeholders are:

- travel and tourism organisations from any of the six sectors of the industry (travel agents, tour operators, transport providers, accommodation providers, visitor attractions and support services)
- tourists — actual and potential customers
- travel and tourism workers, and their trade unions
- local residents and concerned individuals who are not tourists
- pressure groups including environmental campaigners, such as Friends of the Earth and Greenpeace, and tourism impact awareness organisations, like Tourism Concern

- non-travel and tourism organisations like developers, construction companies and governments

## Case study: The continued growth of budget airlines

Budget airline growth has occurred since the mid-1990s. Figure 1.10 shows the number of new routes launched by easyJet (**www.easyjet.com**) each year from 1995 to July 2006. In 2006, easyJet's scheduled routes numbered 267. The biggest single year for new additions was 2004 and the trend is of continued growth. Will easyJet and other budget airlines continue to grow, and if so will they continue to grow at the present rate?

Budget airline flights are a travel and tourism product that continues to develop. So, this is a product development issue for the travel and tourism industry. Not only does it affect other airlines, which need to consider how to adapt their products to meet the threat from continued budget airline growth, but other providers, such as hotel companies, may see budget airline travel as a marketing opportunity. They may see a chance to develop products such as short-break packages to attract the tourists brought to their destination by the budget airlines.

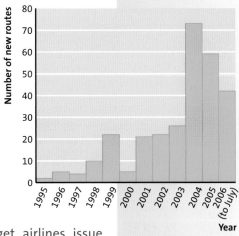

**Figure 1.10**
*The number of new routes launched by easyJet, 1995–2006*

Stakeholders in the continued growth of budget airlines issue include:

- a variety of travel and tourism organisations from different sectors of the industry, as shown in Table 1.2
- passengers of budget airlines and of other transport providers whose services may be affected by their growth (non-budget airlines and cross-channel ferries, for example)
- employees of budget airlines and other transport providers whose jobs may be affected by the continued growth of the budget airlines
- local residents near regional airports in the UK and overseas whose air traffic may increase if budget airlines continue to grow
- Climate Care, an organisation concerned about the rise in air traffic. It invites passengers to put money into carbon replacement projects to neutralise the carbon dioxide emissions from their flights
- local governments of areas with regional airports served by budget airlines which welcome the positive economic benefits brought by extra tourists

| Travel agents which sell airline tickets | Tour operators which arrange packages including charter flights |
|---|---|
| Budget airlines themselves | Non-budget (flag carrier) airlines and charter airlines |
| Providers of other competing forms of transport | Accommodation providers including hotel owners in budget airline destinations |
| Visitor attractions in destinations opened up by budget airlines | Support services, including tourist information offices and guides in destinations opened up by budget airlines |

**Table 1.2** *Travel and tourism organisation stakeholders in the budget airlines issue*

## Case study: Surfing at Newquay

Examples of current issues in the travel and tourism industry also occur at the local scale. An example is a proposed tourism development at Newquay in Cornwall. Newquay is a seaside town with a reputation for surfing because of the Atlantic Ocean waves that break on its shore. The waves can be unreliable, however, and if Newquay is to develop further as a surfing destination (a controversial issue locally) building an artificial reef offshore might be the answer (Figure 1.11).

**Figure 1.11**
*The proposed artificial reef at Newquay: stakeholders' views*

**Local fishermen**
Oppose altering the natural flow of the tides, which may affect fish stocks and alter currents, making it more difficult to steer trawlers safely

**Surf shop owner**
Favours the scheme, feeling it would make Newquay a potential world-class surfing destination

**Scheme developer**
Favours the artificial reef, claiming it would attract marine life as well as surfers and would be a sustainable tourism development

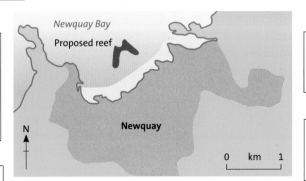

**Travel and tourism organisations locally**
Mixed attitudes; some favour the boost to tourism, while others are concerned at the effect on non-surfing visitor numbers

**Government agencies (Environment Agency and South West Tourism)**
Favour the scheme

**Surfers**
Favour the scheme, seeing it as a new and exciting opportunity for the sport

**Newquay Rowing Club**
Opposes the reef, claiming it would spoil the long-established rowing course and cost too much

**Local council**
£5 million cost — not a spending priority

**Cornwall Wildlife Trust**
Favours the scheme

Stakeholders in the artificial reef issue and their views are summarised in Figure 1.11. Stakeholders' attitudes are often coloured by their roles and the values that go along with them. It is not surprising that surfers generally favoured the Newquay scheme and that organisations with local council-tax paying members worried about the cost. People have their own values and when faced with an issue are likely to respond with an attitude based on those values.

People are, however, not always stereotypical in their views and may have conflicting thoughts themselves. Travel and tourism facility owners are largely commercially motivated. They value the tourist trade. Stereotypically, they might be expected to have views driven by the amount of business a development would bring. However, the case of the Newquay surfing reef (Figure 1.11) shows that some stakeholders thought it would bring them more trade, while others thought that it would bring less. Individuals can belong to more than one stakeholder group and find themselves torn, or having an attitude that is an exception to the norm for their group. Surfers who are local residents might be expected to favour the reef but their local residency may also make them concerned about the cost for council-tax payers and about the influx of outsiders the reef might bring. In some cases, individual people hold views that are simply exceptions from the general stance taken by their stakeholder group.

**Discussion point** ⬤

Are there current travel and tourism issues in your local area?

## Future impacts

Issues that are current remain unresolved and the impacts they will have on the future of travel and tourism are uncertain. The issue of climate change related to atmospheric pollution, caused in part by increased air travel, could have a number of outcomes. There may be limits placed on the numbers of flights people can take, or increased taxes on aeroplane fuel, or air travel may simply continue to grow without such checks.

Nevertheless, the likely effects of the responses made to the issue by some stakeholder groups can be evaluated. Environmental pressure groups are likely to continue raising public awareness of the air-travel pollution issue. Newspaper headlines such as that in Figure 1.9 will influence air passengers' attitudes and make government tax or flight-quota measures to limit air travel more politically acceptable. On the other hand, demand for travel remains high and is growing.

Passengers will continue to want the freedom to travel the globe, and that means flying.

## Your own values and attitudes

Which way do you think air travel will go? Will it continue to grow with no checks such as increased tax on fuel or limits on the numbers of flights tourists are allowed? Or will the environmental argument prevail? No one can be certain, but your own values and attitudes about air travel may affect how you judge what is likely in the future. If you are an environmentally concerned person you might take a view different from the one you might hold if you value the freedom that cheap air travel gives you. You may find yourself torn between the two views. In general, our perceptions of the impacts that stakeholder responses to travel and tourism issues will have on the future are likely to be coloured by the values and attitudes we ourselves hold.

## Support your learning

### Information sources

1 The local media (newspapers, radio and regional televison) are a source of local-scale issue material.

2 Stakeholder organisations may be accessible as primary sources.

### Skills builder

Develop your empathy skills by placing yourself in the roles of opposing stakeholders in a current travel and tourism issue.

### Activities menu

1 For the budget airlines issue, explain why travel and tourism organisations from any three sectors of the travel and tourism industry are stakeholders.

2 Compile a list of stakeholders in the issue of how the travel and tourism industry should respond to increased environmental concerns over the climatic effects of increased air travel.

3 Research and analyse the views of stakeholders in one local-scale travel and tourism issue.

4 *Vocational scenario*
Imagine you are a consultant advising the developer of the proposed artificial reef at Newquay. Evaluate the effects of the values and attitudes of stakeholder groups.

# 1.3

# Researching travel and tourism issues

As Chapter 1.1 showed, issues that are current in travel and tourism arise from changes that can be technological, socioeconomic, environmental or political, or else be a change in consumer demand or brought about by product development. Issues are current and therefore are unresolved. Even so, a researcher can reasonably evaluate their likely future impacts (see Chapter 1.2). Issues may arise at any scale from the local to the global. At any sub-global scale, current travel and tourism issues may be UK-centred or relate to an overseas destination.

This chapter lays out an approach for investigating a current issue affecting travel and tourism. It does this by suggesting some current issue ideas, providing some guidance on sources of information and giving some suggested research targets. It then provides a case study to illustrate the breadth of information that research may elicit.

## Ideas

The issues you research have to be current and they have to affect the travel and tourism industry. Table 1.3 lists some researchable issues for each of the six main categories of change that were identified in Chapter 1.1. These are just suggestions, as many other possibilities exist.

The issues presented in Table 1.3 are phrased in general terms. Research may focus on a tighter subject than the table suggests at first sight. For example, one or two destinations might be the focus of the political change issues identified and one form of new transport or the urban tramway system(s) in one or two destinations could be the focus of a transport issue enquiry.

Local current issues in travel and tourism are often convenient to research when and where they arise. Chapter 1.2 referred to the

| Change | Issue: how will/should the industry be affected/respond? |
|---|---|
| Technological | • The advent of new forms of transport (e.g. super-jumbos, new-generation cruise ships, high-speed rail links, new urban tramways)<br>• The continued development of ICT and of online booking |
| Socioeconomic | • The increasing grey market<br>• Rising demand from non-family customer groups<br>• Rising disposable incomes |
| Consumer demand | • Ongoing demand for new destinations<br>• Increasing demand for short breaks as second and third holidays in a year<br>• More desire for responsible tourism<br>• Higher quality standards being demanded alongside value for money prices |
| Product development | • The continued growth of budget airlines<br>• Hotels geared to certain market segments<br>• The rise in self-packaging |
| Political | • Changing political stability in destinations<br>• The ongoing terrorist threat<br>• Perceptions about the security of destinations |
| Environmental | • Pollution from increased air travel<br>• Negative environmental impacts of mass tourism developments<br>• The rise in ecotourism |

*Table 1.3* Types of change and examples of related issues in travel and tourism

example of a proposed artificial reef at Newquay — this could be an environmental change. It might also be argued that the proposal was born of what technological change made possible or that it was a surfing adventure tourism product development. Which type of change the issue reflects is not important. What makes it a relevant example is that it is an issue, current at the time (2005), that did affect the travel and tourism industry, in that local area.

## Sources of information

While research into any current issue in travel and tourism is likely to uncover useful and particular sources en-route, some broad guidelines are given below about the kinds of places to look.

- National and regional media, such as newspapers and television, feature controversies in articles and documentaries. These are potentially relevant when they relate to travel and tourism.
- Travel press and media such as *Travel Weekly*, *Travel Trade Gazette* and the online *TravelMole* give an industry perspective on changes the industry considers important.

- Pressure groups such as Tourism Concern can be a starting point for issues related to the impacts of tourism in tourist receiving areas. Locally based issues may give rise to organised opposition in the form of pressure groups.
- Ecotourism websites, such as **www.responsibletravel.com**, provide case-study material and background information on sustainable and environmentally friendly tourism.
- Stakeholders themselves, especially in locally based issues, can be approached for interview.
- Developers' publicity materials, laying out details of a tourism development scheme, are a foundation from which to understand the views of other stakeholders.
- The Office of National Statistics (**www.statistics.gov.uk**) has data on social trends and on travel and tourism in the UK.
- The Foreign and Commonwealth Office travellers' advice webpages (**www.fco.gov.uk**) give an insight into the UK governments' view of political stability and security in countries around the world.

**Discussion point**

Why is it good to use different information sources?

## Research targets

A research project into a current issue affecting travel and tourism should aim to collect information about:
- change — the processes that have caused the current issue to arise
- stakeholders — their values, attitudes, responses and actions
- future impacts and your own values

Chapter 1.2 discusses stakeholder identification and the future impacts of current issues, including the continued growth of budget airlines. The case study below relates to the processes of change that an investigation might uncover. Its purpose is to illustrate the breadth that might be expected of an A2 Travel and Tourism student enquiry.

## Case study: The continued growth of budget airlines

It is not just UK budget airlines that have continued to grow in recent years. German-based Air Berlin is one example to add to the UK list of companies such as easyJet, Jet2 and Flybe. Ryanair is, of course, of Irish origin.

Investigation might uncover the following processes of change leading to this ongoing product development:

- the competitive (cheap) pricing policies which are part of the marketing mix of no-frills carriers compared both to flag-carrier airlines and to other transport modes such as rail
- the post-1979 UK political culture of economic liberalism and its relaxed regulatory framework in which open competition is valued and encouraged
- the impetus of the postwar growth of outbound tourism which made overseas travel commonplace, along with the growing familiarity of air travel to more middle-income households that began in the 1950s and 1960s. This left the children (or, in some cases, grandchildren) of the first package-holiday generation seeking a less insulated, more 'authentic' travel and tourism experience
- the intervention of key entrepreneurs such as Freddie Laker with his Laker Skytrain in the 1970s, and Stelios Haji-Ioannou of easyJet and Michael O'Leary of Ryanair in the 1990s
- the growth of the internet
- the rising demand for independent travel and consequent growth of travel and tourism organisations supporting flexible packaging, including travel agencies such as Trailfinders and travel publishers such as the Rough Guide and Lonely Planet series
- changing youth culture, including the increasing phenomenon of non-family group travel, the long-running fashion for backpacking and the increased take-up of gap years among the student population
- the recent relative strengths of the Irish and UK economies. This has allowed available income for travel, especially among social groups such as DINKYs (dual-income no kids yet), and increased their spending power abroad, notably in recently developed budget destinations in eastern Europe such as Prague, Budapest and the Baltic republics
- the lowering of political barriers to international travel following, for example, the collapse of communism in eastern Europe and the settling of the Yugoslav conflict
- the enthusiasm of local and regional authorities for promoting travel to and from lesser-used airports in the UK and overseas

This list illustrates a broad range of the processes of change behind the rise of budget airlines. The various processes are interlinked; consider, for example, changing youth culture and the increased use of the internet.

## Support your learning

### Information sources

1 The mass media (television and newspapers) and travel trade media including *Travel Weekly*, the *Travel Trade Gazette* and the daily *TravelMole* newswire are good secondary sources.

2 Stakeholders themselves can be a primary source and their websites and publicity material secondary sources.

### Skills builder

Develop your presentation skills by delivering the PowerPoint presentation from Activity 1.

### Activities menu

1 Produce a PowerPoint presentation on reasons behind the growth of budget airlines.

2 Brainstorm the processes of change that have led to one issue affecting travel and tourism (other than the growth of budget airlines).

3 Research and analyse how three socioeconomic trends in the UK currently affect travel and tourism.

4 *Vocational scenario*
Imagine you are a travel journalist. Evaluate the extent to which budget airlines are likely to remain distinct from flag-carriers in the near future.

# 2

# Managing people in travel and tourism

Managing people
in travel and tourism

# *Starter:* **managing the human resource**

The **human resource** is the staff of a travel and tourism organisation.

*Figure 2.1*
*A company's staff is*
*its human resource*

## People and quality

People who work in a travel and tourism organisation contribute, sometimes directly and sometimes indirectly, to the customer service the organisation provides. In a traditional high-street travel agency, for example, travel consultants work on a face-to-face basis with customers, advising them on holidays and making bookings for them. Other staff roles may take place behind the scenes, including making payments to tour operators and travel providers, maintaining the customer records database and managing the agency's stock of brochures. These are known as 'back office' functions because they may (but by no means always) take place in an office behind the shop. (The public access space in a travel agency is basically a shop.) Tasks like these support the travel agency's customer service standards.

Travel and tourism managers, including high-street travel agency managers, need to manage the people who work for them to maximise the quality of customer service provided. External customers (members of the public and other organisations) experiencing high-quality customer service are more likely to spend money, return with repeat business, and tell other people, providing free word-of-mouth marketing. All of this generates more business for the agency or for other travel and tourism organisations.

## Travel and tourism employment

People who work in the travel and tourism industry do so under a variety of contracts, both full-time and part-time. Seasonal ups and downs in the flows of tourists (the volume of customers) mean that many temporary (as opposed to permanent) staff are seasonal employees. This ebb and flow of work opportunities creates issues of motivation that travel and tourism managers must deal with to ensure that the expected quality of customer service is maintained.

### Seasonal employment

In the UK and Europe, the main tourist season is the summer (except in winter sports resorts, for example in the Alps and Pyrenees). So the main time for employment is also the summer, despite the sometimes successful attempts to extend the season. An example of extending the season is the winter seaside holidays on the Spanish costas, marketed at the 'grey market' of more mature/retired adults.

*Table 2.1 Employers in the six sectors of the travel and tourism industry*

Employers are the owners and managers of travel and tourism organisations such as accommodation providers, for example hotels, and visitor attractions, for example theme parks. Table 2.1 illustrates the range of employers belonging to the six sectors of the travel and tourism industry. It can only show the tip of the iceberg — in reality there is large and varied range of employers.

| Sector | Examples |
|---|---|
| Transport providers | Airlines, train, ferry and coach operators, car-hire companies, airport transfer service providers |
| Accommodation providers | Hotels, guesthouse owners, caravan and campsite owners, self-catering providers |
| Tour operators | Traditional and online tour operators, tailor-made specialists, coach excursion operators |
| Travel agents | High-street and online travel agencies |
| Visitor attractions | Theme parks, historic and cultural tourism sites, major sporting venues |
| Support services | Tourist boards and information offices, specialist support providers |

In the UK, hotels in seaside resorts, such as Scarborough, and in National Parks, such as the Lake District, employ more staff in their busy summer season. Some staff are local people, while others may be migrant workers coming to the destination in search of seasonal work. One of the economic impact issues of tourism is the seasonal unemployment that can occur in the off-season (usually the winter). The 'migrant worker' category also includes some people who are tourists themselves, for example gap-year students from Australia spending an extended working break in a hotel in the Lake District.

City hotels have a different market, largely business tourists visiting London, Birmingham or any of the UK's other major cities for conferences, exhibitions and sales meetings. This type of business is less seasonal (indeed high summer may be a relatively quiet time because it is when business tourists take their own holidays) and so employment is also less seasonal.

In Europe, a tour operator's resort representative working on a Greek island such as Cephalonia in summer may hope to be retained for the winter season and perhaps re-assigned to a 'winter sun' destination such as Lanzarote in the Canary Islands. Having a breadth of skills to offer may help them find work at a snow sports resort in the Alps over the winter. Tour operator company managers want to retain good staff from one summer season to the next and seek to find winter posts for employees whose work they rate highly.

**Discussion point** ●
Would you enjoy being a resort rep? Justify your answer.

Away from northern hemisphere destinations such as those of the UK and Europe, the seasonal patterns differ. The islands of the Caribbean, for example, attract many tourists from North America in the northern hemisphere winter. This is their peak season. This means that UK tourists holidaying in St Lucia and Jamaica during the northern hemisphere summer may find some hotels relatively empty because this is the Caribbean quiet season. While the water parks of large all-inclusive hotels such as Beaches in Negril, Jamaica may be busy all year (see Figure 2.2), the swimming pools of smaller establishments such as Jamaica Heights guesthouse in Port Antonio (Figure 2.3) may be empty in August. Staff in such organisations may work on a relatively informal basis. The chef at Jamaica Heights, for example, works

**Figure 2.2**
*The location of Negril*

on a self-employed basis, buying food for the guests, cooking meals and keeping his profits. This is motivational at busy times, but when there are no guests at times in the quiet season he has no income, so he retains a subsistence smallholding to live off then.

*Figure 2.3* Jamaica Heights' swimming pool: empty in August

Stephen Rickerby

## Managing people and quality

Travel and tourism managers need to manage the people for whom they are responsible so that high-quality customer service is provided. Phases in this process are summarised in Figure 2.4 — the 'people and quality cycle'. The phases are:

1 dealing with new staff — including the induction and training of newly appointed people (both temporary and permanent) into the practices and procedures of the organisation
2 managing and motivating staff teams to maintain the standard of customer service they have been trained to deliver, including monitoring and evaluating people's performance against set quality targets and discovering what customers think about staff
3 ensuring the health, safety and security of employees and customers in a controlled, well-managed environment — including implementing consumer

*Figure 2.4* The people and quality cycle

- New staff: induction and training
- Motivating staff teams and monitoring customer service
- Ensuring health, safety and security
- Managing complaints and issues
- Performance-managing staff

protection measures such as those laid down by the Consumer Protection Act 1987 and employee rights such as those relating to equal opportunities

4  managing complaints and issues that arise so that staff feel fairly treated and maintain motivation, while addressing customer concerns to protect the organisation's reputation and future business potential. Dissatisfied customers spread bad news about an organisation quickly and can put off other potential customers

5  performance-managing staff, appraising and, if necessary, terminating their employment in a fair manner

## Case study: GNER

Great North Eastern Railways (GNER) is a train-operating company belonging to the transport providers sector of the UK travel and tourism industry. It is a good example of the increasing integration of the industry, in that GNER is owned by the Sea Containers Group (a mostly US-owned international company with headquarters in Bermuda). The business interests of the Sea Containers Group include passenger transport, mainly ferry services in the Baltic and Mediterranean, and the containers used for sea-borne cargo.

Table 2.2 relates GNER's management of customer service to the phases of the people and quality cycle (Figure 2.4). This is a summary — more details are provided in the following chapters.

| People and quality management phases | GNER examples |
|---|---|
| 1 Dealing with new staff | A 3-day Corporate Welcome course and an additional 10 days of induction training for on-train customer service staff |
| 2 Motivating staff teams | Staff performance awards including GNER Employee of the Month and the annual customer service awards ceremony — the 'GNER Oscars' (see Chapter 2.2) |
| 3 Ensuring health, safety and security | Training provision from induction onwards, including train evacuation procedures |
| 4 Managing complaints | Conflict avoidance training<br>Members of staff named in complaints given the opportunity to put their side to Customer Relations Department |
| 5 Performance management | Annual Performance Partnership review of all employees and managers by line managers |

*Table 2.2* GNER and the people and quality cycle

## Support your learning

### Information sources

1 People are the best information source about people. This chapter is about managing people to ensure good customer service. Managers with human resources responsibilities are good people to talk to. Types of organisation to approach include travel agencies, transport providers, hotels, caravan and campsites, tourist information centres and visitor attractions.

2 Chapters 5.3 and 5.6 of this book provide useful information too.

### Skills builder

Develop your formal letter-writing skills by composing a letter of introduction to the manager of a travel and tourism organisation, explaining what information about their management of customer service you would find useful for your course.

### Activities menu

1 a Explain what is meant by 'human resources management'.
  b Explain why it helps achieve good-quality customer service.

2 *Vocational scenario*
  Imagine you are a customer service trainer for a travel and tourism organisation other than GNER. Develop a PowerPoint presentation to illustrate the people and quality cycle as applied to that company.

3 Research and analyse the seasonal employment needs of a hotel located in a UK seaside resort.

4 Evaluate the benefits to the owner of a small guesthouse or hotel of engaging the services of a self-employed chef.

# 2.1

# Dealing with new staff

Induction and training programmes are one of the aspects of human resources management designed to ensure high-quality customer service standards. Travel and tourism organisations introduce new staff to their ways of working and train staff in their approach to delivering good customer service.

## Approaches

Different travel and tourism organisations approach the induction and training of new staff differently. There are various tools available, as shown in Table 2.3.

*Table 2.3 Approaches to training new staff*

| Approach | Description |
|---|---|
| Induction training | Courses are made available to new staff to welcome them to the organisation they have joined and instil in them the approach to good customer service that the management requires. Table 2.2 shows that the train operator GNER provides its staff with a 3-day induction package that is followed up, in the case of on-train customer service staff, by a further 10 days of training. The case study later in this chapter adds more detail |
| Mentoring | Mentoring is a form of on-the-job training in which an experienced member of staff leads a new recruit by example, providing advice and help to ease them into their role and helping them handle new customer service situations |
| Coaching | Coaching is a more direct approach, again involving on-the-job training by a senior staff member. The experienced colleague watches the new staff member deliver customer service and provides advice before, during or after the situation on how to improve their service to the standards the organisation expects |
| Apprenticeships and Modern Apprenticeships | Apprentices were traditionally young people taken on by an organisation to 'serve their time' by observing and following the guided example of experienced skilled workers. Opportunities to attend day release work-related courses at a local college would be available. Modern Apprenticeships are an up-to-date version run by the Learning and Skills Council (see Figure 2.5) |

These courses and programmes may be delivered either by in-house and on-the-job training or else via external and off-the-job training. Training programmes in general provide travel and tourism employees

*Figure 2.5*
*An extract from the Learning and Skills Council website*

with the added benefit of transferable skills they can apply in other work situations within the same organisation or which they can take with them if they change employers.

Different travel and tourism organisations adopt different attitudes towards induction and training that arise from the values of their managements. When used appropriately, induction has the effect of motivating staff and heightening their willingness to train further and provide high standards of customer service.

## National training structures and qualifications

### Investors in People

Investors in People is a standard, which the management of a travel and tourism organisation works to achieve. It does so by planning, delivering and reviewing staff development, including training, to improve the quality of customer service delivered. Organisations reaching the Investors in People standard are entitled to display the Investors in People device (Figure 2.6). They often do this on their premises (in a hotel reception or entrance lobby for example) and on stationery, such as their letterheads.

INVESTORS IN PEOPLE

*Figure 2.6*
*The Investors in People logo*

### NVQs and GCEs

Nationally recognised qualifications in customer service and travel and tourism include NVQs (National Vocational Qualifications) and GCEs,

(General Certificate of Education). National Certificates and Diplomas are a third qualification route by which recruited staff can show performance in line with the National Occupational Standards. The National Occupational Standards are sets of competencies (lists of things people can do) that have been developed by travel and tourism industry experts on behalf of the government for travel and tourism organisations to use.

A2 Travel and Tourism (a GCE) is one qualification that travel and tourism organisations can use to gauge the quality of staff they recruit. NVQs can be used by travel and tourism organisations as part of people and quality training and development programmes. GNER, for example, makes use of Customer Service NVQs as part of the development training it makes available to its staff.

## Case study: GNER staff induction routes

Train operator GNER's induction programmes vary according to the intended role of the new member of staff. For GNER staff who will be based at railway stations (other than in Travel Centres) there is local induction, allowing existing staff to introduce new staff into their team. Figure 2.7 shows the customer service situations for GNER staff at Darlington railway station.

*Figure 2.7*
*Darlington railway station — customer service situations*

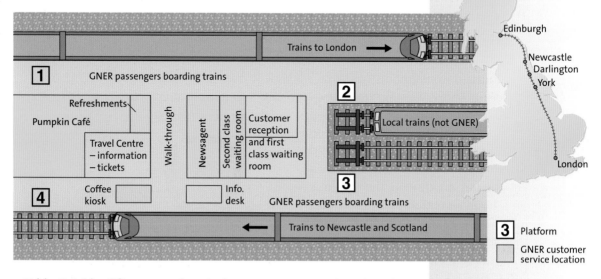

Table 2.4 identifies some face-to-face customer service situations involving GNER staff and Table 2.5 summarises the induction training programmes the company provides for new staff.

**Table 2.4** *Some face-to-face customer service situations*

| On-train | On-station | In a Travel Centre |
|---|---|---|
| • Checking tickets<br>• Answering customer queries and providing information<br>• Serving food and drink at the café-bar (buffet), from the trolley or in the restaurant car<br>• Assisting passengers with specific needs | • Answering customer queries and providing information<br>• Assisting passengers with specific needs<br>• First class lounge reception duties | • Answering customer queries and providing information<br>• Selling tickets |

**Table 2.5** *GNER staff induction programmes*

| 3-day Corporate Welcome programme for all new staff | | |
|---|---|---|
| • Learn how GNER provides customer service<br>• Discuss and deal with hopes and fears about the job<br>• Learn about team work<br>• Find out about health and safety procedures and company policies on issues such as drugs and alcohol, and assaults at work | | |
| **For on-train staff** | **For station staff** | **For Travel Centre staff** |
| An additional 10 days:<br>• Customer service, including uniform, teamwork, personable skills, the GNER Passenger's Charter<br>• Food hygiene<br>• Product knowledge and selling skills<br>• Providing service on the train<br>• Train evacuation<br>• Avoiding conflict | An additional 9 days:<br>• Customer service, including uniform, teamwork, personable skills, the GNER Passenger's Charter<br>• Geography and timetables<br>• Avoiding conflict<br>• Local induction | An additional 12 days:<br>• Customer service, including uniform, teamwork, personable skills, the GNER Passenger's Charter<br>• Geography and timetables<br>• Product knowledge<br>• Selling skills<br>• Avoiding conflict |

# Support your learning

### Information sources

Travel and tourism organisations often publish in-house training manuals for new staff and to help existing staff induct new recruits. These explain how the organisation provides high-quality customer service.

### Skills builder

Develop your interviewing skills. Find a member of staff from a travel and tourism organisation who has had experience of induction training. Ask the member of staff how their organisation helps staff deliver good customer service.

**Activities menu**

1  a  Use Table 2.5 to compare GNER's induction programmes for on-train, station and Travel Centre staff.

   b  Suggest reasons for two differences between programmes.

2  *Vocational scenario*

   Imagine you are a junior manager in a hotel. You have been asked by the general manager of the hotel to prepare an outline induction programme for new reception desk staff. Apply the good practice shown by GNER (see Table 2.5) to your situation.

3  Research and analyse the induction programme of a travel and tourism organisation other than GNER.

4  Evaluate the extent to which you think either the GNER induction programme for on-train staff or another programme prepares people to deliver high-quality customer service.

# 2.2

# Customer service standards and staff motivation

## Staff motivation

People working in the travel and tourism industry often deliver customer service as members of a team. To help ensure their customer service quality is the highest they can make it, successful travel and tourism organisation managers try hard to motivate their customer service teams.

If the people delivering customer service are motivated about the product they are selling or the service they are providing, customers are more likely to feel positive and to spend money and enjoy themselves. This is good for business because it increases revenue. It also encourages future business from the customers served and from other people they tell about their positive experience in dealing with the organisation's staff.

## Customer service standards

Since customer service is so important to travel and tourism organisations, managers want to make sure that the quality of service delivered is actually meeting customer needs. Figure 2.8 shows one common approach to assessing this — customer comment cards. Cards such as these are widely used in all six sectors of the travel and tourism industry.

Managers set quality standards based on customer feedback. During induction and training, staff are made aware of what these standards are. They may relate to:

■ value for money — customers should perceive they are being asked to pay a fair price

*Figure 2.8* *The Beaches guest questionnaire*

## Beaches
*A part of the Sandals family*

Negril guest questionaire

Dear Friends:

Welcome to Jamaica and thank you for choosing Beaches Negril as your home away from home. Now that you are here, we want you to relax, enjoy yourselves and have a great vacation.

It is important to us that you are treated with utmost courtesy and efficient service. We place great value on your impressions, suggestions and comments, and we would appreciate if you would take a moment to complete this questionnaire and drop it in to the "Guest Comments" box at the front desk.

Thank you for helping us to attain a higher level of service.

Enjoy and relax
*The Management and Staff*

Is this your first visit to Jamaica?
Is this your first visit to Beaches?

Code:
E - excellent   G - good   F - fair   P - poor

**Transfer from the airport**
How was your greeting from Beaches staff at the airport?

**Overall assessment**
Taking everything into account how would you rate your vacation?

**Reception desk**
Efficient
Courteous
Check in
Check out
Telephone operators
Bell service
Comments/suggestions _____

**Guest accomodations**
Decor
Clean

- accuracy of information
  — customers need to be confident that
  staff know what they are talking about and that they consistently provide them with accurate, up to date information
- reliability of customer service staff — customers should be able to rely on a member of staff to be present, available quickly, and have good product knowledge and a friendly competent manner
- quantitative level of staffing — there should be a sufficient number of staff available to deliver reliable and accurate customer service
- qualitative level of staffing — the correct people must be present to deliver customer service, including sufficient senior experienced staff to help deal with unexpected situations and provide a fund of deep product knowledge
- enjoyment — travel and tourism's chief purpose is leisure, business or visiting friends and relations; people judge the quality of their experience by how enjoyable, or at least unstressful, it was
- health and safety measures need to be at least in line with legal requirements

- cleanliness and hygiene of accommodation and food need to meet legal requirements and be perceived by customers as achieving high standards
- accessibility and availability of service to the customer — information points, for example, need to be open or it should be clear to customers what they can do to find out what they need to know
- provision for special (specific) needs — access must be provided and comfort afforded to the widest possible range of customers

## Benchmarking

Benchmarking is a tool that travel and tourism organisation managements use to assess the quality of performance of staff in delivering customer service. The idea is to set a level (or **benchmark**) against which performance can be measured. An example for a hotel would be 'every customer in the hotel restaurant will be approached by a waiter within 3 minutes of sitting down'. This benchmark is quantified and measurable — sample observations can be used to determine how often it is met and how much longer it may take for a customer to be served.

Travel and tourism managers can use the performance of competitors (or of similar organisations not in direct competition) to help set benchmarks. The National Passenger Survey has been carried out every 6 months since 1999 by the Department for Transport. The survey measures customer satisfaction with the service they receive from organisations operating across the UK railway network. Managers of train operating companies (TOCs), such as GNER and Wessex Trains, use these data to judge their own company's performance. They value the findings of the National Passenger Survey because they are independently researched and can be regarded as objective evidence of what customers think.

TOC managements use the data to determine two key benchmarks — the average performance and that of the top performing company. They also look at their own organisation's performance — always hoping to improve on it. Following the survey of autumn 2005, GNER's in-house employee newspaper *Newsline* contained an assessment of the latest results. The conclusions are shown in Table 2.6.

Once they have reached a quality assessment, managers can use the information benchmarking generates to identify possible improvements and then set about training and motivating their staff teams accordingly.

**Discussion point**

For any one travel and tourism organisation, consider what special access it should provide.

**Table 2.6** *Aspects of GNER customer service assessed against industry benchmarks*

| Performance criterion | GNER | Benchmark | Assessment |
|---|---|---|---|
| Overall customer satisfaction | 87% | Highest achieving TOC (Midland Mainline) = 89% | Highest ever GNER score, but aim to do better and be top |
| Value for money | 58% | TOC average = 53% | 58% may not seem high but it is better than the average and the highest GNER has ever had, so this is encouraging |

**Forward aim**
To regain top of the TOCs status by continual quality improvement especially on punctuality and reliability of trains, because customers rate these issues very highly
*Source*: National Passenger Survey and GNER *Newsline*, March 2006

## Technical reports

In customer service situations where technology is used — for example telephones in a train operator's call centre or the website of an online booker — it is possible to use technology to generate technical data on quality assurance measures. Examples are call response time (the length of time a customer waits before their call is answered) and the numbers of website 'hits' recorded relative to the numbers of bookings taken.

The printouts (interpreted or not) of such automatic data collection methods are known as **technical reports**. Travel and tourism managers use them to assess customer service quality against company targets and to reward or identify weaknesses in staff performance. Managers may also revise quality targets in the light of technical reports. For example, if the percentage of calls being answered within the target time is greatly improved they may feel that even better service could be delivered by reducing the expected call response time. On the other hand, if staff are struggling to achieve the target, they may need to ask whether the target is too ambitious. Over-ambitious targets can stress staff and cause customer service telephone dialogues to be rushed and less than fully satisfying to the customer. It is not good customer service to conduct a lot of telephone-based customer service conversations that customers do not experience as high quality.

## Feedback from people

Travel and tourism managers can use feedback from both customers and staff team-members to inform their assessments of the quality of customer service delivery. On the basis of these assessments, they may go on to make changes to the organisation's practice.

In addition to the customer comment card approach illustrated by Figure 2.7, travel and tourism managers can choose from a range of feedback-gathering techniques:

- informal feedback
- suggestion boxes
- focus groups
- mystery shoppers
- observation

## Informal feedback

Managers of facilities such as hotels and visitor attractions can talk quite easily with customers on a face-to-face basis. They can also conduct 'walkabouts' — observing the running of the facility and the quality of customer service delivery. As they go, they can gather comments from customers and staff who approach them or by engaging the customers or staff members in conversation.

**Discussion point**

What methods of customer feedback could a Tourist Information Centre best use?

Such an approach is impressionistic. It is not scientific and it is possible that the conclusions drawn may not be entirely accurate. However, impressions do count. It is the impressions that customers have which inform their decisions as to whether or not to make a return visit, bringing repeat business to the organisation.

Novotel Hotels, which belongs to the Accor Group, has a policy of striving always for the best customer service. It calls this *Service Extraordinaire*. As part of this, the general manager of the Novotel in York takes daily walks around the hotel, speaking to customers to gather their informal feedback.

## Suggestion boxes

The point of a suggestion box is to collect good ideas that managers may not have thought of or that may not be elicited by methods such as the questionnaire-like approach of the customer comment card. Customer comment cards collect information in a way that is driven by questions and quality standards that the management thought to ask about. The suggestion box, in contrast, may capture some 'off the wall' or 'blue sky' thinking.

For a staff member, a suggestion box also affords the possibility of anonymity. If a suggestion might be seen as critical of a supervisor, the suggestion box allows the ordinary staff member to communicate ideas to the senior management team without comeback.

### Focus groups

A focus group is a discussion group made up of a relatively small number of customers: 8–10 is a typical size. The 'focus' is the subject under discussion. Travel and tourism organisations use focus groups to debate issues relating to the quality of customer service.

Ascertaining what customers regard as a fair price for a product or service is one example of the way in which a focus group might be used. Members of the group share their own thoughts based on their experiences of competing organisations and their prices, taking into account issues of differing quality. For instance, a group may discuss the basic room rate a hotel chain should charge. Members of the group may have paid more or less money elsewhere but hold views on whether a proposed price is fair that are coloured by the levels of luxury and staffing offered by the different providers.

The chair of the focus group may be a manager from the travel and tourism organisation commissioning the research or a representative of a marketing or public relations consultancy. Whoever is chairing the discussion will not express their own views. The role of the chair is to steer the discussion to keep it focused and to capture the views of the group, passing this record on for management-team discussion later.

Video-conferencing technology, or a bespoke e-mail chatroom, can allow focus group meetings without the need for members to physically congregate in the same room. However, aspects of interaction, including body language, may be lost.

### Mystery shoppers

A mystery shopper is an anonymous person pretending to be a real customer. It is important that members of staff serving mystery shoppers do not recognise them or realise that they are anything other than bona fide customers. The mystery shopper goes through the motions of purchasing or accessing a travel and tourism product or service, for example booking a hotel room by telephone. They record and analyse the experiences they amass for the organisation's management, in order to provide a snapshot of the experience that a genuine customer would have. The underlying principle is that the member of staff providing the customer service is unaware of anything unusual and so will treat the mystery shopper 'customer' the same way they treat others.

### Observation

Watching people is always subject to the possibility that the presence of the observer will affect the behaviour of those being watched. A member of staff who knows a manager is watching them may behave differently from normal and they may put on a show. The customer, if aware of the observation, may also be affected and behave other than normally. Technology such as CCTV can allow a slightly greater degree of detachment between observer and observed.

Observation may be conducted formally, perhaps as part of a training programme, with a checklist being followed by the assessor. However, informal observation is part of the routine behaviour of a successful travel and tourism manager, for example as they go walkabout around their facilities.

## Motivating teams

Travel and tourism managers motivate staff teams so that:
- high quality customer service is provided
- legal rules (for example, health and safety regulations) are fully complied with — unmotivated teams may lose vigilance over such matters

Team-motivating approaches and techniques at the disposal of the travel and tourism manager are summarised in Table 2.7.

*Table 2.7*
*Team-motivating approaches*

| Approach | Comment |
|---|---|
| Clear management style | Teams are motivated when managements set clear targets. Inclusive managers involve teams in the target-setting process |
| Rotating jobs and duty times among team members | Teams work best when members feel equally treated. To avoid feelings that one member has the most interesting job or the most socially convenient work schedule, tasks and schedules are rotated among team members |
| Empowering team members | Delegating authority to teams encourages trained people to act on their own initiative and yet, within the culture of the organisation, brings about higher-quality customer service |
| Offering incentives (including financial ones) | Awards and rewards, especially for overall team performance |
| Creating a positive work environment | Providing not only a stimulating physical environment (although that does matter) but a positive culture means people feel comfortable to be themselves when serving the organisation's customers |

GNER runs an annual GNER Customer Service Awards scheme at which 'GNER Oscars' are awarded to the best performing teams on a special gala night. The GNER Customer Service Awards engenders a sense of competition between teams, with the intention of motivating them to provide high-quality customer service. It encourages team members to work together and demonstrates that the management of the company values and appreciates the quality provided by customer service teams.

## Support your learning

### Information sources

1 The National Passenger Survey provides twice-yearly data on customer satisfaction with Britain's train operating companies.

2 Large travel and tourism organisations publish in-house newspapers and magazines for staff which feature quality incentive schemes.

### Skills builder

Devise a 'mystery shopper' checklist suitable for use in one type of travel and tourism facility.

### Activities menu

1 Explain why the 'GNER Oscars' night can help improve customer service quality.

2 Apply the 'mystery shopper' technique to a travel and tourism organisation in your area or online.

3 *Vocational scenario*
Imagine you are the editor of the in-house magazine of a new train operating company. Research and analyse one aspect of the performance of existing TOCs and use your results to set a justified benchmark.

4 Evaluate the quality of customer service provided by one travel and tourism organisation or department.

# 2.3

# Health, safety and security

Ensuring the health and safety, and the security of people (whether they are external customers, staff or the general public) is vital for the travel and tourism industry. Both are central to the quality of customer service provided.

## Health and safety

Travel and tourism organisations have to provide an environment for staff and customers that is safe and healthy. To do this managers have to understand the requirements of the regulations that affect their organisations. Table 2.8 outlines the principal pieces of legislation and other measures with which managers have to comply.

***Table 2.8*** *Legislation relevant to the travel and tourism industry*

| Legislation/regulations | Main aim | Key provisions | Implications for travel and tourism organisations |
|---|---|---|---|
| The Health and Safety at Work Act, 1974 | To keep people safe at work | Employers must safeguard the health and safety of staff | Train staff. Make sure that premises and equipment are all safe. Be prepared to be inspected by and respond to actions requested by the Health and Safety Executive (HSE) |
| The Reporting of Injuries, Diseases and Dangerous Occurrences Regulations (RIDDOR), 1995 | To allow for the monitoring of hazards to help maintain health and safety at work | Issued by the Health and Safety Executive | Report any work-related accidents, diseases and dangerous occurrences to the Incident Contact Centre of the 'enforcing authorities' — the HSE and local authorities |

| Legislation/regulations | Main aim | Key provisions | Implications for travel and tourism organisations |
|---|---|---|---|
| Consumer Protection Act, 1987 | To protect the interests of the customer | Prices must be clearly displayed. Products and services must be safe to use. The supplier is liable if something goes wrong | Tour operators, for example, are responsible for ensuring that holidays they package are safe and the price is known upfront by the customer. They must follow the EU Package Travel, Holidays and Tours Directive 1993, by producing accurate brochures and clear emergency help and compensation procedures for customers |
| Data Protection Act, 1998 | To protect customers from inaccurate information held about them on databases | All organisations holding electronic data must register with the Data Protection Agency | Make sure customer records are accurate and allow customers access to information kept about them, putting any inaccuracies right and compensating for any loss |
| Licensing laws | To protect people from the negative effects of alcohol abuse | Facilities selling alcohol to be consumed on the premises must be licensed. 18-year-olds can buy alcoholic drinks and 16-year-olds can buy some drinks for consumption with a meal if accompanied by an adult | Organisations running hotels, transport and visitor attractions that include bars and restaurants have to comply with the Licensing Act, 2003 |
| Civil Aviation Authority (CAA) procedures | To keep airline passengers and others safe | Aircraft need to be safe and safely operated and air traffic safely controlled | Air transport providers must operate flights safely and under licence from the CAA |
| Sex Discrimination Act, 1975 | Both genders to be treated equally | Recruitment, training and promotion of staff to be equal, regardless of gender | Staff of both genders should be equally recruited and have equal access to training and promotion |
| Disability Discrimination Act, 1995 | To allow disabled people to be treated the same as everyone else | Disabled people to be treated (recruited, promoted and disciplined) the same as the non-disabled | Adjust duties, working hours, procedures, equipment and the work environment (removing physical barriers to access) |

Laws and rules affecting health and safety change, and travel and tourism managers in all sectors of the industry need to keep up to date with them. Some laws or regulations apply more to one type of travel and tourism organisation than to others. For example, Civil Aviation Authority (CAA) procedures are of most relevance to airlines, although the CAA administers the ATOL (Air Tour Operators Licensing) scheme to protect customers from the collapse of tour operators. This ensures for example, that if a company goes bankrupt when customers are abroad on holiday they will not be stranded.

Within an organisation, some staff members need to have more detailed knowledge of particular rules and procedures than others. Table 2.5 in Chapter 2.1 shows that food hygiene training is needed as part of the induction package for on-train customer service staff employed by GNER but not for those who work in Travel Centres. Only the former may be involved in the preparation and handling of food as part of their job role, whether in the galley kitchen, café-bar (buffet), on the trolley, as part of at-seat service or in the restaurant car.

Figure 2.9 shows the layout of one of GNER's trains, with locations for food handling identified and annotated.

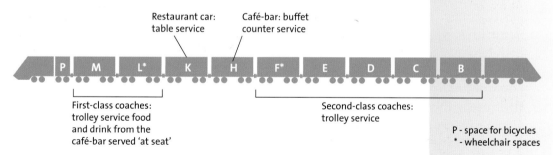

**Figure 2.9** *Food and drink service locations on a GNER 'Mallard' train*

## Security

Security is distinct from safety. Security management is concerned with affording protection to property and people from the malevolent or negligent intentions of others or from accidents.

Customers of travel and tourism organisations (including the internal customers who are its staff) may need to be protected from the following security hazards:

- acts of violence and antisocial behaviour by external customers and others, including those which are alcohol- or drugs-related
- accidental damage to property

- terrorism and sabotage which is not politically motivated
- theft (of property and of information — including electronic information held on computers) and fraud

Travel and tourism organisations seek to protect customers from the security risks associated with making online bookings and payments using credit cards over the internet and via call centres. Organisations such as hotels, airports and train operators offer wireless internet access to their customers and need to protect their security in that context too. Requesting credit card number, card type, security code and often a customer password offers some protection from fraud for online credit card bookings. Secure servers are used; you can see this by the 's' in 'https://...' when you visit a secure site. Figure 2.10 shows the typical information requested of a customer making an online booking payment.

**Figure 2.10**
*The online payment form for the airline Flybe.com*

Terrorist acts have had significant impacts on security and customer service in the travel and tourism industry. On 11 September 2001 terrorists deliberately flew two passenger airliners into the World Trade Center Twin Towers in Manhattan causing over 3,000 deaths (Figure 2.11). More than any other single event, this galvanised the US government into adopting tighter security procedures. The intention of increased 'homeland security' has primarily been to protect the USA and its citizens, but it has affected travel and tourism organisations globally.

**Figure 2.11** *The 9/11 terrorist attack*

Increased security measures a tourist to New York City post-9/11 might experience include:

- more rigorous checks of people and baggage (and passports and other documentation) at points of entry, such as the gateway airports of JFK and Newark
- the global banning of all sharp objects from hand luggage on aircraft
- airport-type X-ray portals and bag checks at key visitor attractions, such as the ferry to the Statue of Liberty in New York harbour

TopFoto

■ the visible presence of armed National Guards at key points, such as the entrance to the Lincoln Tunnel linking New Jersey (where Newark Airport is located) to Manhattan Island

Airport security can seem heavy-handed to tourists. This is especially so if they are on holiday but experience damage to their property or brusque treatment by security personnel (who do not interact with them using the kind of user-friendly approaches adopted by customer service staff). Travel and tourism organisation staff, for example working for a tour operator arranging package holidays to New York, need to balance their clients' frustration against the importance of security. They may need to provide tourist education to help their customers understand the issues involved if they complain about security measures. (Chapter 2.4 is about how travel and tourism organisations manage the handling of customer complaints and issues.)

**Discussion point**

What travel and tourism security measures have you encountered? How do you feel about them?

## Support your learning

### Information sources

1 People in the travel and tourism industry are very aware of the health and safety and security issues that affect them. This applies to managers and to operational-level staff.

2 Travel and tourism organisations produce health and safety information material that is available to customers and for training staff.

### Skills builder

Develop your presentation skills by preparing and delivering a short staff training talk on one aspect of health and safety or security for one travel and tourism organisation.

### Activities menu

1 Choose one piece of legislation or regulation measure:
   a describe its key provisions
   b explain its implications for travel and tourism organisations

2 *Vocational scenario*
   Imagine you are a staff trainer for a named travel and tourism organisation. Make a PowerPoint presentation to explain the implications of one piece of legislation or regulation to one group of travel and tourism staff.

3 Research and analyse the health and safety or security implications for tour operators of one recent major news event.

4 a Evaluate the extent of adjustment the Disability Discrimination Act 1995 caused any one travel and tourism organisation to make to its operations.
   b Recommend any further reasonable adjustments the organisation could make in the future.

# 2.4

# Managing complaints and issues

Travel and tourism organisations receive complaints from customers. Complaints may originate from external or internal customers. Those that concern products and services are more likely to come from external customers while those that are about staff may emanate from either source.

Customer feedback may raise issues without explicitly being a complaint. This can come about through low scores given by customers completing customer comment cards (such as that shown in Figure 2.8) or critical comments received via other mechanisms such as focus groups, informal feedback and suggestion boxes.

It is important to realise that customer complaints are not always justified. The customer can be wrong. The investigation of complaints involving members of staff needs to take this into account. The train operating company GNER, for example, is careful to allow staff to give their side of the story when reporting an incident to the Customer Relations Department.

Managers train staff to follow established procedures when dealing with customer complaints. Part of the procedure for customer-facing personnel is normally to pass on serious issues to a senior member of staff or manager. Procedures allow trained staff to deal with an awkward and potentially stressful situation calmly and in a way that the company can support. They mean staff can deal with problems without allowing their own values and attitudes to influence their handling of the situation in a direction that the company could not later support.

However, blind following of procedure can lead to a rather humourless and sterile interchange with a customer that may not achieve the goal of providing customer satisfaction. A rigid procedure may not suit every situation. So, good complaint-handling procedures allow a degree of flexibility and an opportunity for the staff member to empathise with the customer where that is appropriate.

## Case study: GNER and conflict avoidance

GNER includes conflict avoidance techniques in its staff training programmes (see Table 2.5, for instance). GNER instructs staff to follow certain steps as good practice to avoid conflict when dealing with a customer:

- listen
- show empathy
- remain calm and respectful
- use support systems
- report it

Central to the approach is the notion that 'behaviour breeds behaviour'. In other words, confrontational behaviour on the part of a customer can be caused by the behaviour exhibited by a member of staff. Similarly, non-confrontational customer behaviour is more likely to follow positive behaviour from staff members.

Delegates on the GNER conflict avoidance training are told that good communication has three components:

- body language (including posture, eye contact and facial expression)
- listening
- verbal communication (including tone of voice, emphasis and pitch)

The acronym 'HELP' summarises the barriers to effective communication:

- **h**earing — not listening properly and hearing wrong messages
- **e**motion — becoming upset or annoyed distorts what we hear and say
- **l**anguage — jargon gets in the way of understanding and staff are trained never to use it with a customer
- **p**hysical — obstacles and differences in position of the two parties (one standing, one sitting) are examples

Good customer service in general includes overcoming or removing such barriers and is especially important in tricky situations, such as a customer having the wrong ticket and then being annoyed at the extra charge they are asked to pay, which could be as much as £100 on a

*Figure 2.12* The GNER
Passenger's Charter.
The cover and one
page of the booklet
are shown

long-distance express service. Staff are trained to assess any particular
situation early and to take an assertive and pro-active approach to
dealing with it, while understanding the effect of their own behaviour
on that of the customer and being aware of the customer's responses.

As part of its customer service, GNER publishes its Passenger's
Charter (Figure 2.12) and makes this available to customers at stations
and on trains. The charter is relevant to GNER's customer complaints
handling in two ways.

1  Customers know what to expect of GNER and therefore know what
   basis they have for pursuing an issue, without needing to initiate a
   face-to-face confrontation at all; see Figure 2.12.
2  Customers know what behaviours GNER expects of them. The
   charter lays out that GNER staff:
   —  are trained to look after all customers fairly
   —  may be busy with safety-critical tasks (such as overseeing the
      safe departure of a train from a station platform) and may not be
      available to help customers with queries immediately —
      however, they will help when the task is done

– GNER 'will not tolerate abuse of our staff...and will take...court action against offenders'

The charter is part of the support that GNER provides for staff. Ultimately, on-train staff have the backing of the British Transport Police, including special constables, if a serious situation develops.

Travel and tourism managers need strategies to deal with serious situations. These often complex situations can be:

- inappropriate or even criminal behaviour by customers, ranging from abuse of staff through to assault or attempt to defraud the organisation (ticket evasion or credit card forgery, for example)
- technical failures, delays or adverse weather conditions

Travel and tourism managers have to put action plans and emergency contingency plans in place so that trained staff have procedures to follow in the event of a sudden crisis — like a fire or major accident at a visitor attraction. The successful resolution of a serious incident is more likely to avoid any subsequent legal action.

## The compensation culture

A social trend of recent years has been the increasing likelihood of aggrieved customers suing organisations they feel have wronged them. This 'wrong' may have been putting their health and safety at risk or simply failing to deliver the promised goods and services. The high level of customers' preparedness to use legal means to seek redress is termed the **compensation culture**. Dissatisfied customers are now more likely to feel that they should receive financial compensation for inadequate service because of a general belief that such redress is appropriate.

Travel and tourism organisation managers are keen to avoid litigation, because it can be expensive and can also generate unwelcome publicity that may put off potential customers. Indeed they may be more likely to make a discrete payment to a dissatisfied customer with a reasonable but not fully watertight case than to fight a case in court. In the normal provision of their service they are also wary of risks; they may prevent customers from taking risks by, for example, prohibiting unsupervised children from activities such as watersports at an all-inclusive hotel.

**Discussion point**

What instances of poor travel and tourism service do you know of? How should the organisation have dealt with them?

Sometimes customers find health and safety precautions irksome. For example, the water flume at the Beaches hotel in Negril, Jamaica (Figure 2.13) can only be used, whether by an adult or a child, if a life jacket is worn. This precaution makes it unlikely that a customer could successfully sue the hotel in the event of accident.

Stephen Rickerby

**Figure 2.13** *The water flume at Beaches Negril: safety is important even in a 'fun' environment*

## Support your learning

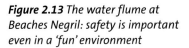

### Information sources

1 Larger travel and tourism organisations have staff training materials such as manuals and PowerPoint presentations.

2 Managers and staff team members can be interviewed to find out about procedures and training for customer complaint handling in an organisation.

### Skills builder

Imagine you are a travel and tourism manager. Now observe two colleagues role-playing a face-to-face customer complaint situation in a travel and tourism context. Advise the server on the strengths and weaknesses of her/his performance in handling the situation.

### Activities menu

1 *Vocational scenario*
   As a staff trainer for a travel and tourism organisation, you have been asked to give a 5-minute talk on ways in which behaviour breeds behaviour in customer service situations. Prepare your notes for the presentation.

2 Discuss examples of customer complaint (or other issue) handling you have seen in travel and tourism contexts.

3 Research and analyse the complaints handling procedures of one travel and tourism organisation.

4 Evaluate the quality of customer service displayed in the examples you discussed for Activity 2.

# Performance management and dismissal

## Quality

Travel and tourism managers want to offer customers the best quality service, so that the customers will be satisfied and want to make more use of their products and services. This will bring increased revenue to the organisation or, in the case of a non-commercial organisation such as a tourist information centre, it will increase use of the facility, helping to achieve its objective of showing best value for money invested from a public sector source such as the local authority.

Satisfied customers are more likely to return and bring repeat business. They are also good advertisers, in the sense that they are likely to tell other people about the good-quality service they have received. These potential customers may then become actual customers, bringing further business to the organisation.

## Appraisal

People are the key to quality in customer service. Travel and tourism managers have to monitor people in their staff teams and provide support so that staff performance is maximised.

It is common for staff performance to be reviewed annually by an employee's line manager in order to evaluate (or appraise) their level of performance and see what can be done to raise it further. Appraisal may reveal issues or weaknesses in overall staff perform-ance, which the travel and tourism manager will seek to address through support mechanisms such as providing training.

## Case study: GNER Performance Partnership

GNER operates two staff review, or appraisal, systems. One is for employees (operational staff) and one for managers. Figure 2.14 shows an extract from the document used to support the employees' appraisal review. To emphasise the two-way nature of the dialogue that takes place GNER uses the title 'Performance Partnership'. Travel and tourism organisations often prefer the term 'dialogue' to 'interview'. An interview is a 'question and answer' session firmly driven by the agenda of the interviewer. A review dialogue is an interchange of ideas driven equally by the line manager (the reviewer) and the employee (the reviewee).

| **Performance Partnership** | G**NE**R |
|---|---|

**Employees – Summary document**                                        **Confidential**

Name _____          Job title _____

Team/department/location _____

Name of reviewing manager _____

Date of last review _____          Date of review meeting _____

**General assessment of last 12 months**          Length of time in job _____

1 What have you enjoyed most about your job in the last 12 months?
*(Please refer to page 5 of the Reviewers Guidelines, section 1 to help you)*

2 What are the areas of your job which have been most difficult over the last 12 months?
*(Please refer to page 5 of the Reviewers Guidelines, section 2 to help you)*

What are the things that would make your job easier?

3 Particular issues raised and agreed actions.
*(Please refer to page 5 of the Reviewers Guidelines, section 3 to help you)*

*Source*: GNER

*Figure 2.14*
*GNER Performance Partnership*

Questions 1–3 are typical of review dialogues. The first gives the reviewee an opportunity to reflect on the year since the last dialogue and share its positive aspects. The reviewee is offered support on the kinds of thing the reviewer is looking for by a separate document (the Reviewers Guidelines), which is available to both parties. After a settling, positive opening, in which the employee's successes, their enjoyment of role and their achievements can be celebrated, the dialogue moves to the second question, which is about difficulties that have been experienced. The manager's intention here is to be positive again — this time by looking for support that GNER might offer the employee to ease these difficulties over the coming year. Training opportunities might be identified or possible changes to working practice flagged up. If the employee has an idea for how an aspect of customer service could be made both easier and better this can be taken away by the reviewer for discussion by management colleagues later. Travel and tourism organisations can gain good ideas from operational staff reflecting on and sharing their experiences of the job in their annual review dialogue.

The third question of the GNER Performance Partnership review deals with what actions are going to be taken. These might be something different for the employee to do, perhaps they could gain experience in another aspect of the company's work (for example, working on a station instead of on board a train). Alternatively, the actions may be for the reviewer to take away and carry out, like arranging a place on a training course for the employee.

Following further discussion in the dialogue, a summary of overall performance is decided on. There are four possible outcomes, which are shown in Figure 2.15.

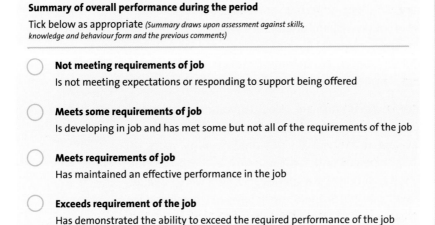

**Summary of overall performance during the period**

Tick below as appropriate *(Summary draws upon assessment against skills, knowledge and behaviour form and the previous comments)*

◯ **Not meeting requirements of job**
Is not meeting expectations or responding to support being offered

◯ **Meets some requirements of job**
Is developing in job and has met some but not all of the requirements of the job

◯ **Meets requirements of job**
Has maintained an effective performance in the job

◯ **Exceeds requirement of the job**
Has demonstrated the ability to exceed the required performance of the job

*Source:* GNER

*Figure 2.15* Summary of performance outcomes

The review dialogue closes by considering the next 12 months.

- Where does the employee see her/himself after 12 months?
- Will s/he be in the same job then?
- What personal job priorities will the next 12 months bring and how will the employee self-evaluate how well things are going?
- What developments do they foresee in their role over the next year?

Both the reviewer and the reviewee make closing comments about the dialogue and its usefulness to them. An interim review meeting may be agreed at a date less than 12 months ahead to look at progress so far towards the goals agreed by the main review dialogue.

**Discussion point**

How do appraisal schemes benefit travel and tourism organisations?

## Termination of employment

Termination of employment means bringing someone's role in the organisation to an end. It can happen voluntarily through resignation (perhaps by mutual agreement) or it can be compulsory, in which case it may be either redundancy or dismissal.

Redundancy occurs when a job role ceases to exist. Traditional high-street travel agents are under pressure from online bookers. If the management of a travel agency chain decides that falling business means a particular branch needs fewer consultants, some jobs are surplus to requirements and staff will need to be made redundant. This may be done voluntarily or it may be compulsory. Figure 2.16 reproduces a news story from the online travel news organisation *TravelMole* about job losses at the Channel Tunnel operator Eurotunnel. Eurotunnel hoped to achieve a staff reduction of 900 people through voluntary redundancy.

**Eurotunnel shed 900 jobs**

Eurotunnel has made 900 staff redundant under its voluntary redundancy programme as talks continue with creditors over its reported £6 million of debt.

A statement said the move will "reinforce the company's financial position without compromising safety or quality of service."

Eurotunnel has committed not to make any compulsory redundancies.

*Source: TravelMole, 21 October 2005*

*Figure 2.16 Redundancy at Eurotunnel*

**Voluntary redundancy** is when staff are asked to volunteer to leave the company's employment. Redundancy often attracts financial compensation. It may suit an individual's personal circumstances to take the money rather than continue in their job. If there are not sufficient volunteers for redundancy, a manager may have to decide who is going to be asked to leave. Someone will have to leave because their job no longer exists — even if they don't want to go.

**Compulsory redundancy**, or its threat, can damage staff morale. Morale is important for good-quality customer service delivery.

Travel and tourism managers prefer a voluntary redundancy scheme if possible. Under such circumstances staff colleagues may understand that the redundant person's employment termination suits their particular circumstances. This may mitigate any lowering of morale.

**Dismissal** (sacking or firing someone) is an extreme step for a travel and tourism manager to take, but one that may occasionally be necessary. Managers have to be prepared for it. Travel and tourism organisations have disciplinary procedures in place. There is normally a series of stages, involving warnings that become progressively more serious. Low-level issues, such as lateness, may initiate a first-level warning. A discussion between the staff member who is coming in late and the line manager can often resolve the situation. This is what travel and tourism organisations want. Staff are the organisation's human resources, in whom they have invested time and money — in recruiting them initially, in their induction and in their training. It is not part of the travel and tourism manager's job to waste the organisation's investment by sacking people. Their role is to support the person in overcoming difficulties, so that the time and money invested in them is not wasted, while still preserving good-quality customer service.

However, persistent or more serious breaches of the organisation's expected code of conduct may escalate the handling of the issue through the higher levels of the disciplinary procedure. In the case of a criminal act, such as defrauding the organisation through credit card theft, an issue may pass straight to the top level — which is dismissal. The travel and tourism organisation's disciplinary procedure is there to clarify the process for the benefit of managers and staff.

**Discussion point**

Under what circumstances would a travel and tourism organisation be justified in dismissing a member of staff?

## Support your learning

### Information sources

1 Travel and tourism organisations in all sectors undertake review dialogues with employees and may be able to supply blank copies of the supporting documentation.

2 *TravelMole* (**www.travelmole.co.uk**) is a news and resource centre for the UK travel industry. You can register to receive a free daily newswire about unfolding stories affecting the travel and tourism industry.

### Skills builder

Role-play a review dialogue to help you develop your people-management skills.

**Activities menu**

1 Explain why:
   a staff appraisal benefits customer service
   b travel and tourism managers regard dismissal as a final resort only

2 Suggest what questions 4–6 of the GNER Performance Partnership might ask (Figure 2.14).

3 Research and analyse recent news stories about job redundancies in the travel and tourism industry.

4 Evaluate the usefulness to GNER of the questions asked in the Performance Partnership review dialogue.

# 3

# Travel and tourism in practice

## Travel and tourism in practice

# *Starter:* **travel and tourism projects and events**

### Trips and tours

In the travel and tourism industry, tours are assembled from the component parts of transport and accommodation. Typical ready-packaged tours sold by tour operators either as main holidays or as short breaks include two travel components:

- transport for the main journey — air flight, coach travel, ferry crossing or rail journey
- transfers (where necessary) from the gateway point of entry (the airport, for example) to the accommodation

Figure 3.1 shows an example of a typical tour operator package arrangement. Customers buying the package shown in Figure 3.1 will benefit from the services of the tour operator's resort representative, who will meet them at the airport, supervise their transfer to their hotel and be an advisor for them during their stay. The resort representative will host a welcome meeting. This is a key opportunity for the representative to market the range of optional trips and events she or he has planned (often in a small team with colleagues representing the same or other tour operating companies). Profitability of any trip or event depends on having sufficient customers. If a coach is involved viability may depend on booking nearly all the seats. To acheive this, cooperation between the reps of different companies based at one hotel, or between those from different hotels in the resort, will be necessary.

Both self-packaging and tailor-made holidays have grown in number in recent years. Online bookers have made self-packaging easier, by

### 9 Days  Swiss Delights and the Glacier Express

**Tour highlights**

*Included excursions*
+ Glacier Express
+ Bernina Express
+ Klosters & Chur
+ Brienz & Lake Thun
+ Interlaken
+ Lucerne

*Optional excursions*
+ Shilthorn Train
+ Lake Lucerne Cruise
+ Lake Thun Cruise

*Figure 3.1* A typical holiday package

using websites that allow the customer a choice of flight, hotel, transfer and excursion options. Travelocity (**www.travelocity.co.uk**) is one example of such an online booker, Expedia (**www.expedia.co.uk**) is another. Figure 3.2 shows the flight options made available instantly by Travelocity to a self-packager intending to fly on 21 November 2006, returning on 26 November, travelling economy class and leading a party of two adults and one child. Users of sites such as this can go on and build their package, including further elements as they wish.

Tailor-made holidays are customised holidays packaged by a tour operator to meet a customer's individual requirements. Trailfinders (**www.trailfinders.com**, see Chapter 5.1) and Cox and Kings

*Figure 3.2*
*Online flight options*

(**www.coxandkings.co.uk**) are examples of travel and tourism providers that deal in the tailor-made market. Staff employed by them assemble the individual packages in consultation with the customer.

Specialist providers can assemble business travel packages that they put together on behalf of their corporate clients. An example of such a provider is Active Incentive Travel (**www.getactive.co.uk**) which markets overseas conference packages and incentive trips to businesses. The incentive trip is a tool that business managers can use to help motivate individual staff and teams. Chapter 2.2 of this book deals with motivating staff teams in the travel and tourism industry and Figure 3.3 gives information about one incentive trip that a business manager, who may be a travel and tourism manager, can buy as a staff motivator — perhaps as a reward for achieving a certain level of performance. The motorsport experience shown in Figure 3.3 is priced for one participant. Team motivation might be achieved by sending all team members on this trip or on another trip that involves working together in an adventure tourism activity (ATA, see Chapter 5.6). A white-water rafting trip could be used, for example, not only to motivate staff teams but also to build team spirit in order to facilitate greater efficiency when working together.

*Figure 3.3*
*An incentive trip*

### Ferrari Racing (Intro)        Price: **105**

No. of People: **1**
No. of Nights: **0**
Board: **N/A**
Availability: **N/A**
Locations: **W Sussex**

Everyone dreams of driving a Ferrari. Now you can in the knowledge that you won't get caught for speeding. Your taster session will last approximately 15 minutes and will consist of three laps around the famous Goodwood Circuit in West Sussex. The course is only available weekdays between March and October.

Includes: **15 minute (approx) session driving a Ferrari, equipment and tuition.**
Restrictions: **Full UK licence required, subject to terms and conditions of the centre. ONLY AVAILABLE WEEKDAYS MARCH TO OCTOBER**

*Source*: www.goactive.co.uk

Group packages are common in the educational tourism market. Operators such as UK Connection (**www.ukconnection.co.uk**, part of the tour-operating company Kuoni) specialise in arranging packages for the school and colleges market (Figure 3.4). To cover the breadth

of its specialist market, UK Connection also markets travel and accommodation packages for educational groups which like to organise their own itineraries. It also offers coach travel-only options for budget and UK/Europe trips.

## Running a trip as a project

Professionals in the travel and tourism industry plan, organise and run trips as parts of their jobs. Travel consultants, tour operators and resort representatives are examples of such jobs. As an A2 Travel and Tourism student you can apply the knowledge, skills and under-standing you have gained from your course to the planning and running of a trip within the UK or abroad. You could plan a one-off event or a residential tour, conference, ATA experi-ence or field trip. To run your own trip can be exciting and rewarding as well as good prepa-ration for the future. It is a chance to put your travel and tourism knowledge into practice.

**Figure 3.4**
*UK Connection brochure*

Chapter 3.1 explains how to compile a business plan for a trip, or other travel and tourism event.

### Other project and event options

Travel and tourism projects and events involve travel and so the customers are tourists. **Tourists** are people who travel from the area where they normally live and work to somewhere else. They do this for leisure reasons (for a holiday), business purposes or to visit friends and relatives (VFR). It is important to bear these first principles in mind when considering project and event options other than running a trip. An event held in your own school or college and attracting local customers would be likely to be a leisure industry event but would not be travel and tourism.

Since a trip involves travelling *away* (probably from your home area), the logical alternative to organising a trip is to consider options that involve travel *to* your area. There are three options:

1 An exchange with a group of students from somewhere else — it may be, for example, that the modern languages department in

your school or college could use your services to help arrange an exchange.

2 Hosting tourists that come to your area, maybe to your school or college — for example visiting sports teams. Candidates for job interviews who do not live locally are business tourists. Accommodation and travel arrangements could be made for either of these groups and leisure-time activities organised, perhaps providing a guide service too.

3 Promoting a tourist attraction or facility in your area. Through your course, you may have good links with a local travel and tourism organisation. Planning, organising and running a promotional event on its behalf would be a travel and tourism project if it is a travel and tourism organisation with tourist customers.

### Teams

Projects carried out by teams work well because the various tasks can be shared out between team members. This means each task can be given sufficient time and attention. Chapter 3.2 deals with team working and suggests how tasks may be distributed among team members.

However, it is important that the work of team members is coordinated. Regular team meetings are held in the travel and tourism industry between staff delivering customer service and such meetings are likely to be part of a successful A2 Travel and Tourism project.

Team size matters. Obviously there needs to be a sufficient number of team members to do the work properly. On the other hand, efficient teams are not overloaded with too many members. For example, a group of three or four people may be all that is needed to plan and organise a trip away. Excessive numbers either generates 'passengers' — members who don't really make much of a contribution — or spreads the work so thinly that no one has a chance to become very involved.

### Viability

Travel and tourism organisations are often commercial operations. Tour operators organise trips that are economically viable. Usually, this means that they are profitable in themselves. For example, a specialist adventure tour operator offering a trip to a new destination may cancel the tour if it does not attract sufficient customers to at least cover the costs of organisation. Disappointed customers will be

**Discussion point**

Which other class members could you best work with in a team?

offered either a place on another holiday or their money back. This may be just their deposit, or, if the company cancels the tour at a late stage, the full amount.

An A2 Travel and Tourism project may well be a one-off trip or event. It is important to establish at an early stage of planning that it is likely to be viable — to attract sufficient customers and take enough money to pay for the costs of running it. If other income is available from elsewhere, such as a subsidy, or money from sponsorship, this can be taken into account. Chapter 3.1 deals with planning the project, including deciding about viability.

## Support your learning

### Information sources

Tour operator brochures, online bookers' websites (and those of airlines) can be explored to discover the range of packages that have been put together for the market.

### Skills builder

Develop your internet research skills by compiling a short leaflet directory of business travel organisers.

### Activities menu

1 Produce a list of types of trip that are organised by the travel and tourism industry and that could be used as an A2 Travel and Tourism project.

2 Use an online booking site to price three different options for a group of four 19-year-old students wanting to spend a weekend in one city destination outside the UK.

3 Research and analyse three methods of travelling from your home town to a tourist town or city within the UK.

4 *Vocational scenario*
Imagine you are a travel and tourism manager responsible for customer service teams. Evaluate three different incentive trips that might help build team skills and motivate a team of six adults.

# 3.1

# Business plans

The viability and feasibility of a travel and tourism project can be evaluated by producing a business plan.

- **Viability** refers to the demand level for the project's product or service. Are there sufficient customers? Is it likely to break even?
- **Feasibility** takes into account what the organising team can deliver; for example is the project realistically within their capabilities?

## Elements of a business plan

The business plan you produce for a travel and tourism project should consist of the elements shown in Figure 3.5.

*Figure 3.5*
*The elements of a business plan*

Figure 3.5 contains quite a long list, which is why it is appropriate to work with others as a team. Once the aims and objectives have been agreed, many of the remaining elements can be researched and presented by individual team members at regular team meetings.

## Aims and objectives

Aims and objectives are related but they are not the same as each other. **Aims** are the project's broad purposes while **objectives** are its clearly identified targets. A travel and tourism project's aims may be broad. They may be to run a viable, safe, fun trip for customers. Objectives are harder-edged and might be seen as the answers to the key question 'How can we know?' that follows the aims. Table 3.1 relates the aims and objectives of a projected trip.

*Table 3.1 The aims and objectives of a trip*

| Aims | → | Objectives |
|---|---|---|
| A viable trip | 'How can we know?' | The trip should break even financially |
| Fun for customers | 'How can we know?' | Customer feedback will show most of them enjoyed the experience |
| A trip that is safe | 'How can we know?' | Conforms to relevant health and safety regulations |

Objectives, once stated and agreed, become the targets to which the whole team should work. For instance, for the trip in Table 3.1, now that viability has been clarified as meaning 'break even', the choice of destination is narrowed down to one that:
- will attract sufficient customers
- can be priced to cover costs while being affordable by the potential customers

Customers, it can be seen, are key. The trip won't be viable without enough of them or without their money. Team meetings early in the project — perhaps even the first meeting — will need to clarify who the customers are (the target market). Market research may need to be undertaken into questions such as:
- What sort of trip, to what destination, would potential customers find attractive?
- How much would they be prepared to pay?
- When would they be able to travel?

## SMART objectives

SMART objectives are targets that are:

- **s**pecific — clearly identified
- **m**easurable — can be quantified and tested to evaluate success
- **a**chievable — the team is capable of meeting each objective
- **r**ealistic — can be expected to work in the project's market and regulatory environment
- **t**imed — are amenable to the setting of a timetable of dates

An example of the SMART objectives of an A2 Travel and Tourism project planned by students from a sixth-form college in the UK is shown in Figure 3.6.

All the four objectives identified in Figure 3.6 are SMART. Look at the first objective.

- Setting a clear date, destination and length for the trip is a specific objective (S). It is more than a broad aim, which is just to run a trip at all. What the project will be is now clearly defined.
- Whether the objective is eventually met will be measurable from the calendar (M).
- March is far enough into the A2 year for the planning team to have a good chance of actually running the trip to a place they can readily research (A).
- The destination is realistic for peer-group customers to afford and sufficiently conservative to attract college management approval (R).
- Having a clear month in mind makes it possible to work out a timetable of dates for the organising stages (T).

1. Run a 2-day city break trip to Dublin in March
2. Break even financially, paying all the costs only from sales revenue
3. Every customer is satisfied (a 100% satisfaction rating)
4. Health, safety and security policies laid down by the college are followed

*Figure 3.6*
*SMART objectives for a trip to Dublin*

The objectives need to be in the forefront of team thinking when putting together the rest of the business plan. Links back to the agreed objectives of the project should be made from every other element of the business plan.

## Customers

There are two types of customers — internal customers and external customers.

**Internal customers** in a travel and tourism organisation are its staff — people within the organisation. So, internal customers in a travel and tourism project team are the team members themselves. They provide customer service for each other. One example of this is if each team member has an allocated role and reports on progress to the regular team meeting. The team member is providing a service to the rest of the team, who are therefore the internal customers.

**External customers** are people who are served and are outside the project team. They may still be people internal to the school or college. The paying customers who would travel on the trip to Dublin (featured in Figure 3.6 and Chapter 3.3) are external customers. Successful planning of the project depends on a clear definition of the customer base in terms of factors including age group, spending power and interests.

An A2 Travel and Tourism project may have external customers such as:
■ other students of the school or college
■ teaching and ancillary staff
■ parents, friends and siblings of students and staff
■ pupils or students of another school (such as a partner feeder school)
■ exchange students and teachers from overseas
■ members of a visiting sports team or music ensemble
■ the management of an attraction that the project aims to promote
■ members of the general public

Once the target customer group has been agreed, it is important to identify the customer service needs particular to that group. When in Dublin, for example, what visitor attractions or leisure activities would most meet their needs and help meet the objective of 100% customer satisfaction?

## Marketing techniques

Market research may be undertaken to help identify the target market segment and to discover the needs of potential customer members, so that project planning can be tailored to meet them. A questionnaire is likely to be one appropriate technique to discover what people want out of a trip or event, what price they will pay and when it should take place. Knowing answers to these questions enables you to consider the 4Ps of marketing.
■ **P**roduct — what trip or event, using what kind of transport and when?
■ **P**lace — where should the venue be, where should a trip start from, where can promotional techniques be most effectively used?
■ **P**rice — how much can be charged that will still attract sufficient customers?

■ **P**romotion — how can the event or trip be most successfully brought to the target market's *attention*, to raise their *interest* and *desire* and lead them to *act* (AIDA) by attending or paying a deposit?

### Promotional techniques

Advertising is one promotional technique that can be used. Market research evidence can be studied to try to establish what advertising messages will grab the attention and interest of the target market. Supposing that the target market is made up, at least partly, of members of the school or college, where might advertisements most effectively be placed? Where could you put poster, flyers and leaflets, for example?

Publicity may also be generated using existing systems of information dissemination such as announcements, daily bulletins and staff briefings. Internally, an intranet system can be effectively harnessed. Advertisements can be posted, announcements made and direct mail e-mails sent. Externally, press releases can be written and public relations firms used by the school/college could be consulted.

Marketing is generally most effective when a campaign is organised from launch onwards, making a series of well-planned and timetabled promotional interventions in the life of the school or college during the promotional phase of organising the project.

### Resources

Table 3.2 summarises the ranges of physical, financial and human resources that may need to be considered. A team will need to think through the entire operation of the project and list all the resources of these three types that are needed. It will need to be clear how and when these resources will be accessed and who will do what. Allocation of responsibilities among team members will help get this task done. However, the team as a whole will need to be satisfied that all the resources needed are in place. For any specific project, resources other than those listed in Table 3.2 may be needed. Chapter 3.3 'Managing your own project' presents practical scenarios that may help you to run your project.

### Systems

The second financial aspect of the business plan concerns budgeting, and the handling of payments (by customers and to suppliers).

**Discussion point**

Where would you place promotional materials and activities in your school or college?

| Physical | Financial | Human |
|---|---|---|
| • Equipment such as display equipment, ICT hardware including VCR, furniture and transport<br>• Space, for example a venue for an event<br>• Materials — for promotion, for instance | • Money<br>• Subsidies<br>• Income from fund-raising events | • Team members running the event<br>• Teaching staff or adult supervision<br>• Expertise — health and safety officer advice, for instance |

*Table 3.2*
*Travel and tourism project resources*

Payment handling goes along with other administrative systems, in particular with record keeping. You need to know who has paid what and when, for example. Records may be kept using paper-based systems, such as a payment card with ledger back-up for an instalment-paid trip, or electronically, perhaps using spreadsheet software.

A budget document should be produced, detailing the categories and amounts of both income and expenditure, balanced to show that income can be expected to cover the total expenditure. In colleges and schools, budgetary advice and documentation can be obtained from office staff and senior teachers.

### The law

The legalities of health and safety, security and insurance need to be considered as part of the business plan. There are potential implications, depending on the nature of the actual project for:

■ the safe provision of food and drink
■ security of customers' belongings
■ keeping customer data secure under the terms of the Data Protection Act 1998
■ fire safety, including not exceeding the safe capacity of the venue
■ the safe use of equipment

As A2 Travel and Tourism students you are not likely to be fully conversant with all these requirements, even if you have studied some health, safety and security legislation and regulation during your course. The best solution is to take qualified advice. Health and safety officers are able to advise on how school events and trips should be conducted and they can provide appropriate documentation, such as risk assessments that members of the team can complete under their guidance.

## Contingency plans

Things go wrong. Projects may be meticulously planned but some unforeseen occurrence outside the control of the organisers can still upset matters. Good business plans consider:

- what could conceivably go wrong
- for each eventuality, what would the organisers do?
- what resources need to be held in reserve — such as a budgeted amount of money or spare staff capacity — in case they are needed

## Time scale

Timetabled stages in the organisation of the project need to be agreed. Team members need to keep to the timetable and, if that is not possible, report to the team as a whole so that contingency arrangements can be made. It is advisable to build in some flexibility so that minor delays can be absorbed without affecting the overall time plan, in particular the date of the actual trip or event.

Critical path analysis is a technique which can be used. It is discussed in Chapter 3.3.

## Support your learning

### Information sources

People are the most important sources for project-planning advice. Staff in your school or college have particular expertise, for example in budgeting or health and safety, which can be tapped.

### Skills builder

Work in a group to hold a meeting. Write a proper agenda and keep formal minutes. This initial meeting can be done as a simulation exercise in preparation for the actual project planning when regular team meetings should be held as a matter of course.

### Activities menu

1 Explain how each of the project objectives given in Figure 3.6 is a SMART objective.

2 a Produce a list of SMART objectives for one travel and tourism project other than that in Figure 3.6.
   b Explain why one of your objectives is a SMART objective.

3 Research and analyse the needs of one customer group for your project idea from Activity 2.

4 *Vocational scenario*
   Imagine you are a resort representative based in a hotel in an overseas destination. Evaluate how well two possible social events could bring families with children closer together.

# Team working

A good business plan is a solid foundation on which to build the project itself. It provides the pathway along which the project should progress and should be referred to frequently along the way. Teamwork is the next essential. This chapter deals with teams, and is based round the context of running an A2 Travel and Tourism project.

## Team purpose

A project is one-off. The purpose of the team is confined to the delivery of the project — its planning, organisation and running, followed by an evaluation of its success. These are four distinct phases and at any one time each is the purpose of the team. It is important to remember that the project is the whole point of the team existing and to avoid distractions such as 'having a bit of fun'. The project will be exciting and stimulating, provided team members are fully involved. This is a good reason to think carefully about who should be in the team and how many — avoid having too many people involved.

During the designing of the business plan, SMART objectives will be determined (see Chapter 3.1). These objectives more clearly define the purpose of the project

## Team structure

Figure 3.7 shows one possible team structure. Tight and well-organised teams work well. If you are organising a simple trip, four team members may be sufficient. The roles and responsibilities of these team members create the structure. Although six job titles appear on Figure 3.7, the project leader and deputy can each effectively undertake one of the other roles as well.

The structure in Figure 3.7 is small but formal. It is hierarchical, with lines of command clearly drawn. The leader and deputy are line-managers of the others and the leader is the line-manager of the

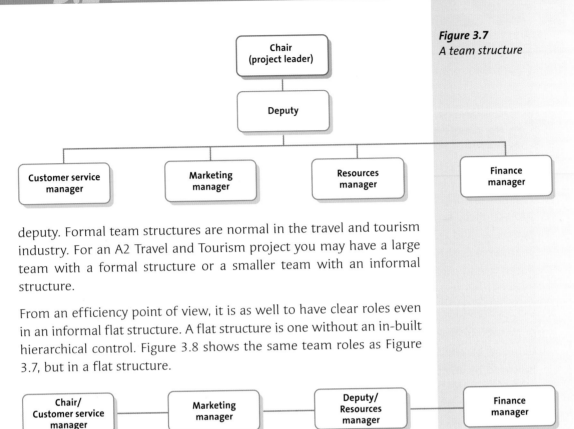

**Figure 3.7**
*A team structure*

deputy. Formal team structures are normal in the travel and tourism industry. For an A2 Travel and Tourism project you may have a large team with a formal structure or a smaller team with an informal structure.

From an efficiency point of view, it is as well to have clear roles even in an informal flat structure. A flat structure is one without an in-built hierarchical control. Figure 3.8 shows the same team roles as Figure 3.7, but in a flat structure.

Team structures can evolve from informal to more formal. During the course of running an A2 project it is common for a natural leader (or leaders) to emerge from teams — individuals whose energy and commitment drive the project forward or whose people skills enable them to motivate others and settle personality clashes that arise.

**Figure 3.8**
*A flat team structure*

Planning, organising and running an A2 Travel and Tourism project is a learning experience — team members learn about themselves and each other and teachers and lecturers learn about team members. In undertaking the project it is sometimes the case that less expected leaders emerge from the team. Their contribution could be stifled by the setting of an over-rigid formal structure early on using an obvious candidate as leader.

The roles of chair and secretary (agenda writing and minute-taking included) can be effectively rotated between the members of an A2 project. This allows all team members to 'have a go' and also provides evidence of their contribution to the planning process. In the travel and tourism industry this would be unlikely to happen because the roles, responsibilities and seniority of individual team members are clearly delineated.

## Team building and interaction

Figure 3.9 shows a typical classroom dialogue when the idea of project teams is first introduced.

**Figure 3.9** *Is this what your classroom is like?*

It is common for pre-existing friendship groups within a class to gel together into nascent teams. Some of these will be effective (those made up of hardworking, already firmly established, small groups of friends), others will not (peers whose influence on each other is not conducive to work). There may be individual class members or pairs who are not part of cells in the travel and tourism class — perhaps their friends do different subjects. They may gel with each other.

Michelle

Extrovert
Plain-spoken
Energetic
A do-er

Daniel

Quiet
Tactful
Hard-working
A thinker

*Figure 3.10*
*Two sides to successful team-leading*

In an A2 situation it is likely that the initial groups will be allowed to assemble themselves by the teacher or lecturer — perhaps with broad guidelines such as how many should be in each group. A teacher may, alternatively, design the teams. Assuming that the teacher does not intervene, however, individual students are well advised to remember that the team's purpose is the delivery of the project on time and on budget and to ask coolly who they would work with best to achieve that end. This might not always be their best friends.

Figure 3.10 profiles two students who were not members of the same friendship group, but worked effectively together in running their team's project and emerged as the team's twin drivers. Michelle, the more obviously dominant, was perhaps considered by other team members to be the leader, but she and Daniel didn't see it like that and worked together at leading the team and ensuring eventual success.

## Tuckman's stages of team building

The American educational psychologist Bruce Tuckman first advanced his model of team building stages in 1965. His basic model (Figure 3.11) has stood the test of time and is worth thinking about as team relationships develop. The four stages are based on observations of what happens in teams. They are still valid because experience since 1965 has shown that teams do, by and large, develop this way.

It will help you form a team if you are aware that these stages are likely to happen, are normal and can be worked through. That does not mean that nothing need be done. Relationships that become strained in stage 2 need to be mended for progress through to stage 3 to occur. The emergent project-driving members of stage 3 are often those who were able to do the mending and so encourage back into the group members who were in danger of dropping by the wayside.

### Teams working to solve problems

Rather as relationship issues are par for the course as teams develop, so problems can be expected during organisation and execution. Teams deal with problems well when they are flexible enough to admit that difficulties happen. You also need to be aware that problems occur in one team member's area of responsibility which are not necessarily the fault of that person. Problems happen. Problems have solutions.

Finding a solution depends on:

- clearly defining the problem
- identifying the options for moving forward
- evaluating the options together and agreeing on the direction to take

Outside expertise from consultants is brought into play by teams when the members of the team realise that, between them, they lack the expertise to see a solution or understand the relative merits of different options. A2 Travel and Tourism teams can and should consult others, including teaching, administrative and senior staff in their school or college, as and when necessary.

**1** *Forming*
- Starting to be a team
- Getting to know each other or beginning to focus on the task
- A nervous time as members interact warily

**2** *Storming*
- Clarifying roles and relationships
- Uneasy and potentially stormy stage (hence the name)
- Members may compete for roles
- Some may dislike the roles they are given and disappoint others by their lack of effort
- People can fall out

**3** *Norming*
- The team gets into gear
- People get on better with each other and start to pull together
- Individual team members may begin to shine

**4** *Performing*
- Now it's getting done
- The project moves along and the event or trip happens
- New relationships emerge, based on mutual respect of colleagues

*Figure 3.11*
*Tuckman's stages in building a team*

## Project success

How successful a travel and tourism project is depends on how well its management team works together in planning, preparing and running the final trip or event. Factors that affect the effective working of project teams are summarised in Figure 3.12.

**1 Communication**

Successful teams keep in touch with each other — not just at team meetings but in between meetings too. Use informal chats, mobile phones and e-mails to help

**2 Leadership**

If there is a formal structure, the leader will need to be given the space to lead. Careful choice of the leader is very important. If there is an informal structure, a natural leader or driver may emerge. Rotate the job of chair between meetings

**3 Personality clashes**

These happen (see Tuckman's stage 2). Leaders may help smooth over clashes between members. Members can help when it is an issue involving the leader — this is a reason for an informal starting structure

**4 Resources**

Planning needs to set SMART objectives (Chapter 3.1). 'A' is for achievable. Resources that are achievable should be planned for

**5 Environment**

Not just physical, though that helps — a suitable room/space to meet. The atmosphere between people is important. Get to know each other and stay focused on the team purpose

**6 Problem solving**

Problems happen. Problems have solutions. Define the problem, evaluate options, consult others

*Success*

**Figure 3.12** *Factors in project success*

## Support your learning

**Information sources**

As in Chapter 3.1, people are key. Team working advice is likely to be available from staff in your school or college.

**Skills builder**

Build team-working skills in advance of the main project you run — perhaps with a preparatory activity like Activity 2 below. Go on to produce an evaluation (Activity 4), so you reflect on improving your skills for the 'real thing'.

**Activities menu**

1 Design a cartoon strip to illustrate Tuckman's four stages (Figure 3.11).

2 *Vocational scenario*
  Work as part of a small team to mount a display suitable for a travel fair that promotes one tourism destination.

3 Research and analyse the structures of two contrasting organisational teams.

4 Evaluate the team's performance in carrying out Activity 2.

# Managing your own project

This chapter presents three practical scenarios to help you manage your own travel and tourism project. These scenarios are:

1 a tour project
2 a guided tour
3 a tourism event

Time management is crucial to successful project management. This chapter also introduces two time-management techniques:

- critical path analysis
- Gantt charts

## Scenario 1  A tour project

Project definition: a weekend tour to Dublin in March for sixth-form students from Darlington, Co. Durham. The route of the trip is shown in Figure 3.13.

### Critical path analysis

Critical path analysis is a tool that helps the scheduling and management of complex projects — such as an A2 Travel and Tourism project. It helps with planning tasks that need doing. Critical path analysis can be the basis for preparing the project schedule and planning the use of resources. During the management of your own travel and tourism project, it allows your team to monitor when project stages have been successfully completed. Critical path analysis can also help you identify when action may need to be taken to put the project back on course after a problem has arisen.

Figure 3.14 shows the application of critical path analysis to the Dublin tour scenario. The approach taken was to start with the period of time available for organising the project (November to March). That gave

**Discussion point**

What would be a suitable A2 tour project originating from your locality?

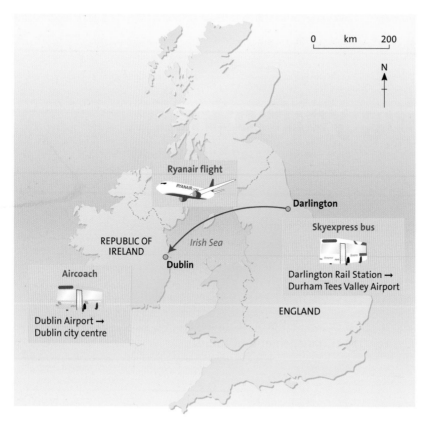

**Figure 3.13**
*The Dublin trip*

five rows, one for each month (plus one for follow up in April). Within each column the tasks that need to be done that month were recorded, using arrows across the months to link the elements of each task together. Completing the analysis in rough first helps identify tasks and sequences that may not be apparent initially.

## Scenario 2  A guided tour

Project definition: plan and deliver a 3-hour introductory tour of Newcastle-upon-Tyne and Gateshead Quaysides and a city centre shopping opportunity in Newcastle-upon-Tyne for a group of seven French exchange students. This will be one of a series of tours for this group that make up the overall project.

### Planning the tour

There are considerations to clarify with the external customer. In this case, during the planning phase, the immediate customer is the head of modern languages. The clarifications needed so far have been noted

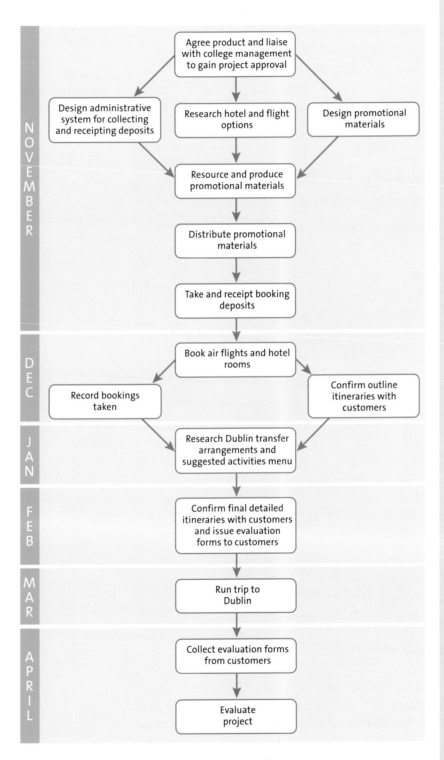

**Figure 3.14**
*An example of critical path analysis*

by Amy, the liaising team member. The relevant page of her notebook (with replies) is shown in Figure 3.15.

**Figure 3.15**
*Clarification notes*

✦ When (date and time)?

*April 5. Morning. Expect to arrive in Newcastle at 10:00.*

✦ How will the group be travelling to Newcastle?

*Train to Newcastle Central Station.*

✦ Should refreshment opportunities be built in?

*A coffee break if convenient. Lunch organised by French teacher.*

✦ Will the group have any specific needs, such as wheelchair access?

*Yes — there is one student in a wheelchair.*

✦ How will responsibility for the group be handed back?

*All meet at some central point in the city centre (Grey's Monument?) French teacher will take them to lunch from there. We're invited.*

Figure 3.16 shows the agenda for the next team meeting.

**Figure 3.16**
*The agenda for a
planning meeting*

French exchange
Guided tours project
Meeting 16 January, 1.15 p.m.
Room 139

### AGENDA

1 Apologies for absence
2 Matters arising
3 Newcastle/Gateshead tour
  a Report from Amy (meeting with French teacher)
  b Places to include
  c Possibility of using bus from Central Station to Quayside
4 AOB

## Scenario 3  A tourism event

An appropriate example is a promotional event for a local tourist facility — such as a museum — that has tourist customers. One such event is a family open day, which is publicised beyond the immediate area.

## Gantt charts

Gantt charts are useful tools for analysing and planning more complex projects. They help you:

- plan the tasks involved
- schedule when tasks will be done
- plan the use of resources
- carry out a critical path analysis (see Figure 3.14, Scenario 1)

Figure 3.18 is an example of a Gantt chart used to plan a family open day at a small steam railway museum run by volunteers.

**Figure 3.17**
*Plan an event for a local tourist facility such as a museum*

| | Nov | Dec | Jan | Feb | Mar |
|---|---|---|---|---|---|
| Agree idea | | | | | |
| Get college approval | | | | | |
| Design and produce promotional materials | | | | | |
| Plan open day activities | | | | | |
| Organise resources | | | | | |
| Ensure health and safety in place | | | | | |
| Run event | | | | | |
| Evaluate event | | | | | |

**Figure 3.18**
*An example of a Gantt chart*

## Support your learning

### Information sources

Other team members, staff at the museum, a local tour guide and your teacher/lecturer are relevant sources for the scenarios here. You might consider using a few other students as a focus group to discuss your marketing and customer service ideas.

### Skills builder

Apply the critical path analysis and Gantt chart techniques.

**Activities menu**

1 Write the report you, playing the part of Amy in Scenario 2, would give your team meeting about your meeting with the head of modern languages.

2 Apply the critical path analysis technique to the museum event (Scenario 3), for which Figure 3.18 is a Gantt chart.

3 Research and analyse places to include in the Newcastle/Gateshead guided tour (Scenario 2).

4 Evaluate the usefulness of the Quayside bus service for the tour in Scenario 2.

**4**

# Managing tourism developments and impacts

# 4 Managing tourism developments and impacts

# *Starter:* **tourism developments and impacts**

## Tourism development

**Development** is change that is planned to be an improvement. Tourism is growing across much of the world and tourism development, or change within a destination, involves the growth of tourist facilities. These facilities belong to different sectors of the travel and tourism industry, including the following:

- hotels (accommodation)
- airports (transport)
- purpose-built attractions such as theme and water parks

A tourism development project in a destination may involve several elements belonging to different sectors of the industry. Tourism development may also be seen as part of the economic growth or regeneration of an area. In that case, it may include elements of development from other industries, such as retail and leisure, or residential development.

The Sands development project in Scarborough is an example of tourism development (Figure 4.1). Scarborough is a seaside resort on the coast of Yorkshire in the north of England. The Sands project includes some elements that are clearly for tourists:

- hotel and conference centre
- covered water park
- open air theatre
- extensive car parking

Some of these elements and the remaining elements of the development cross over into other industries and into the residential sector:

- sports facilities
- health and fitness club
- casino
- shops
- bars and restaurants
- apartments

**Figure 4.1** *The Sands development in Scarborough*

Many of the elements of the Sands development have been planned with the intention of attracting customers from the local area as well as tourists, who by definition must live and work elsewhere. There are close links between the leisure and the travel and tourism industries in the UK, and developments such as restaurants, car parks and sports facilities often attract local leisure customers as well as tourist visitors. For example, the residential apartments at the Sands are intended for sale to customers who may buy them to live in permanently or as second homes. They might also buy to let — meaning they will rent them out, perhaps to workers in the resort or to tourists.

## Impacts

What is intended to happen does not always occur, and tourism developments intended to bring economic gain to a place can have negative as well as positive impacts. Table 4.1 shows how the impacts of tourism are classified. Social impacts are sometimes called sociocultural impacts. **Culture** refers to a society's way of life and this can be impacted upon by tourism — often, but not necessarily, in a negative way.

**Table 4.1** *Examples of impacts of tourism*

|  | Economic | Environmental | Social |
|---|---|---|---|
| **Positive** | A tourism development brings employment | Landscaping improves the appearance of a destination | There are improved leisure facilities for local people to use too |
| **Negative** | There is economic leakage, with profits going somewhere else | Extra pollution is caused by tourist transport vehicle exhaust emissions | The traditional way of life of local people is disrupted |

The direction of impact (positive or negative) can be in the eye of the beholder. While foreign observers and older local people may bemoan the loss of traditional life patterns in rural areas caused by tourism development, younger locals may enjoy the new, more sophisticated life brought by the tourists. Tourism developments are issues because they attract differing points of view. They are often the focus of controversy and conflict.

## Economic impacts

### Positive economic impacts

The economic impacts of travel and tourism are those connected with wealth and money. On the positive side, tourism developments create jobs, and the local people employed in those jobs are paid wages that they spend in the destination that is their home. This benefits the local economy. Other local businesses, which may not be travel and tourism businesses, prosper in consequence, feeding more money into the local economy and creating more jobs. This is called the **multiplier effect** because jobs and money multiply as a result of travel and tourism development.

A major tourism development like the Sands project in Scarborough can act as a **growth pole**. This means that other new tourism developments are stimulated because of the overspill trade from the major development. It acts as a growth pole, attracting tourists to itself. These tourists then venture further into the destination and become a market, encouraging other tourism-related developments such as bars, restaurants, hotels and visitor attractions to soak up the new business that has been generated.

In the case of the Sands project, such facilities are already incorporated within the development. In other situations, tourism development may occur spontaneously on the doorstep of a planned development. In Chapter 4.3 the section about Negril, Jamaica, describes an example of spontaneous tourism development in a less economically developed country (LEDC). Figure 4.2 shows an example of spontaneous tourism development in the seaside resort of Port de Pollença in Mallorca.

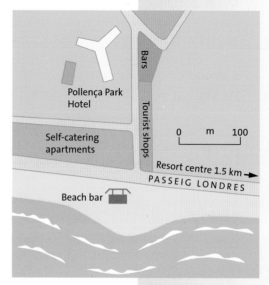

**Figure 4.2** *Pollença Park Hotel, Mallorca — a growth pole*

Local governments, for example in parts of the less economically developed world (LEDW) in South and Central America, the Caribbean, Africa, the Indian Ocean, south and southeast Asia and the islands of the Pacific Ocean, are often keen to encourage tourism development because of its economic benefits. In more economically developed countries (MEDCs) such as the UK, similar positive economic impacts are often the hope of tourism development agents. Such agents are active stakeholders in tourism developments in areas of economic regeneration, as explained in Chapter 4.1.

### Negative economic impacts

In some cases the jobs brought to a destination by tourism development are seasonal. This is a problem traditionally experienced by seaside resorts in the UK, such as Scarborough, where the winter unemployment rate has risen. The residential, retail and leisure elements of the Sands tourism development project attempt to address this issue by providing the opportunity for year-round revenue.

A second negative impact is **economic leakage**. This occurs where the wealth brought to a destination by tourism development leaks away again to somewhere else. Economic leakage is a problem that has been experienced in some LEDW countries, for example where foreign-owned hotel chains have established themselves. Although the hotel company may pay taxes locally, its profits belong to a large organisation whose headquarters may be overseas (often in a MEDC in western Europe, North America, Japan or Australasia). Profit may leak away from the destination and go overseas. This is examined in more detail in Chapter 4.3.

## Environmental impacts

The very act of travelling can have negative environmental impacts. Aircraft, ships, trains, cars and coaches all consume fuel. Emissions from road transport and aircraft in particular can have damaging effects on the environment through atmospheric pollution. Tourism developments, such as airports and the new highways connecting them to increasingly developed tourism destinations such as beach resorts, can have a negative environmental impact, as shown in Chapter 4.2. Pollution caused by noise and by waste disposal can also be downsides of tourism development if they are not properly managed. Tourist destinations with coral reefs, for example in the Maldives, have experienced some damage as a result of water pollution when untreated shampoo from hotel showers is emptied into the sea.

Clearing land for the building of tourism facilities such as hotels changes the natural environment in ways that may be seen as detrimental. For example, natural vegetation and animal habitats may be lost and there may be impacts on the land's natural drainage system, increasing the risk of flooding.

However, tourism can also bring environmental benefits. Landscaping often accompanies tourist developments such as hotels, seaside resorts and purpose-built resorts such as the Disneyland complexes. This leads to artificial environmental change that may be judged as a positive impact. In hot countries, coastal marshes may be breeding grounds for mosquitoes and a health risk for the transmission of diseases such as malaria. The drainage of such swamps adjacent to tourism developments can be beneficial to local inhabitants as well as tourists and will probably be seen by them as an environmental improvement.

## Sociocultural impacts

**Sociocultural impacts** are impacts on people's ways of life. On the one hand, tourism brings people from different places and cultures into contact with each other, creating the opportunity for increased understanding between different social groups. On the other hand, conflicts and frictions can sometimes result. For example, domestic tourism development in the UK has sometimes led to conflict between local customers and tourist visitors in the bars and clubs of seaside resorts.

Tourists from places with very different cultural standards to those held by local people in a tourist destination can cause offence, often unintentionally. For example, the wearing of beachwear in town centres and on sightseeing trips to religious sites may be viewed as inappropriate in some countries. This is more likely when tourism development brings significant numbers of tourists to a destination where the host population is unused to their ways — often in an LEDW setting. Sensitive management can mitigate such effects, as explained in Chapter 4.4.

**Discussion point**

What can the travel and tourism industry do to avoid conflicts between locals and visitors?

# Sustainable tourism development

**Sustainable tourism** development tries to allow tourism and tourist facilities to grow in ways that will have minimal negative impact on a destination. In this way the destination is not spoilt — either for local people or future tourists. The tourist appeal of a destination is often a result of attractive natural environments. Beach resorts such as Negril in Jamaica (see Chapter 4.3) initially became developed for tourists because of the presence of a beach. In Negril, there is a continuous 11 km (7 mile) sweep of sand north from what was originally a small fishing village on Jamaica's western tip (Figure 4.3).

*Figure 4.3
Negril's beach*

Natural environments are often fragile and tourism development in such places can be damaging if sufficient care is not taken. Sustainable tourism development management attempts to conserve the environment so that tourists will keep coming to the destination in the long term. Where this is successful it means that both the environment and the tourism development itself can be sustained into the future.

*Figure 4.4 Examples of ecotourism holidays*

## Ecotourism and responsible tourism

**Ecotourism** involves visiting a destination because of its natural environment, while causing minimal impact on that environment. Ecotourism developments focus on not upsetting the balance or harmony of life in the ecosystem that is the attraction. Accommodation, for example, is low-rise and designed to fit in with the natural surroundings. It is serviced in an environmentally friendly way and staffed by local people. Ecotourism has an ecological ethos — hence the name. Figure 4.4 shows examples of ecotourism holidays marketed to UK tourists by one online booker that specialises in responsible tourism in the natural and rural environments (**www.responsibletravel.com**). Further details of ecotourism and responsible tourism are given in Chapter 4.4.

**Responsible tourism** involves visiting any destination (whether a natural attraction or not) in such a way as to cause minimal negative impact on its environment and the culture of the host community. Responsible tourism tour operators attract customers who are sympathetic to this notion. They package their holidays so that their customers' impact on the destination is positive. For example, local suppliers and local labour are used wherever possible. In this way the economic benefits of tourism feed directly to the local people and tourists and locals come into contact in positive and mutually beneficial ways.

## Support your learning

### Information sources

1 Media articles in the UK feature newly proposed tourism developments and views about their impacts.

2 Websites of responsible travel companies, such as **www.responsibletravel.com**, and tourism pressure groups, such as **www.tourismconcern.org.uk**, cover mass tourism's negative effects and the positive benefits of sustainable tourism.

### Skills builder

Debate the likely positive and negative impacts of a tourism development such as the Sands project in Scarborough.

### Activities menu

1 a Explain what is meant by each of the following:
   * tourism development
   * sustainable tourism
   * ecotourism
   b Distinguish ecotourism from responsible tourism.

2 Suggest the likely positive and negative impacts of one tourism development project, such as the Sands project in Scarborough.

3 *Vocational scenario*
   Imagine you are a researcher for an ecotourism pressure group. Find out about and analyse a range of ecofriendly tourist accommodation available to UK customers travelling to the Amazon region of South America.

4 Evaluate the extent to which any one responsible tourism holiday would appeal to a family of two adults and three children.

# 4.1

# Tourism development

**Tourism development** is a change in the facilities provided by the travel and tourism industry for the delivery of its products and services. Such change is planned with the intention of bringing what providers see as improvement — growth in, or maintenance of, tourist custom. Tourism developments may involve the enhancement, upgrading or refurbishment of current facilities or the creation of new ones, either in an existing tourism destination or as part of establishing a new destination.

## Agents of tourism development

Agents of tourism development are the individuals and organisations involved in developing tourism in a specific place. They include construction companies, private-sector travel and tourism organisations such as hotel owners, and public-sector organisations such as local councils. In a tourism development project, individuals and organisations from the commercial and non-commercial sectors often work together in partnership. Rundown inner-city areas in the UK, often in dockland and-riverside locations, have been regenerated in recent years. Tourism development has played a major part of that process in cities, including Edinburgh, Manchester, London, Bristol, Belfast, Cardiff, Newcastle-upon-Tyne and Liverpool. Figures 4.5 and 4.6 show tourism development along the River Tyne in Newcastle/Gateshead.

*Figure 4.5* Tourism developments, Quayside, Newcastle/Gateshead

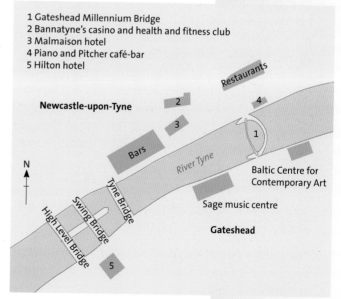

1 Gateshead Millennium Bridge
2 Bannatyne's casino and health and fitness club
3 Malmaison hotel
4 Piano and Pitcher café-bar
5 Hilton hotel

TopFoto

**Figure 4.6**
*The Gateshead
Millennium Bridge*

Urban redevelopment schemes like those in Britain's major cities have the aim of broad economic regeneration. Elements of the total development package may be travel and tourism facilities in themselves or may serve a customer base that is part local and part tourist visitor. For example, the Gateshead Millennium Bridge is a tourist attraction but it is also a bridge used by local people to cross the River Tyne. Similarly, the Baltic art gallery and the Sage music centre are widely used by local people as well as attracting tourists. The hotels on both banks of the River Tyne (including the Malmaision and the Hilton) are more overtly travel and tourism facilities, attracting business and leisure tourists. Leisure facilities such as Bannatyne's casino and health and fitness club and restaurant/bars such as the Piano and Pitcher have many local leisure customers and are facilities belonging to the leisure industry. However, they also attract tourists. All these and other facilities on the Newcastle and Gateshead Quayside create a locality with an ambience and visual appeal attractive to many tourists.

## Tourism development overseas

Tourism development projects vary widely in the MEDW. Table 4.2 gives a range of examples; these are discussed below.

The South Street Seaport scheme in Manhattan is a waterfront economic regeneration scheme similar to many urban regeneration schemes in Britain. It is located immediately south of Brooklyn Bridge, in a previously declining part of New York's old port (Figure 4.7).

| Tourism development type | Example |
|---|---|
| Urban economic regeneration | South Street Seaport development in the former docks area of southeast Manhattan, New York City |
| Purpose-built resorts and theme parks | Disneyland Hong Kong |
| Major infrastructure schemes | Hong Kong international airport |
| Heritage tourism development in historic locations | St Benezet Bridge attraction development, Avignon |
| 'Greenfield' resort developments | Negril, Jamaica |

*Table 4.2 Examples of tourism developments overseas*

TopFoto

*Figure 4.7 South Street Seaport, New York*

Disneyland in Hong Kong, China, is the Disney Corporation's first theme park outside the MEDW. Hong Kong is in a special economic zone of China, where development is fast-tracked to help drive the country's rapid economic growth. The theme park is linked to Hong Kong international airport. The airport is a major investment in the area's infrastructure, designed to fuel growth by attracting large volumes of business tourist traffic. Leisure tourists are an added bonus. Inbound tourists to Hong Kong, including those from southeast Asia, are attracted to visit Disneyland, as are tourists from China's rapidly expanding domestic market.

The St Benezet Bridge tourist attraction in Avignon, southern France, is the surviving four-arch span of the original 22-arch twelfth-century medieval bridge made famous by the song '*Sur le pont d'Avignon*'. To develop the bridge as a visitor attraction in what was already a major tourist city, coach parking has been provided beside a visitor centre containing a gift shop and exhibition, and connected to the bridge itself by a walkway. Personal audio-guides, on which tourists can access a recorded commentary about the bridge during their visit, are provided.

## Support your learning

### Information sources

1 Internet search engines such as Google provide a gateway for researching tourism development projects. The websites listed can be selectively browsed to cover the range of promotional material posted by the developers and the views of other stakeholders.

2 Visitor centres, educational centres and exhibitions mounted during and following development work often accompany such projects. Promotional literature may be available as hard copy and can be ordered via the internet.

### Skills builder

Develop your research, editing and information synthesis skills by compiling a PowerPoint presentation about one tourism development scheme other than those showcased in this chapter.

### Activities menu

1 Produce a PowerPoint presentation comparing the tourism development at the Sands, Scarborough with either the Newcastle/Gateshead Quayside or the Negril, Jamaica, schemes.

2 a Explain the main purposes (aims and objectives) of a tourism development project other than the developments featured in this chapter.
   b Explain the roles of three key agents of development involved in the scheme.

3 Research and analyse the roles of key agents of development in one tourism development project.

4 *Vocational scenario*
   A local authority, such as your local council, is investigating possible sites for tourism development in its area. Evaluate one such site and report on its likely suitability for a tourism development project.

# Environmental impacts of tourism

Tourism developments affect the natural environment. Travel itself, in particular vehicle emissions, affects the environment adversely. However, there are positive environmental impacts of tourism as well as negative ones. For example, since the grounds and surroundings of tourist destinations and facilities affect their tourist appeal, travel and tourism authorities and organisations attend to the landscape. They do this by making use of environmental management techniques including drainage, planting, irrigation and gardening. Landscaping is one way in which tourism has a positive impact on the environment.

## Positive environmental impacts

### Landscaping

Landscaping of urban environments, such as seaside resorts and tourism cities (Figure 4.8), is one positive impact of tourism on the environment. As Figure 4.9 shows, landscape improvement increases the appeal of destinations to tourists, stimulating more visits, bringing more economic success, and so allowing more environmental improvements to be made. Landscaping improvements, such as gardens, fountains, clean, planted and well-maintained verges, cobbled and rustically paved heritage streets and squares have a benefit for everyone — locals and visitors alike.

*Figure 4.8*
*Hyde Park in London*

Corel

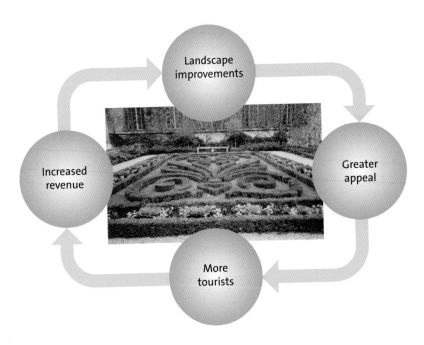

*Figure 4.9* A positive feedback loop

## Management and designation

Management of the rural environment can encourage ecotourism. **Ecotourism** involves visiting a destination because of the appeal of its natural environment while minimising any negative impacts (environmental, sociocultural and economic) on the place and its people. Ecotourism is dealt with specifically in Chapter 4.4 and some examples are included in Topic 5.

Conservation of the environment is a primary goal of managing the rural landscape, but is also important in urban heritage and historic city destinations. Note that conservation is not preservation.

- **Preservation** is maintaining a place exactly as it is, not allowing for development.
- **Conservation** allows for developments that do not damage the character of a tourism destination.

Conservation in tourism destinations begins with the designation of an area as a place to be carefully managed. The result of designation is that development is controlled to protect the environment, whether urban or rural, in the LEDW or MEDW.

## National Parks

Rural areas may be designated as National Parks. This is a designation applied to large areas of land that national governments recognise as special. Usually they are scenically attractive areas or they have unusual and interesting wildlife. Some examples from around the world are the Lake District National Park in the UK (Figure 4.10), the Yosemite National Park in the Sierra Nevada Mountains of the western USA, the Kruger National Park in the Republic of South Africa (Figure 4.11) and the Blue and John Crow Mountains National Park in Jamaica.

Corel

*Figure 4.10* The Lake District National Park

*Figure 4.11* Tourists in Kruger National Park

Gallo Images/Corbis

The national governments in individual countries may give other designations to countryside areas that they wish to protect. Designation not only protects the environment, it also encourages people to visit — literally putting the designated environment 'on the map'. Sometimes it is the growing popularity of a beautiful place that prompts the authorities into thinking that conservation is necessary. Figure 4.12 shows the locations of Britain's National Parks.

There are additional rural environment conservation designations in the UK:

■ Areas of Outstanding Natural Beauty — more than 30 parts of the countryside whose landscape is considered so special that it needs to be conserved, varying in size from 16 km² to over 2,000 km². Examples include the North Pennines and the Scilly Isles.

■ Heritage Coasts — coastlines to be conserved for their natural beauty while allowing access to them by tourists. Examples include the white cliffs of Beachy Head in East Sussex and Flamborough Head in East Yorkshire.

In the USA, the heritage tourist attractions of the Statue of Liberty and Ellis Island in New York harbour (see Figure 5.42) are designated as a National Monument. Note that Liberty Island is actually across the state boundary in New Jersey. In New York City itself, the Historic Districts Council (HDC) protects urban heritage areas. The HDC is non-governmental organisation that acts as an advocate for sympathetic development in the architecturally historic neighbourhoods of New York. Figure 4.13 shows a row of brownstone houses in West Village, typical of the historic architecture of that neighbourhood.

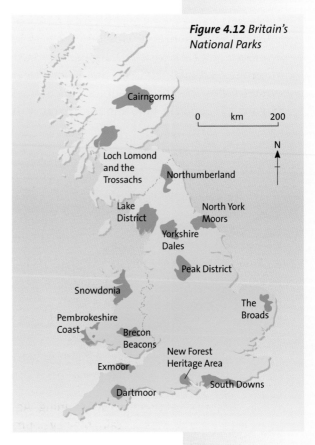

*Figure 4.12* Britain's National Parks

0    km    200

N

Cairngorms

Loch Lomond and the Trossachs

Northumberland

Lake District

North York Moors

Yorkshire Dales

Peak District

Snowdonia

The Broads

Pembrokeshire Coast

Brecon Beacons

New Forest Heritage Area

Exmoor

South Downs

Dartmoor

Jane Buekett

*Figure 4.13* Historic housing in New York City

## Case study: an LEDC — Jamaica

The Jamaican government has established three National Parks:

- Montego Bay Marine Park
- Negril Marine Park
- Blue and John Crow Mountains National Park

Figure 4.14 shows the locations of these parks. A further six sites have been designated for future protection.

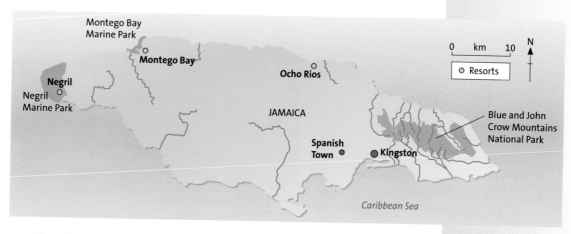

*Figure 4.14 National Parks in Jamaica*

The National Environmental Planning Agency has overseen the Jamaican government's sustainable development strategy since 2001, while the Jamaica Conservation and Development Trust has management responsibility for the National Parks (**www.greenjamaica.org**).

The two marine parks arise from the need to conserve the coral reef environments off Jamaica's shores. They need protecting from damage, including over-fishing and industrial pollution as well as damage by mass tourism. However National Parks are still parks — the idea is to encourage sustainable levels of visits by tourists but to manage tourism so that the environment is protected. The designation of these parks is a positive environmental impact of tourism. It is the desire of tourists to visit and the need to conserve the environment to attract future tourism that drives the designation and management process.

### World Heritage sites (WHS)

The United Nations Educational, Scientific and Cultural Organization (UNESCO) lists historic and natural sites that are designated as being of 'outstanding value to humanity'. Such a designation transcends a national government's concerns with bringing tourists to its country while conserving the environment so future tourists continue to bring revenue. Inclusion on the World Heritage list is global recognition of the site's importance to all people. Clearly tourism to such places can draw them to the attention of UNESCO. However, in LEDCs in particular the designation of a building, a natural environment or a monument as a WHS may be seen by governments as a key to bringing more tourism development, with its attendant economic benefits (see Chapter 4.3). The desire to have tourism creates the positive environmental impact of protecting internationally valuable historic and natural assets.

*Figure 4.15* *The Old Bridge, Mostar*

WHSs are found in MEDCs too. There are over 20 sites in the UK. The recent growth of tourism to eastern Europe has gone alongside the designation of more WHSs there, including the historic tourism destination of Mostar in Bosnia Herzegovina (Figure 4.15).

## Case study: The Old Bridge and Old City at Mostar

In 2005 the Old Bridge and Old City at Mostar, in the former Yugoslav republic of Bosnia Herzegovina, were added to the World Heritage list. The historic town of Mostar was a frontier of the Ottoman empire in the fifteenth and sixteenth centuries and part of the Austro-Hungarian empire in the nineteenth and early twentieth centuries. Mostar has long been famous for its old Turkish-style houses and the Old Bridge. During the Yugoslav Civil War in the 1990s, however, most of the historic town and the Old Bridge were destroyed. They have since been rebuilt.

UNESCO sees the Mostar Old Bridge area, with its pre-Ottoman, eastern Ottoman, Mediterranean and western European architecture, as an outstanding example of a multicultural city. Its designation as a WHS will conserve the city's heritage as tourism to the area increases.

### Spin-off effects

Positive spin-off effects occur where tourism facilities are economically successful, as in Mostar. The buildings themselves are well maintained and freshly painted. This is partly for marketing purposes — to encourage customers — but it also improves the built environment for everyone. One of the positive economic impacts of tourism (see Chapter 4.3) is the **multiplier effect**, by which the money generated from successful travel and tourism enterprises finds its way into the general local economy. As a consequence, the overall prosperity of a tourist destination increases. This is reflected in environmental improvements which are a result of the cumulative effect of building and landscape improvements made by individual householders and businesses, as well as the planned and deliberate efforts of local authorities.

**Discussion point**

How does money from tourists boost the local economy of a destination?

### Impacts on tourism planning

Authorities in historic tourism destinations like Mostar need to develop long-term strategies for the planning of tourism development to ensure that the development is sustainable. Sustainable tourism development is examined in Chapter 4.4. Sustainable approaches to tourism development seek to minimise the negative impacts that tourism may have. Some of these negative impacts are environmental.

## Negative environmental impacts

### Pollution

Travel and tourism are contributory factors in land, water and air pollution. The waste from tourism developments which outstrip corresponding developments in infrastructure such as sewage and waste disposal systems, can cause pollution of the land. While the rubbish generated is not generally toxic it is often non-biodegradable (plastic bottles, for example). The physical disposal of waste can be a major problem in the LEDW, especially when tourist facilities are located on small islands — in the Maldives for example. In the MEDW, Spain's Balearic Islands briefly introduced a tourist levy of 1 euro per day to pay for the disposal of waste generated by the tourist industry. However, tourist numbers fell shortly afterwards and so the levy was removed.

Tourist destinations are also susceptible to water pollution — from hotel bathrooms for instance. Apart from sewage, there is the issue of soap and shampoo washed down the drains and sometimes piped into the sea. Used water from sinks, showers, baths and laundry is termed **grey water**. In fragile coral-reef ecosystems damage can be caused by the injection of such effluents from large hotels. Cruising is a form of tourism that is increasing. A cruise ship releases large volumes of grey water into the sea.

Air pollution can be caused by land and air transport. Busy tourist destinations, both tourist cities and seaside resorts, generate a lot of road traffic (cars and buses). Apart from the congestion caused by such traffic the polluting exhaust gases it emits can be a danger to the health of local people and tourists. Air traffic has increased significantly in Europe in recent years with the advent of budget airlines, and there has been a growth in long-haul holidays too. Any plane journey has an atmospheric pollution impact and jet aircraft travel makes a significant contribution to global warming.

Air travel is the most rapidly growing source of greenhouse gas emissions. An aeroplane on a typical holiday flight from the UK to Spain emits 1,300 kg of carbon dioxide ($CO_2$) into the atmosphere per passenger. Noise is an additional negative environmental impact of air travel which is often the cause of local opposition to plans for new or extended airports. The sound of an aeroplane taking off is typically 120 db (decibels) — sufficient to be an intrusive nuisance to local people.

## Landscape quality and land clearance

The development of tourist facilities and the necessary supporting transport infrastructure often leads to the clearance of natural vegetation. Development sites for mass tourism projects will often be drained and levelled to make building easier. Ecotourism developments, which are lower key, strive to fit in more with the environment that is already there — hotels and guest-houses are low rise and set among woodland rather than clearing the woodland away (Figure 4.16). In comparison, high-rise hotels are an example of tourism developments with a relatively high environmental impact (Figure 4.17).

*Figure 4.16* Ecotourism accommodation in a desert resort in United Arab Emirates

Ludovic Maisant/Corbis

Alan Schein/Corbis

*Figure 4.17* *High-rise hotels on Miami Beach*

The aesthetic impact of tourism development can be negative when dense high-rise buildings alter the appearance of a place. Fear that the quality of the landscape will suffer from development can lead to local protests. For example, a proposed new highway on Ibiza, linking the island's capital city, main airport and the town of San Antonio, led to a protest rally attended by 20,000 local people in 2006. Protestors felt strongly that the highway (up to six lanes wide in places) would scar the landscape and be too high a cost to justify, even with the convenience and economic benefits that would be brought by easing tourist traffic flow. In remote areas with little economic development, however, the arrival of tourism can be seen by local people as a source of much-needed employment. As a result, they may be prepared to put up with some negative impacts, judging the economic benefits to outweigh the environmental costs.

Environmentally attractive destinations popular with countryside tourists can still suffer negative impacts from excessive tourism. The French Iles d'Hyères (Figure 4.18) have suffered damage to rare plant species and a reduction in bird numbers associated with too many walkers. One proposed solution is to reduce the numbers of tourist visitors by making car parking more difficult at the mainland ferry ports. Visitors are already warned not to smoke in the countryside of the islands (because of the risk of fire sweeping across the dry vegetation in the summer months), or to pick flowers or drop litter.

**Discussion point** ◯

Which should come first? Jobs or the environment?

In coral-reef environments, snorkelling and diving can lead to damage if tourists are not aware of how to behave. Figure 4.19 shows a sign erected by the Negril Coral Reef Preservation Society on the beach at Negril in Jamaica, advising tourists of the possible negative environmental impacts that may result from thoughtlessness.

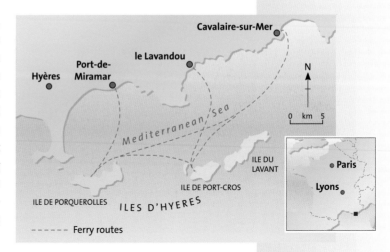

*Figure 4.18* The Iles d'Hyères

*Figure 4.19* Eric the eel says...

# Support your learning

## Information sources

1 The UNESCO World Heritage website (**http://whc.unesco.org**) provides a gateway to WHS information.

2 Media articles about environmental issues relating to travel and tourism and the websites of ecotourism pressure groups and operators are other useful information sources. **www.responsibletravel.com** is an example and **www.chooseclimate.org** is another that calculates the environmental cost of an aircraft journey between two points.

## Skills builder

Debate the environmental costs of a tourism development in comparison to the economic benefits it may bring.

## Activities menu

1 a Describe, with examples, three different types of conservation designation.
  b Explain why designating a destination for environmental protection is an environmental impact of tourism.

2 a Use the UNESCO World Heritage website (**http://whc.unesco.org**) to discover the World Heritage sites in a region or country of your choice.
  b *Vocational scenario*
  Imagine you are a local government tourism official in the area you have chosen. Put forward the case for an unlisted natural or heritage attraction to be made a World Heritage site.

3 Research and analyse the ways in which one ecotourism holiday is designed to minimise negative environmental impacts.

4 Evaluate the environmental impacts of travel and tourism to one destination.

# 4.3

# Economic and sociocultural impacts

## Economic impacts

In one way or another, the economic impacts of tourism are to do with money. Tourists spend money on travelling, while travelling and when in their destination — whether they are leisure, business or VFR visitors. Some of their money is spent with travel and tourism organisations, for example travel agents, tour operators and online bookers in their country of origin, some is spent en-route, with transport principals such as airlines and ferry operators and overnight stay hotels, and the remainder is spent in their destination (or destinations if they are engaged in itinerant tourism, see the Starter chapter of Topic 5).

Money that tourists spend in their destination (or destinations) on the products and services of travel and tourism industry providers will pass into the hands of one of three broad groups of provider:

1 locally based enterprises (often small- and medium-sized), such as locally owned hotels and guesthouses and taxi cooperatives (a collection of individual taxi owners who work together to provide a reduced cost service and share the profits)

2 internationally owned enterprises (often large), such as hotel chains and large car-hire companies

3 individual service providers, such as local tour guides

Figure 4.20 categorises some of the people and organisations that received a tourist family's money during a holiday in an LEDW country (in this case, Jamaica). It is tempting to imagine that the economic impacts of tourism are more keenly felt in LEDCs than MEDCs. There is some truth in this, but in remote and relatively less developed regions of the MEDW tourism can be just as significant in changing people's lives both economically and, as shown later in this chapter, socioculturally.

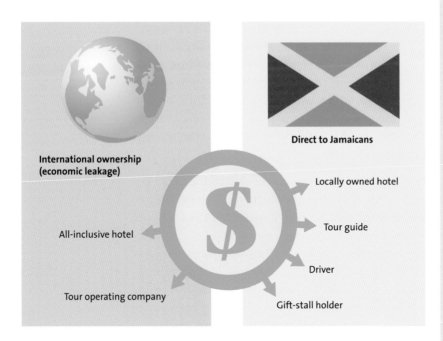

*Figure 4.20* *Spending on a holiday to Jamaica*

International ownership (economic leakage)

All-inclusive hotel

Tour operating company

Direct to Jamaicans

Locally owned hotel

Tour guide

Driver

Gift-stall holder

In Europe this is particularly true of peripheral regions such as Atlantic Portugal and Spain, southern Italy, Malta and other-less visited island destinations such as northern Cyprus. In eastern Europe, where the tourism industry is rapidly expanding in the Balkans and the Baltic republics, the impacts of tourism are considerable. In contrast, in large LEDC cities, such as São Paulo in Brazil and Mumbai in India, international leisure tourism is a relatively small fraction of the local economy.

Travel and tourism organisations such as tour operators and hotels spend large sums of money in destinations too. Tour operators buy rooms from hoteliers. Hotel-owners invest money in land and buildings and may employ local people and source supplies (including food) locally. Alternatively, they may import a large proportion of their workforce and supplies. Clearly, there will be reduced economic benefits for the destination if they do this.

The economic impact tourism has on a place varies between tourist-receiving and tourist-generating areas (see below) and, in the case of the former, according to the extent to which tourism is dominant or not in the total economy of the destination.

## Tourist-generating and tourist-receiving areas

Tourist-generating areas are regions where tourists normally live and work and from which they travel for business or leisure purposes, or to visit friends and relatives. Tourist-receiving areas are the opposite. It is possible for an area to be both tourist-generating and tourist-receiving. New York City is an example. New Yorkers travel throughout the USA (traditionally to Florida in the winter, for example) as well as visiting destinations in the wider world. London is in a similar position. Although London's economy is a broad mix of different industries, inbound tourism brought £28 billion of spending to the city in 2004 — a major economic benefit.

Traditionally, densely populated urban areas in industrialised MEDCs were tourist-generating areas. Mass foreign tourism developed in the twentieth century as the citizens of countries such as the UK, USA and Germany enjoyed higher disposable incomes, more paid holidays, the availability of package holidays provided by tour operators and the development of jet aircraft. Florida in the USA and Mediterranean resorts in Europe grew as tourist-receiving areas. In the case of Florida, US tourists travelling south for the warmer weather fuelled this growth first, but by the late twentieth century Florida had become a long-haul tourist-receiving area for people from other parts of the world, including the UK.

The growth of mass tourism to Mediterranean Europe created a north–south divide, with colder northern European industrial and urban regions acting as tourist-generating areas and warmer southern European seaside locations being tourist-receiving areas. The expansion of long-haul tourism transferred this pattern, at least to some extent, to the world, with the often colder but relatively affluent North (the MEDW) containing the tourist-generating areas and countries of the South (the LEDW) developing more tourist-receiving areas. However, the real picture is less simple, with tourists flowing in both directions. Jamaica, for example, is an island in the major tourist-receiving area of the Caribbean, but Jamaican tourists visit the USA and European countries, including the UK, for leisure, business and VFR.

**Discussion point** ⬤

Globally, how true is it that the North generates tourists for the South?

## Positive economic impacts

Tourism creates jobs, and the local people employed in those jobs are paid wages that they spend in the destination that is their home, to the benefit of the local economy. Other local businesses, which may not be travel and tourism businesses, prosper in consequence, feeding more money into the local economy and creating more jobs. This is called

*Figure 4.21* Small tourism businesses, Negril beach

*Figure 4.22* Tourism development, Negril, Jamaica

the **multiplier effect**, because jobs and money multiply as a result of travel and tourism development. LEDW governments are often keen to develop tourism for this reason. In MEDCs, similar positive economic impacts are often the hope of agents of tourism development in areas of economic regeneration. In the UK such areas are often rundown inner cities, typically in dockland and riverside locations, which have been regenerated in recent years (see Chapter 4.1).

Major tourism investments in a destination, such as hotels, can create spin-off opportunities for local entrepreneurs. Figure 4.21 shows some small tourism businesses established on the beach at Negril in Jamaica. As Figure 4.22 shows, these small businesses are located just to the south of a series of large all-inclusive hotels. Although many all-inclusive hotel customers stay close to the hotel for much of their holiday, enterprising small business owners, for example Premium Parasailing, use direct selling to attract custom. They patrol the beach promoting their products and put on

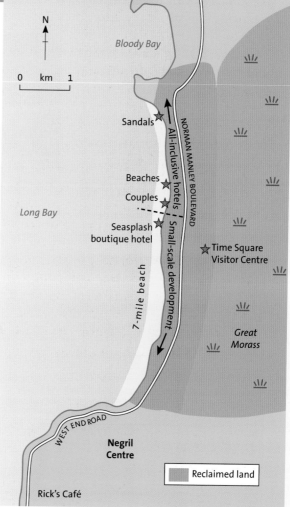

demonstrations. The establishment of the internationally owned hotels has led to the negative economic impact of leakage. However, these hotels do provide direct employment for local people and they also provide an opportunity for the marketing of these small beach-shack-based enterprises. This spin-off effect is an example of a positive economic impact.

The 7-mile beach at Negril is a continuous sales-strip for beach vendors who sell cigarettes, handicrafts, sunglasses and hats to tourists on the sand. Such vendors sometimes live in rural, inland parts of Jamaica, in St Elizabeth parish for example, and so there is an economic transfer of the income they earn from the beach to benefit communities which tourists rarely visit. Figure 4.23 shows a tourism business in the informal sector. The informal sector is very important in LEDCs. It is the part of the economy that is not regulated and for which there are often no paper records. Individuals (often poorer people) simply start providing and selling a product or service direct to customers (tourists), usually without any permanent premises. Belinda's Canteen is a riverside café and gift stall set up on a river beach on a meander of the Rio Grande

Stephen Rickerby

**Figure 4.23**
*An informal tourist enterprise*

Stephen Rickerby

**Figure 4.24** *Tourists and locals interact at Belinda's Canteen*

in Portland, Jamaica (Figure 4.24) where raft trips for tourists regularly pass by. Belinda sells soft and alcoholic drinks, home-cooked local dishes such as jerk chicken and rice and peas, and craft gifts to tourists passing by on raft trips. The money she makes is transferred to her inland village community in the nearby hills — a place little visited by tourists.

One of the main ways in which tourists can pass money directly into the hands of local people (in both MEDW and LEDW destinations) is by employing a local guide or driver themselves. Figure 5.35 (Chapter 5.6) shows a local guide escorting tourists on the Gordon Town trail in the Blue Mountains of Jamaica. The guide works for himself. The tourists pay him directly in cash. He lives locally (in Redlight) and so some of that cash finds its way into the local economy.

Destinations in MEDCs and LEDCs are sometimes well-known for particular craft goods or types of artwork. Chania in Crete is famed for leather goods, Thai resorts for silk, French villages for wine and olives and St Lucia for batiks. Money that tourists spend on gifts and souvenirs to take home has positive economic impacts not only in benefiting retailers but also the manufacturers of such products. Factories making traditional parasols in Thailand, for example, are kept going by tourist spending — money which keeps their workforces in employment.

## Negative economic impacts

In some cases the jobs brought to a destination by travel and tourism organisations are seasonal. This is a problem traditionally experienced by seaside resorts in the UK, such as Scarborough where the winter unemployment rate has risen. The Sands development in Scarborough, featured in the starter chapter of this unit, is partly aimed at counteracting that effect.

A second negative impact is **economic leakage**. This occurs when the wealth brought to a destination by travel and tourism leaks away again to somewhere else. It is a problem that has been experienced in some LEDCs, for example where foreign-owned hotel chains have established themselves. Although the hotel company may pay taxes locally, its profits belong to a large organisation whose headquarters may be overseas (often in an MEDC in western Europe, North America, Japan or Australasia). If profits return to the overseas parent company they leak away from the destination.

In the case of Negril, Jamaica, the large hotels shown on Figure 4.22 are foreign-owned. However, many, if not all, the staff are local people. In the Sandals-owned Beaches Negril all-inclusive, for example, staff from the general manager downwards are Jamaican. Their wages benefit these individuals, their families and the general economy through the multiplier effect. In addition, there are spin-off opportunities for local entrepreneurs. There may be leakage abroad of some of the economic benefit, but some remains in Jamaica. If migrant workers, whose permanent home is elsewhere in the country or abroad, are used then the problem can be worsened, since they are likely to send some of the money they earn home. Arguably, if their homes are in LEDCs this is less of an issue. In the Maldives, where hotels are located on islands uninhabited by local people, flows of money like this are clearly a benefit to the country as a whole.

However, wages are sometimes not good. Staff engaged in kitchen and laundry work may be paid minimal wages. Travel and tourism industry providers seek to keep costs down in order to keep prices low. In less developed regions of the MEDW and in the LEDW labour is often plentiful and so lower wages still attract staff. The pressure group Tourism Concern, which highlights issues raised by tourism impacts, has recently found examples of low pay among tourism industry staff (some of whom work in quite luxurious four-star hotels), in destinations including Egypt, the Maldives, Mexico and the Canary Islands. The Canary Islands, for example, have the third lowest salaries in Spain but, partly due to tourism, the highest cost of living. Low-grade local employees in the travel and tourism industry there can sometimes find it difficult to make ends meet.

**Discussion point**

To what extent is it true that all-inclusive hotels do not benefit local economies?

## Sociocultural impacts

Sociocultural impacts affect people and their way of life. Tourism brings people from different places and cultures into contact with each other, creating the opportunity for increased understanding between different social groups. However, conflicts and tensions can sometimes result from interactions between tourists and local people. In domestic tourism in the UK, for instance, there can be conflict in bars and clubs of seaside resorts between some local customers and tourist visitors. Tourists from places with very different cultural standards from those of local people in a tourist destination can cause offence, often unintentionally. For example, the wearing of beachwear in town centres and on sightseeing trips to religious sites may be viewed as inappropriate.

The Maldives is a country with a high degree of segregation between the tourist hotel islands and those where local people live. Tourists on day excursions to the capital Male, to see the golden-dome mosque for example, are expected to conform to the more conservative dress of the townspeople. The same is true in MEDCs. Visits to places of religious worship that are also tourist attractions, such as cathedrals, require dress codes such as head-covering; local people can be upset when such dress codes are not followed.

Sensitive management of such issues by travel and tourism organisations, and by tourists themselves, can usually avoid friction before it arises. Travel and tourism organisations, such as tour operators, can reduce the risk of friction by providing customers with information in brochures and at welcome meetings.

In tourist-receiving areas of LEDCs, visits to local markets or watching performances of local dances and rituals can be part of the tourist experience. This may help keep such events and activities alive, but there is a risk of them becoming distorted in order to provide for the needs of the tourists. For example, dances intended for certain special occasions may be adapted or performed at other times to fit in with tourist schedules. Such corruption of traditional culture is widely regarded as a negative impact. Sustainable tourism (see Chapter 4.4) seeks to allow local people to benefit economically from visits by tourists without damage to their traditional way of life.

**Discussion point**

Does tourism help preserve local traditions or inevitably destroy them?

Tourism to resort towns can increase the range of social facilities available for local people's own leisure. Hotels intended primarily to cater for tourists at UK seaside resorts, such as Scarborough, inland conference centres, such as Harrogate, and National Park towns, such as Ambleside in the Lake District, provide facilities such as restaurants, function rooms for events (for example wedding receptions) and sport and fitness clubs. Local people can use these facilities, which would not exist were it not for the tourist trade. This happens in LEDCs too. Beach hotels in destinations such as St Lucia in the Caribbean feature evening entertainment spectacles that are popular with local people who can afford an evening out in a large hotel. The weekly street party at Gros Islet on St Lucia attracts tourists from nearby hotels, but is a focus for fun for local people too.

Chapter 5.7 of this book deals specifically with cultural tourism and makes the point that cultures move with people. Tourists bring elements of their culture to a destination and take elements of its culture home with them. International all-inclusive hotels like Beaches Negril cater for a wide variety of nationalities. Figure 4.25 shows the range of foods from different cultures that its restaurants provide. While many tourists may stick to food from their country of origin, others learn and experience a little of Jamaican culture through the food they eat. This builds some understanding of other people's lives, which is a positive sociocultural impact. Clearly that impact is all the greater where direct contact is made between tourists and ordinary people — as at Belinda's Canteen for instance (see Figure 4.24).

## Restaurants

**Mill Restaurant**
Open daily, buffet style
Breakfast: 7:30 –10 a.m.     Lunch: 12:30 – 2 p.m.     Dinner: 6 – 9:30 p.m.

**Seville Restaurant**
Serves Jamaican cuisine, open 6 –10 p.m.

**Teppanyaki Restaurant**
Serves Oriental cuisine, reservations required

**Last Chance Saloon**
Serves Tex-Mex cuisine, open 6 –10 p.m.

**Blazing Paradise Beach Grill**
Serves burgers, fries, chicken, etc.

**Café Carnival**
A full service pasta bar; serves freshly baked brick oven pizzas and made to order pasta, open daily from 11 a.m.

*Figure 4.25*
*Restaurants at Beaches, Negril*

On the other hand, tourists can feel intimidated by local people offering products and services for sale in what seems to be quite an aggressive way. The perception that they will be hassled keeps some tourists to LEDW destinations like Jamaica inside the safety of the all-inclusive hotel, venturing out only on excursions organised by the hotel itself. Some of what is perceived as hassle and pressure selling is driven by the restricted size of the market. If many tourists avoid contact with locals, then some locals will want to make sure they do not let the opportunity of a sale walk by. Such tension constitutes a negative sociocultural impact. It is not confined to LEDCs. Touts outside bars in Mediterranean seaside resorts, hawkers at major urban attractions like the Eiffel Tower and the Battery Park ferry landing for the Statue of Liberty, and streetfood sellers in London markets are treated with similar nervousness by some tourists.

The pressure group Tourism Concern's 2006 campaign 'Sun, Sea, Sand and Sweatshops' highlighted issues of poor working conditions among tourism workers in a range of destinations in MEDCs and LEDCs. Figure 4.26 is a quote from Carmen, a room cleaner in a hotel in the Canary Islands. As well as the economic issue of Carmen's level of pay, there are social issues here and a suggestion that the hoped for positive impact of understanding between people is not always achieved.

*Figure 4.26* Carmen's story

> The people in higher positions treat us as inferior human beings. They think we are machines while we work as hard as we can. Working as a room cleaner is very hard. I have to clean 23 rooms, but if a workmate is off, I have to clean 26 rooms instead. My job is physically and emotionally tough, and many young people leave the job, but I have no choice. Some of the tourists we see are educated and have consideration towards us, but others think we are their slaves, and don't treat us well. Going on holiday is a luxury I could never afford.
>
> Source: www.tourismconcern.org.uk/campaigns

## Support your learning

### Information sources

Tourism Concern is a pressure group which highlights negative tourism impacts. Its website is a useful source for such information (**www.tourismconcern.org.uk**).

### Skills builder

Develop your empathy skills. As an informal tourism business owner in an LEDC destination (like Belinda in Jamaica), explain how you regard the development of an all-inclusive hotel in your area. To develop interview skills, work with a partner and role-play an interview between a local radio presenter and the owner of the informal business.

### Activities menu

1 Produce a chart to summarise the positive and negative economic and sociocultural impacts of tourism. Use examples from both LEDCs and MEDCs.

2 *Vocational scenario*
Imagine you are a resort representative in an all-inclusive hotel. Explain to a concerned customer how they can help local people while they are on holiday.

3 Research and analyse the economic impacts of tourism in one MEDC destination.

4 Evaluate the positive and negative sociocultural impacts of tourism in one LEDC destination.

# 4.4

# Ecotourism and sustainable development

## A sustainable approach

**Sustainable development** is an approach to tourism management that can be used to:

- conserve and manage the environment in which tourism takes place
- conserve traditional ways of life enjoyed by host peoples in tourism destinations

Sustainable developments are changes that are not only improvements on balance (between costs and benefits), but are actively planned to minimise negative impacts on the environment and on local cultures. The environment and culture that constitute the appeal of a destination should be conserved by appropriately managing developments. Today's tourist visit will be arranged so it does not cause undesirable change in either the environment or the culture that might spoil the destination for the future tourist.

## Case study: Gospel tours in Harlem

Harlem is an African-American neighbourhood in New York City (Figure 4.27). Cultural tourism to Harlem is increasing; one of the most popular visits is to attend a Harlem gospel choir service. Some tours include an opportunity to walk in the area, spend money in a local restaurant or shop and meet local people. These are sustainable tours. Responsible tourists participate in the service, realising that it is an act of worship, and dress conservatively for church, as local people would.

Unsustainable tours have taken place in the past. Tourists left gospel services before the end to continue their schedule, arriving and leaving by bus without meeting local people or contributing to the local economy at all. As a consequence, some churches segregated visitors from the rest of the congregation — restricting them to the upper floor for example — so that they did not interrupt the service. The tours that caused this to happen changed the tour experience for the worse for those that followed and negated a possible sociocultural positive impact.

*Figure 4.27* Harlem

TopFoto

## Ecotourism

**Ecotourism** is a type of tourism — a way of visiting and organising visits to a destination. The natural environment is key in two senses:
- the appeal is the environment — the scenery and/or the wildlife
- visits are conducted sustainably so that the environment is not adversely affected and is conserved for its own sake and to retain its appeal for local people and tourists in the future

## Case study: A raft-trip on the Rio Grande, Jamaica

Figure 4.28 shows a raft being poled downstream on the Rio Grande in Jamaica. Rafts like this were once used to transport bananas from inland plantations to Port Antonio for export. Refrigeration ended that. Nowadays, the rafts and the raft captains who propel them have a new cargo — tourists. The Rio Grande may appear peaceful and benign to tourist passengers but this is largely because of the skill of the raft captains and the knowledge they have acquired (often over many years) of the river, its currents and rapids. Raft captaincy is a skilled profession. The traditional way of life of Rio Grande raft captains can continue because of this sustainable tourism.

*Figure 4.28*
*Rafting in Jamaica*

Tourists are taken downstream in small groups. Only two adults can be safely carried per raft. The bamboo used to make them is harvested from the forest by the captains who build their own rafts and make model rafts to sell to tourists for extra income. The rafts leave singly and, when possible, with long time gaps between them, so that the peace of the forest through which the Rio Grande meanders is not disturbed. The river and its scenery are essential parts of the appeal to tourists in the first place. The tourists can enjoy the environment by swimming in the river en-route and learn about the forest from tales told by the raft captain. This is an example of ecotourism.

Stephen Rickerby

Figures 4.23 and 4.24 in Chapter 4.3 show examples of responsible tourism during the 3-hour raft trip down the Rio Grande.

## Responsible tourism

**Responsible tourism** is about the behaviour of tourists and travel and tourism organisations in tourism destinations. A responsible tourist will seek to avoid negative impacts on the place and people they visit and will try to pass on positive impacts, including economic ones, as much as they can. For example, a responsible tourist will employ local people as guides, eat locally grown food when they can, patronise locally run facilities such as bars and restaurants, and where possible stay in locally owned hotels. The net result will have been to pass money directly to local people so that it has maximum benefit in the local community.

## Case study: responsibletravel.com

**www.responsibletravel.com** is an online travel agent specialising in holidays that benefit local people and have minimal impact on the environment. Figure 4.29 gives information about the beginning of a typical responsible ecotourism holiday. The growth of responsible travel websites is part of the sustainable approach to tourism development.

---

Country: **Vietnam**
Destinations: **Hanoi and the Sapa mountains**

---

Itinerary (5 days in total)
Day 1:
**Ha Noi arrival and Sapa.** Arrive by aeroplane. Welcome dinner at a local restaurant in a colonial building. Overnight sleeper train to Sapa.

Day 2:
**Sapa–Ta Van.** Morning trekking 15 km with local guide on a small path down the valley to the Muong Hoa River and from here to a small village. Lunch with a local family in the village. Continue trek to Ta Van to visit the Zay people. Stay overnight with a local family in Ta Van and have dinner there.

*Figure 4.29*
*A responsible-travel.com holiday*

Tourists on the trekking holiday trip are visiting a poor but scenic area in northern Vietnam. The tour is operated with the aim of keeping negative impacts to a minimum. Tourists stay in local stilt houses and are escorted by local guides. They eat in local restaurants and have the chance to buy local products along the way. This exemplifies responsible tourism.

Of course, the aeroplane journey from the UK to Hanoi and back has a negative environmental impact. Based on a return trip for two people, the flight contributes 5.17 tonnes of carbon dioxide (a greenhouse gas) to atmospheric pollution. Some long-haul travellers pay a holiday supplement to organisations which undertake projects such as reforestation to reduce atmospheric carbon dioxide. This is aimed at making their travel carbon neutral. For the return air flight from the UK to Hanoi, two tourists would pay a supplement of about £40.

## Support your learning

### Information sources

Tourism Concern (**www.tourismconcern. org.uk**) is a pressure group concerned to minimise the negative impacts of travel and tourism.

### Skills builder

Develop your skills of argument. Prepare a short opening speech suitable for a debate on whether tourism can really be sustainable.

### Activities menu

1 Explain why the Jamaican raft trip is an example of ecotourism.

2 *Vocational scenario*
Prepare a brochure or website page suitable for a tour operator to use to promote an ecotourism holiday.

3 Research and analyse similarities and differences between an ecotourism holiday in an MEDC and one in an LEDC.

4 Evaluate the extent to which either of the holidays you researched for Activity 3 can be regarded as responsible tourism.

# 5

# Special interest tourism

# *Starter:* **the range of special interest holidays**

A **special interest holiday** is a holiday that is focused on one particular activity or pursuit. The point of the holiday is to give the customer the chance to spend significant amounts of time on a leisure interest. Special interest holidays include those based on physical activities, such as skiing, walking and diving. Some of these come under the heading of adventure tourism (see Chapter 5.6). Other types of special interest tourism are:

- sports spectating — holidays centred on a football or athletics tournament, a cricket tour or a Grand Prix motor race
- ecotourism holidays — for example bird-watching and wildlife safaris
- cultural tourism — such as attending an artistic or musical event or festival
- heritage tourism — including visits to places of historic or architectural importance
- wedding holidays
- working holidays — such as working at a children's summer camp in the USA, on a kibbutz in Israel or volunteering to help in environmental conservation, such as in a UK National Park
- educational tourism — taking classes in leisure activities such as painting, cookery and dance, usually in a pleasant setting such as the French or Italian countryside
- religious tourism — pilgrimages, retreats and visits to shrines
- spa holidays — originally for 'taking the waters', these are now more likely to include massage, pampering and physical health regeneration

Example of these types of holidays are given in Table 5.1.

| Type of holiday | Example |
|---|---|
| Snowsports | Skiing in the French Alps |
| Walking | Rambling in Ireland's Ring of Kerry |
| Diving | Scuba-diving in the Red Sea |
| Sports spectating | Following the England team to the football or cricket world cups |
| Ecotourism | Seeing mountain gorillas in Rwanda and Uganda |
| Cultural tourism | Attending the Glastonbury Festival |
| Heritage tourism | Touring the pyramids and temples of ancient Egypt |
| Working holidays | Picking grapes in the French countryside |
| Educational tourism | Painting classes in Tuscany |
| Religious tourism | Taking part in the Haj pilgrimage to Mecca |
| Spa holidays | Taking health treatments in Baden Baden, Germany |

*Table 5.1*
*Examples of special interest holidays*

## Niche tourism

Because special interest holidays focus on particular activities, they have a narrower target market than general interest holidays. **Niche markets** are small markets that deal in a specialised product or service — such as a particular type of special interest holiday or travel to a specific place (usually not a mass tourism destination). Sample advertisements from tour operators that provide for niche special interest tourism markets are shown in Figure 5.1. Such small classified advertisements are often used to promote niche tour operators and can be readily found in the travel supplements of weekend newspapers.

*Figure 5.1 Niche market tour operators*

Specialist holidays sold by niche market tour operators are not mass tourism. Nevertheless, some specialised holiday markets, such as skiing, are large enough to attract large-scale tour operators. By 2005 the UK snowsports tourism market had grown to almost 1.3 million participants, according to the Ski Club of

Great Britain's annual Snowsports Analysis. Because of this number of potential customers, major tour operators from the general interest holidays market publish their own ski brochures.

## Itinerant holidays

**Itinerant holidays** involve tourists travelling around during their trip — not just to and from a single destination but between different destinations. Sightseeing tours and cruises are two examples of itinerant holidays. Others include backpacking and rail holidays, for example a trip on the *Orient Express* or along the Garden Route in South Africa.

Some special interest holidays are itinerant. Examples include trekking, safaris and sports tours, such as following the England cricket team on a test match tour abroad. Figure 5.2 shows an example of a special interest itinerant holiday.

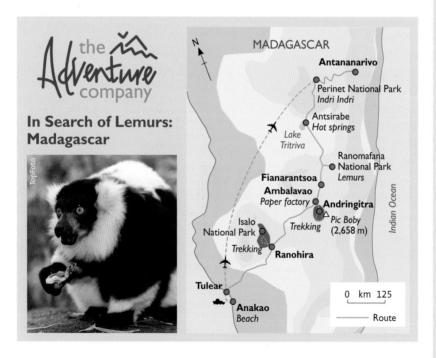

*Figure 5.2* A special interest itinerant holiday

## Adventure tourism

Holidays that involve daring, risk or excitement in the natural environment, or travel to a remote or exotic destination are **adventures**. Much adventure tourism involves physical activity, usually outdoors.

Diving, mountain biking and horse-riding holidays are examples of adventure tourism.

Adventure tourism activities (ATAs) can be classified into three main groups:

- water-based activities, such as canoeing and sailing
- land-based activities, including trekking and mountain biking
- air-based activities, for example paragliding and hang-gliding

Some companies and educational institutions send staff and students on ATAs to increase self-esteem and help team building and the development of skills such as problem-solving. Holidays to raise funds for charity have become more popular recently. An example is sponsored challenges, such as walking the Inca Trail in Peru. Figure 5.3 is an example of an internet advertisement to encourage tourists to attempt a sponsored walk for cancer research.

**Figure 5.3** *A walking holiday for charity*

# Funding cancer research

How far would you go for someone with cancer?

Join us for this amazing trek along the Inca Trail to the world famous lost city of Machu Picchu, and through the sacred valleys and picturesque towns and villages of the Andes.

Chapter 5.6 covers adventure tourism in more detail.

## Cultural tourism

Figure 5.4 shows the city of Cartagena on the Caribbean coast of Colombia in South America. The city hosts the Cartagena Literary Festival in January and the Caribbean Music Festival in March. Tour operators selling travel for UK visitors to either event are dealing in the international cultural tourism market. The Cartagena Literary Festival is linked to the Hay Festival, held annually in Hay on Wye — a UK cultural tourism destination. Stratford upon Avon, birthplace of William Shakespeare, has three theatres where the Royal Shakespeare Company perform and is another UK cultural tourism destination.

There is more detail about cultural tourism in Chapter 5.7.

## Special interest destinations

### Geographical distribution

Figure 5.5 shows some examples of destinations that are associated with particular types of special interest holidays.

The geographical distribution of special interest holiday destinations, such as those shown in Figure 5.5, depends on several factors, which are summarised in Table 5.2. Since some types of tourism depend on

*Figure 5.4 Cartagena, Colombia*

Jeremy Horner/Corbis

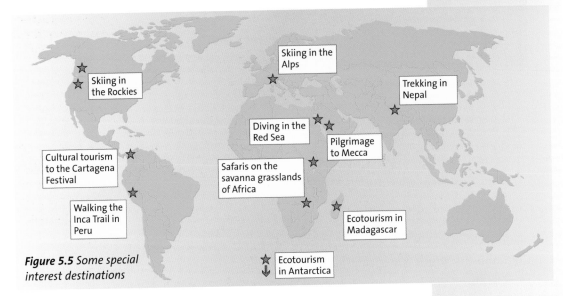

Skiing in the Alps

Skiing in the Rockies

Trekking in Nepal

Diving in the Red Sea

Pilgrimage to Mecca

Cultural tourism to the Cartagena Festival

Safaris on the savanna grasslands of Africa

Walking the Inca Trail in Peru

Ecotourism in Madagascar

Ecotourism in Antarctica

*Figure 5.5 Some special interest destinations*

certain geographical environments, their distribution is limited. Trekking holidays are concentrated in the world's more remote mountain ranges, while skiing holiday destinations cluster in mountainous regions that are easily accessible for tourists from affluent source regions such as the urban areas of western Europe and North America.

| Factor | Examples |
|--------|----------|
| Climate | The tropical climates of Madagascar and Costa Rica and the polar climate of Antarctica support the flora and fauna that attract ecotourism |
| Landscape | Savanna grasslands on the African plains encourage safari tours; mountainous regions such as the Andes, Rockies and Himalayas support trekking |
| Culture and heritage | Musical heritage in the American South (for example country and western in Nashville, jazz and blues in New Orleans and Elvis Presley in Memphis) encourages cultural tourism |
| Accessibility | Mountainous regions that are easily accessible from tourist-originating regions, such as the Rockies in North America and the Alps in Europe, have developed skiing facilities |

*Table 5.2 Factors in the distribution of special interest holidays*

## Features of destinations

Figure 5.6 shows the features of destinations that support special interest tourism.

*Figure 5.6 Features that support special interest tourism*

**Discussion point**

What special interest holidays can tour operators market to 17–19-year-olds?

## Case study: Ecotourism holiday to Madagascar

Figure 5.2 gives information about an ecotourism holiday to see lemurs in Madagascar. The list of features in Figure 5.6 can be applied to this holiday.

Madagascar's tropical climate and sparsely populated, rainforest-filled interior landscape create the habitat of the lemurs that are the ecotourism focus of this holiday.

The relative absence of easy transport into the interior of the island has made it inaccessible and helped preserve the natural environment that attracts today's tourists. In contrast, the availability of air transport to Madagascar makes it sufficiently accessible to develop ecotourism.

The availability of Western-standard accommodation and of local services to cater for the needs of tourists (including food and drink, clean water and hygienic sanitation) are other vital features of the island that have allowed the development of Madagascar as an ecotourism destination.

Other attractions include the isolated and idyllic beach at Anakao, accessible only by boat, that is built into the tour as a rest and recuperation stop at the end of the trekking.

Events and entertainment are not major selling points of a tour such as this, but ecotourists like to soak up local culture and heritage as they travel. The overland treks that are parts of this tour bring the tourists into contact with local people and customs.

Activities like trekking and swimming are integral to the tour, and facilities along the way are sufficiently developed to cater for Western tourists with an environmentally aware attitude.

## Support your learning

### Information sources

While the brochures and websites of major tour operators do feature special interest holidays, those of smaller niche tour operators are invaluable. The small classified advertisements placed by such companies in the press (see Figure 5.1) are useful information gateways.

### Skills builder

Develop your communication key skills by researching a range of special interest tourism brochures and websites to gain an understanding of how operators try to make their products attractive to potential customers.

**Activities menu**

1 Explain what is meant by each the following terms:
   - niche market
   - itinerary
   - ecotourism
   - adventure tourism
   - cultural tourism

2 Apply the list of features given in Figure 5.6 to a special interest destination other than Madagascar to explain why its features have helped it develop special interest tourism.

3 Research and analyse the customer base of one type of special interest tourism.

4 *Vocational scenario*
   Imagine you work as a tour operator for a special interest tour company that is seeking to cater more for the family market. Your manager has asked you to evaluate a long-haul destination to include in next year's brochure. Produce a report that evaluates how well such a destination is likely to meet the needs of your company's special interest family customers.

# 5.1

# Tour operators in the specialist market

A wide range of tour operators package and sell holidays in the specialist tourism market. Different operators' products (i.e. their holidays), and different products within their range, appeal to different types of tourist.

## Case study: The Adventure Company

The Adventure Company specialises in adventure tourism (see Chapter 5.6 for more information on adventure tourism). The company markets its products with a range of potential customers in mind (see Figure 5.7):

- worldwide adventure holidays for tourists seeking excitement and challenge (more likely to be singles and couples)
- family adventures for customers with children, which can also be offered to childless adults, including 'empty-nesters' (mature adults whose children have grown up and left home)
- 'The Adventure Collection' for 'off the beaten track' experiences with more upmarket accommodation, such as safari lodges in African destinations including Kenya and Namibia, and colonial-era hotels in South American countries such as Ecuador and Peru

Adventure holiday packages, such as those marketed by the Adventure Company, are operated for small groups of customers

*Figure 5.7 The Adventure Company website*

(12 is a typical maximum size). A single customer, a couple or a family joins others to make up the party. This appeals to some potential customers and not to others. For small families, or those that include children of different ages, one of the selling points is that there will be other, similar-aged, children in the party on a family adventure.

Varying its appeal beyond the straightforward adventuring tourist allows The Adventure Company to push back the edges of its niche market — to widen its customer base.

Large-scale mass market tour operators such as Thomson, Kuoni and First Choice, whose brochures are distributed through travel agents, cater for specialist markets either through some of the holidays in their main brochures or using brochures specifically for a narrower market range, such as winter sports holidays. These operators use their websites as an additional promotional tool and as a means of direct selling.

## Independent tour operators

Smaller independent tour operators proliferate in the specialist holidays market place. Such operators are 'independent' in the sense that they are not owned by larger, major companies.

## Case study: the skiing specialist market

Independent Ski Links (Figure 5.8) is a small independent tour operator based in the UK that arranges skiing packages in Europe and North America. Like many niche operators, it is affiliated to a larger body in order to build confidence in potential customers that access its website. As Figure 5.8 shows, Independent Ski Links is affiliated to the Ski Club of Great Britain (**www.skiclub.co.uk**) and is a member of the Travel Trust Association (see page 137).

Small operators such as Independent Ski Links often use partner organisations to provide support services. They are unable to do everything themselves and tend to stick to their own specialism (skiing), using the expertise of other small specialist companies to provide ancillary services. In this case, Airport Transfer Service provides a supporting transport service for Independent Ski Links customers by meeting them at the gateway airport and taking them on to their ski resort accommodation. Small niche tour operators such as

**Discussion point**

Why do small tour operators feel the need to build customer confidence?

Independent Ski Links have specialist expertise which they use to provide for the needs of their enthusiast customers. They aim to build a loyal clientele of repeat customers.

The internet has increasingly become a means by which niche tour operators can market their products and services to potential customers. As well as tour operators such as Independent Ski Links, specialist travel agencies do business online. An example of such an organisation is packyourskis.com (Figure 5.9), which acts as a portal for customers to access skiing holidays in Europe and North America provided by a variety of tour operators.

**Figure 5.8**
*Independent Ski Links website*

**Figure 5.9**
*packyourskis.com*

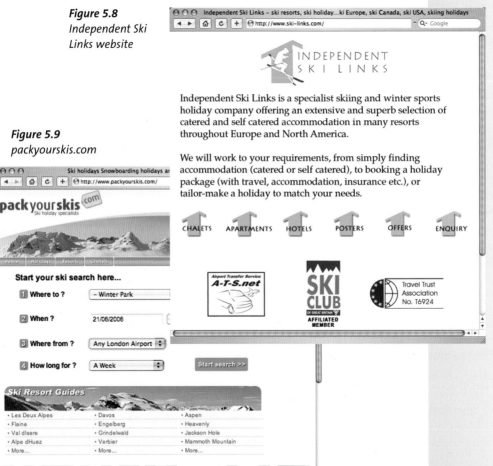

## The Travel Trust Association

Five hundred of the UK's independent travel agents and niche tour operators are members of the Travel Trust Association (TTA). Membership enables small companies to offer their customers financial protection, such as compensation, in the event of a problem such as unavailable or double-booked accommodation. Potential customers are sometimes wary of dealing with an independent operator which does not have a household name. TTA membership helps independent operators market their products because they can use the association's logo (as in Figure 5.8) to promote consumer confidence.

## Tailor-made holidays

Independent travellers make their own arrangements for travel and accommodation (self-packaging), while traditional package holiday customers are sold pre-packaged 'off-the-peg' holidays. Some tour operators assemble tailor-made holidays to order, using elements of travel and accommodation that best meet a customer's particular requirements, and selling them the completed, specifically tailored package.

**Tailor-made holidays** are customised holidays put together for an individual customer. In the niche markets of special interest tourism, tailor-made holidays are one of the varied products on offer. As Figure 5.8 shows, Independent Ski Links uses its website to market its tailor-made service. Increased internet use by potential customers has facilitated online tailor-made services provided by tour operators. Exsus Travel makes use of the internet for this purpose, but it also operates three offices — in London and Edinburgh — where customers are served on a face-to-face basis.

Cox and Kings is another tailor-made holiday tour operator, while Trailfinders is a travel agency which packages tailor-made itineraries for retail customers. Trailfinders runs shops called travel centres in city-centre locations such as Manchester (Figure 5.10), as well as operating online and by telephone. Trailfinders one-stop travel shop in Kensington, London, offers additional support such as a travel clinic where customers can take specialist medical advice and obtain products such as anti-malaria tablets and services such as travel vaccinations.

**Discussion point**

Can tour operators market tailor-made holidays more effectively in specialist markets than in general interest markets? Explain your answer.

**Figure 5.10** *Trailfinders' travel centres in the British Isles*

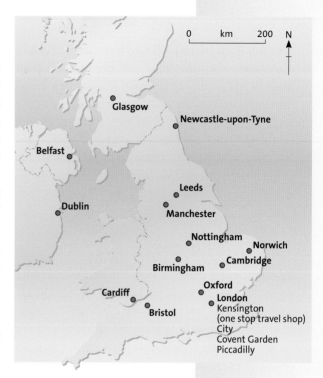

Large travel and tourism organisations sometimes publish brochures in the specialist market under a brand name different from their own. For example TUI, which owns the Thomson brand (and publishes ski brochures under that name), is also the parent company of Crystal Ski. Such specialist brands are often trading names of subsidiary companies operating with some degree of autonomy — able to make their own day-to-day business decisions without frequent reference to the parent organisation. For example, Crystal Ski is a limited company in its own right even though it comes under the TUI umbrella.

## Vertical integration

Specialist providers exist in different sectors of the travel and tourism industry. For example, packyourskis.com is a ski specialist belonging to the travel agent sector and Independent Ski Links belongs to the tour operator sector. Like all classification systems, the convention of categorising travel and tourism organisations in this way has strengths and weaknesses. One issue is that some travel and tourism organisations cross the boundaries between the sectors. Large companies, such as Thomson, provide products and services across the different sectors, having subsumed previously separate brands, such as the former Lunn Poly travel agency chain. This process is referred to as **vertical integration**. There are also crossovers between pairs of sectors. For example, Trailfinders acts partly as a retail travel agent with branches 'in the high street' (in other words, in city centres), but also assembles travel and holiday packages, acting as a tour operator. In the case of Trailfinders, the distinction between the travel agent and tour operator sectors is not so clearly defined as the apparently simple distinction of travel agents selling packages assembled by tour operators.

**Discussion point** ◯

How appropriate is it to regard travel agents and tour operators as separate sectors of the travel and tourism industry?

## Transport principals

**Transport principals** are travel companies that provide transportation for tourists. Airlines, cruise lines, train-operating companies, ferry operators, coach firms and car-hire businesses are examples. Transport principals may diversify into the packaging of special interest tourism products. For example, British Airways sells wedding packages to destinations in the Caribbean such as St Lucia and Antigua and to the Indian Ocean island of Mauritius. In such cases, transport principals are crossing over into the tour-operating sector of the industry. The travel and tourism industry has become increasingly integrated in recent years, and there is a greater degree of interdependence among its sectors.

## Other specialisms

Tour operators can specialise in particular types of special interest holiday (see above). Alternatively, some organisations have adopted specialisms involving:

■ specific market segments — dealing with particular types of customer (student groups on educational visits, corporate clients on team-building activity breaks or attending conferences, for example)

■ focusing on a particular destination, perhaps at the national scale or with a narrower focus on one or a few resorts

Examples include UK Connection (the schools and colleges arm of the tour operator Kuoni) and Journey Latin America that specialises in travel to South and Central America.

## Support your learning

### Information sources

1 The internet is a valuable source of up-to-date information on the companies mentioned in this chapter and others that operate in the different specialist markets listed at the beginning of the Starter chapter.

2 Supplement the internet by referring to guidebook series such as Lonely Planet and the Rough Guides to specialist tourism destinations.

### Skills builder

Build your IT research and presentation skills by collecting internet information about a specialist tourism provider and choosing an appropriate means of presenting a summary of your findings.

### Activities menu

1 Make a display to show the range of tour operators dealing in any one specialist tourism market.

2 *Vocational scenario*
Imagine you are the owner of a recently established small tour-operating business catering for a niche specialist market. You are to meet a range of travel industry professionals from the relevant sectors of the industry in order to provide transport, insurance and accommodation options for your clients. Prepare a short presentation to explain the nature of your business.

You should include reference to your:
• specialist focus
• customer base
• destination/s used

3 Research and analyse the variety of tour operator products available to independent travellers in any one specialist tourism market.

4 Evaluate the extent to which the products and services offered by two contrasting tour operators in any one specialist tourism market meet the needs of families with teenage children.

# 5.2

# Specialist holiday itineraries and planning

**Itineraries** are schedules that tourists follow. Specialist market holidays have programmes that are assembled by tour operators or, in the case of independent travellers, by the tourists themselves. Figure 5.11 gives an example of a special interest itinerary featured by a tour operator in its brochure. Tour operators may also develop individual, customised itineraries for the tailor-made market.

## Planning itineraries

A special interest itinerary may be for a single destination holiday or for one that has two centres. Alternatively, it may programme a multi-centred or 'itinerant' holiday. Examples of itinerant holidays include cruises and some walking and cycling holidays.

The following must be considered when planning an itinerary:
- the customer — the needs of individual customers vary within those expected for each customer type; needs that may need to be taken into account are listed in the 'Customer needs' section of this chapter (page 144)
- the dates of travel, both at the beginning and the end of the trip, and of any staging posts or excursions scheduled during its course
- the timing of the stages that make up the holiday programme — for example, 3 days at the first destination, 2 at the second and so on
- activities and excursions
- accommodation
- details of useful contacts, such as the accommodation and transport providers involved
- details of the destination itself, such as the attractions it offers
- any optional extensions

## Kenyan Safari

*Price:* from £1,499

*Game parks:* 2 nights in Tsavo West, 2 nights in Amboseli, 2 nights in Masai Mara, 2 nights at Lake Naivasha

*Beach:* 4 nights

**Day 1 London to Mombasa**
Flight from Heathrow via Nairobi

**Day 2 Mombasa**
Transfer to resort hotel for 1 night

**Day 3 Mombasa to Tsavo West**
Drive from Mombasa through the National Park to Tsavo Camp. This beautiful camp lies in the shadow of Mt Kilimanjaro and on the banks of the River Sante. See hippo and crocodile in the river and enjoy an afternoon game drive in the park.

**Day 4 Tsavo West**
Early morning and later afternoon game drives in the park, with time to relax in the camp in the afternoon. Enjoy a night game drive in the late evening.

**Day 5 Tsavo West to Amboseli**
Drive to the lodge at Amboseli, followed by an afternoon game drive in search of elephant roaming the open plains.

**Day 6 Amboseli**
Two nights are spent at the lodge

**Day 7 Amboseli to Naivasha**
Drive north through the Rift Valley to Naivasha Lodge, overlooking Lake Naivasha.

**Day 8 Naivasha**
A boat trip on the lake and a visit to Lake Nakuru National Park.

**Day 9 Naivasha to Masai Mara**
Descend to the plains and drive to Masai Mara, staying at beautiful Siana Springs.

**Day 10 Masai Mara**
Early morning and later afternoon game drives in search of plains wildlife such as zebra, wildebeest and lion. Another night at Siana Springs.

**Day 11 Masai Mara to Mombasa**
Drive to Nairobi and fly to Mombasa.

**Day 12–13 Mombasa**
Three nights at the beach resort.

**Day 14 Mombasa to London**
Overnight flight to Heathrow via Nairobi.

Itineraries presented in travel brochures are often general summaries and may not include full details.

*Figure 5.11*
*A brochure itinerary*

Figure 5.12 is an example of a special interest holiday itinerary. It was compiled by a tour operator for a group of middle-aged UK rock music fans attending a stadium concert in Milan. Figure 5.13 gives a pen portrait of one of the customers, showing her needs and circumstances.

**Figure 5.12**
*A rock concert break*

**Friday 27 June**
Make your own way to Manchester Airport.
Meet for check-in at Terminal 2, 14.30.
Flight: Al Italia Express 261 to Milan Malpensa Airport departs 16.35, arriving 19.50 local time. Flight duration is 2 hr 15 min.
Transfer by train (Malpensa Express). Trains run every 30 minutes, costing €11 per person to Milan city. Alight at Cadorna station. Journey time 34 minutes.
Taxi transfer to Hotel Concorde, Viale Monza.
Relax. Meet for drinks and a buffet supper in the hotel from 22.00.

**Saturday 28 June**
Breakfast in hotel.
Morning at leisure: suggested city centre sightseeing – Duomo (cathedral), La Scala (opera house), shopping and lunch: the Galleria Vittoria Emanuele II.
Afternoon: make your own way to the San Siro Stadium by public transport (allow up to 1 hour). Use the Metro (€1 per ride) line MM1 (direction Molino Dorino). Alight at Lotto-Fiera2 station and walk along Viale Caprilli (about 1.5 km).
San Siro Stadium – doors open at 18.30 for concert to start at 20.30.
Expected finish time 22.30.
Return to hotel by Metro, alighting at Turro station on line MM2 (direction Sesto).

**Sunday 29 June**
Breakfast in hotel.
Morning: time for a lie-in or perhaps a leisurely stroll and coffee in a pavement cafe in the Brera quarter of the city.
Mid-morning: make your own way back to Malpensa Airport by taxi from the hotel or city centre in time for the 11.27 (suggested departure time), Malpensa Express to the airport.
Meet for check-in at Malpensa Airport Terminal 1 at 12.30.
Flight: Al Italia Express 260 to Manchester, departs 14.35 local time, arriving Manchester Terminal 2 at 15.50 (UK time).
Return home.

**Customer name**
Brenda O'Toole

**Circumstances**
Previous customer, visited Milan once before
Mature female adult
Single parent, leaving child at home
Lives in Teesside, travelling to and from airport by train from Darlington
Mobile phone number on record

**Specific needs**
Single room at hotel (non-smoking)
Vegetarian
No specific access needs
Female customer alone – requested non-ground floor room
Requests hotel be informed she be contacted at once in the event of telephone call from her brother (child minding)

**Figure 5.14** *A ticket for the concert*

**Figure 5.13**
*A customer pen portrait*

# Customer needs

Special interest holiday customers may have needs that are linked to one or more of the following:

- sport
- leisure
- education
- relaxation
- religion
- special travel requirements, facilities or services
- high quality

The prime purpose of the holiday may be to participate in a sport or to watch a particular event. Sports tourism itineraries that are well planned include alternative activities for members of a tour group who do not share the enthusiasm of others. For example, a golfing holiday in Portugal is an example of a special interest holiday. Within a family group, one person may be a keen golfer happy to play at least a round a day and not concerned about alternative experiences. Other family members may be less enthusiastic and, for them, alternative activities are important elements of a well-constructed itinerary.

*Figure 5.15 Tourists visting the Bob Marley Museum*

Leisure activities such as cookery, dance and painting are the basis of other special interest holidays. Alternative activities may again be appropriate. The customers of a tour operator organising a culinary-based holiday in Tuscany or one focused on painting in the Provence countryside would be likely to organise excursions to major sightseeing locations like Florence and Aix-en-Provence.

For school and college groups, education is the primary motivator for travelling. A school skiing trip to the Italian Alps is one example. Educational opportunities may arise out of special interest holidays with other declared purposes. For example, the parents of a family enjoying an ecotourism holiday in the Blue Mountains of Jamaica may think it educational to show their children the Bob Marley Museum in Kingston (Figure 5.15).

Stephen Rickerby

Some people go on holiday just to relax. Spa holidays (Figure 5.16) are a special interest for those who want relaxation in connection with health and beauty goals. The opportunity to unwind is a feature of other special interest itineraries. Parties, discos, restaurants and bars cater for the après-ski relaxation of snowsports participants for example.

*Figure 5.16* Beach massage on a spa holiday

Catherine Karnow/Corbis

Religious events can be the main reason for travel — pilgrimages to Mecca and Rome, for instance. However, requirements of certain religions (such as kosher food) and opportunities for worship may need to be borne in mind by the itinerary planner, especially if the timing of a tour means that it includes the Sabbath or a particular religious festival.

Special travel requirements may need to be written into an itinerary. These may arise from the specific needs of customers — wheelchair accessibility, for example — or they may be customised features of the itinerary. For example, the middle-aged rock fans following the itinerary in Figure 5.12 may require a private transfer from the airport rather than following the travel plans proposed in the itinerary. Such optional extras may be expected to add to the price of the tour.

Specific customer needs, such as mobility, may require special services. This might be accommodation arrangements such as ground floor rooms for elderly customers or the laying on of transport between locations on a cycling tour for a participant who has sustained an injury.

High-quality standards or exclusivity may be expected by some customers. For example, a group of US lawyers on a literary tour of Ireland, organised by a Northern Ireland tour operator, expected (and were provided with) four- and five-star hotels and executive private mini-coach transport throughout their visit.

## Support your learning

### Information sources

Compiling an itinerary requires the combination of information from diverse sources:
* websites of airlines, hotels, online bookers and destinations
* travel guides and maps, available from libraries
* tour brochures
* customer profiles (including pen portraits)

### Skills builder

Assembling an itinerary for a particular special interest trip for particular customers will help build your key communication skill of synthesising information from diverse sources, as well as developing the vocational skill of itinerary planning.

### Activities menu

1 Explain how the rock concert holiday itinerary in Figure 5.12 matches the needs of the customer profiled in Figure 5.13.

2 a Plan a holiday itinerary for a group of three 19-year-old UK motor sports fans who want to attend the first of next season's Grand Prix races at a budget price.
   b Justify your recommended itinerary.

3 *Vocational scenario*
   Imagine you are a tour operator working for a large tour operating company. Your manager has asked you to help investigate a possible diversification into operating diving holidays.
   a She has asked you to research a destination that supports diving holidays. Analyse the key features of diving holidays to draft a sample itinerary to meet the needs of the perceived target market of affluent 30-something couples.
   b Justify the recommendations you make.

4 Evaluate the extent to which your draft itinerary from Activity 3 would be likely to meet the needs of customers belonging to the perceived target market.

**5.3**

# Health and safety

The health and safety of their customers is of prime importance to travel and tourism providers from all sectors of the industry. This is as true of specialist markets as it is of any other. Indeed, the nature of special interest holidays that may include adventure, small group size, physical activity and off the beaten tracks destinations bring health and safety issues to the fore, not least in the planning of itineraries (see Chapter 5.2).

## Health and safety legislation

Health and safety legislation has major implications for travel and tourism organisations operating in special interest markets. Staff have a primary duty of care for the health and safety of customers, both external (the organisation's clients) and internal (staff colleagues), including themselves. Any holiday carries with it some degree of risk. Risks need to be assessed and procedures for managing them established.

### Staffing issues

Travel and tourism organisations have a duty of care that prioritises the health and safety of their customers. Special interest tour operators recruit and train staff so that they are appropriately qualified to standards laid down by any appropriate governing bodies. Table 5.3 lists some UK sport governing bodies that tour operators may need to contact. Travel and tourism organisations should also ensure that staff receive appropriate first aid and health and safety training.

*Table 5.3 Some UK sports governing bodies*

| Sport | Governing body |
| --- | --- |
| Canoeing | British Canoe Union |
| Caving | National Caving Association |
| Cycling | British Cycling Federation |
| Golf | English Golf Union |
| Sailing | Royal Yachting Association |
| Skiing | British Ski and Snowboard Federation |
| Sub aqua (diving) | British Sub Aqua Club |

## Adventure tourism activities (ATAs)

Adventure tourism activities are leisure pursuits that are exciting for participants and involve a degree of physical challenge. Diving, abseiling, paragliding and white-water rafting (Figure 5.17) are examples, as are skiing and snowboarding.

*Figure 5.17*
*White-water rafting*

TopFoto

Some ATAs are subject to regulation by national governing bodies or other authorities, whose roles have grown to include the assurance of the health and safety of ATA participants.

## Case study: Sub aqua (scuba) diving

The British Sub Aqua Club (BSAC) has been the UK governing body involved with the ATAs of sub aqua diving and snorkelling since 1954. The Professional Association of Diving Instructors (PADI) is a global organisation based in the USA whose system of scuba diving training and qualifications is well recognised and is the standard adopted by tourist diving centres in resorts around the world.

To help ensure proper safety standards, the BSAC Safety First Programme is designed to help all grades of diver keep up to date with safe diving practices by following ScubaWISE courses. The BSAC Divers' Code of Conduct supplements this by laying out guidelines for sub aqua divers so that their activities do not conflict with those of other water users or damage the environment.

Both the BSAC and the PADI publish magazines that help promote and encourage participation in scuba diving. *Dive* magazine (**www.divemagazine.co.uk**) is the BSAC's official journal (Figure 5.18).

As a national sport governing body, the BSAC has a diver-training programme operated by its branches and by BSAC dive schools, leading to qualification awards at four levels:

- Ocean Diver
- Sports Diver
- Dive Leader
- Advanced Diver

The awards build in a sequence as divers become more experienced and proficient. The last two are leadership grades.

*Figure 5.18* Dive *magazine website*

PADI scuba diving proficiency and leadership awards range from PADI Scuba Diver (a restricted level of certification within the PADI Open Water Diver Course that suits the first-timer tourist) to more advanced programmes like the PADI Divemaster course. Many tourists take scuba lessons that lead to PADI qualifications either at their resort or in the UK before travelling abroad, knowing that the qualification is universally recognised.

## ATA regulatory authorities

Within the UK, travel and tourism organisations that promote adventure tourism activities such as scuba diving, or land-based recreations such as climbing and skiing, are subject to regulation by official government agencies including the Health and Safety Executive and the Adventure Activities Licensing Authority.

### The Health and Safety Executive (HSE)

The role of the HSE is to protect people's health and safety (customers, the public and staff). The HSE guides, inspects and advises travel and tourism organisations, including those offering ATAs to their customers, making sure that what they do is healthy and safe and that they are complying with the law (and with European Union regulations), on health and safety. The key piece of UK legislation is the

Health and Safety at Work Act, 1974 (travel and tourism professionals are 'at work' when their jobs involve them with ATAs).

Under the Health and Safety at Work Act, all travel and tourism organisations have a duty to safeguard, as far as is practical, the health and safety of their staff and customers, as well as members of the public and anyone else who comes into the organisation to do some work (a building contractor, for example). For a travel and tourism organisation running an adventure tourism activity this means that:

- equipment being used is safe
- practices and procedures followed by staff are safe
- the environment in which the activity is to take place is regularly checked to ensure that it is healthy and safe
- any potentially dangerous substances (fuel, for example) are safely stored
- the organisation must produce a written health and safety statement which is brought to the attention of its staff
- the organisation must keep staff informed about health and safety, and offer them proper health and safety training

To help small businesses, the HSE provides a free Workplace Health Connect link on its website (**www.hse.gov.uk**) that can be used to access free and impartial practical advice.

### The Adventure Activities Licensing Authority (AALA)

The AALA is funded by the UK government's Department for Education and Skills. It aims to operate a licensing scheme for providers of ATAs that:

- enables customers (specifically, young people) to enjoy adventure challenge activities such as white water rafting, canoeing (Figure 5.19) and abseiling safely
- commands the respect and trust of the public — well-publicised media stories about accidents on adventure activities that were parts of school trips provided a background against which the government judged it necessary to introduce the scheme

The AALA inspects providers such as outdoor activity centres and assesses their safety management. A licence is granted when the provider can show that it complies with accepted standards — without the licence the provider cannot offer ATAs to its customers. Potential customers, which may include the organisers of an outdoor activities course, are able to search the AALA website (**www.aala.org**) to find licensed providers for particular activities, such as water sports, trekking and caving, in different regions of the UK.

The Activity Centres (Young Persons' Safety) Act 1995 ensures that facilities that provide adventure tourism activities for young people aged under 18 are regulated and are required by law to introduce safety practices and procedures to meet government standards. For example, activity centres must be licensed by the Adventure Activities Licensing Authority.

*Figure 5.19 Canoeing*

## Local authorities

The Education or Children's Services Departments of local councils sometimes choose to operate their own outdoor education centres. As providers, they need to be licensed under the terms of the 1995 Activity Centres Act by the AALA. For example, education services in Bradford are provided for the local authority by a company — Education Bradford — which undertakes what would normally be the local authority's role. Education Bradford supports Bradford Metropolitan District Council partly by operating three outdoor education centres. Two of these (Buckden House and Ingleborough Hall) are in the Yorkshire Dales National Park and offer educational adventure activity programmes as well as residential accommodation. Both have been inspected and licensed to comply with the Activity Centres (Young Persons' Safety) Act 1995.

In other cases, local authorities may be customers of activity centres or else regulatory bodies for schools and colleges in their areas. When considering ATA-focused trips, schools and colleges may be subject to health and safety and risk assessment rules, practices and procedures laid down by the local council.

Topic 3 of this book is about travel and tourism in practice and includes information about the planning of an effective ATA.

## Support your learning

### Information sources

1 The websites of the Health and Safety Executive and the Adventure Activities Licensing Authority are sources of further information on these bodies.

2 Websites of the governing bodies of different sports (see Table 5.3) are gateways to researching ATAs that fall under their auspices.

### Skills builder

Develop your ICT presentation skills by making an ICT presentation about the proficiency and leadership awards made available by the governing bodies of sport(s) other than sub aqua.

### Activities menu

1 Produce a 1-page revision aid about ATA regulatory authorities.

2 Describe the range of proficiency and leadership awards run by the UK governing body of a sport other than sub aqua diving.

3 Research and analyse the outdoor ATA education facilities of one UK local authority.

4 *Vocational scenario*
A tour-operating company running adventure holidays for families in Europe is considering expanding its operation on a Caribbean island. Imagine you are a staff member. Prepare an evaluation of two ATA options that the company may consider.

# 5.4

# Tourism flows

**Tourism flows** are the volumes of people travelling to tourist destinations. Tourism flow intensities vary between places and according to time of year.

Figure 5.20 is a proportional flow map showing volumes of outbound tourists from the UK flowing to countries abroad. This map shows the top five most visited countries and the width of each arrow is proportional to the numbers travelling.

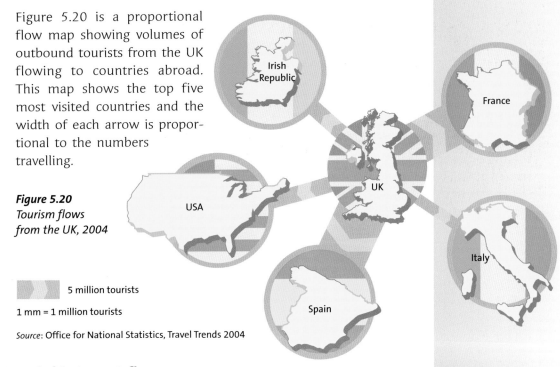

*Figure 5.20*
*Tourism flows*
*from the UK, 2004*

5 million tourists

1 mm = 1 million tourists

*Source*: Office for National Statistics, Travel Trends 2004

## Special interest flows

Special interest holiday markets can be seasonal. The snowsports market is one obvious example. More UK tourists go on skiing and snowboarding holidays in the northern hemisphere winter months than at other times of the year. Psychologically, their own winter seems to be the 'natural' time to ski. In addition, northern hemisphere destinations in Europe and North America are the most accessible from the UK. Ski holidays, or winter sports as parts of holidays, are available at other times of year, for example to southern hemisphere destinations such as New Zealand, but such tourism flows are relatively light.

Travel to events and festivals that take place at or around certain calendar dates is part of the special interest market. The Muslim Haj pilgrimage to Mecca in Saudi Arabia, the Rio de Janeiro carnival in Brazil and holidays to see the New England fall colours in the USA are some examples. Actual dates may vary from year to year (as with the Haj for instance).

*Figure 5.21 A family adventure holiday*

Pete Saloutos/Corbis

The UK school holidays significantly affect the pattern of tourism flows in and from the UK. The ebb and flow of this tourist tide is reflected in the range of holidays on offer during school holiday periods and in prices charged by travel and tourism organisations such as tour operators and accommodation providers. Figure 5.21 shows a family adventure holiday. Figure 5.22 relates the departure dates for such a holiday with those of a UK local authority's schools. Note how some of the departure dates (e.g. 1 April, 15 July, 14 October and 16 December) mean that children may miss a week of school.

## Tourism flows and destinations

Individual destinations experience varying tourism flows. These variations in tourism flow may be:

- qualitative (type of tourism)
- quantitative (numbers of tourists)

An example of somewhere that experiences qualitative variation is the Alps. This is predominantly a winter sports region when the snow is on the ground, but it transforms into a sightseeing and physical/mountain activities destination (walking, climbing, cycling, hang-gliding) when the weather is warmer.

## 2006 CALENDAR

**January**

| M | 30 | 2 | 9 | 16 | 23 |
|---|----|---|---|----|----|
| T | 31 | 3 | 10 | 17 | 24 |
| W |    | 4 | 11 | 18 | 25 |
| T |    | 5 | 12 | 19 | 26 |
| F |    | 6 | 13 | 20 | 27 |
| S |    | 7 | 14 | 21 | 28 |
| S | 1  | 8 | 15 | 22 | 29 |

**February**

| M |   | 6 | 13 | 20 | 27 |
|---|---|---|----|----|----|
| T |   | 7 | 14 | 21 | 28 |
| W | 1 | 8 | 15 | 22 |    |
| T | 2 | 9 | 16 | 23 |    |
| F | 3 | 10 | 17 | 24 |   |
| S | 4 | 11 | 18 | 25 |   |
| S | 5 | 12 | 19 | 26 |   |

**March**

| M |   | 6 | 13 | 20 | 27 |
|---|---|---|----|----|----|
| T |   | 7 | 14 | 21 | 28 |
| W | 1 | 8 | 15 | 22 | 29 |
| T | 2 | 9 | 16 | 23 | 30 |
| F | 3 | 10 | 17 | 24 | 31 |
| S | 4 | 11 | 18 | 25 |    |
| S | 5 | 12 | 19 | 26 |    |

**April**

| M |   | 3 | 10 | 17 | 24 |
|---|---|---|----|----|----|
| T |   | 4 | 11 | 18 | 25 |
| W |   | 5 | 12 | 19 | 26 |
| T |   | 6 | 13 | 20 | 27 |
| F |   | 7 | 14 | 21 | 28 |
| S | 1 | 8 | 15 | 22 | 29 |
| S | 2 | 9 | 16 | 23 | 30 |

**May**

| M | 1 | 8 | 15 | 22 | 29 |
|---|---|---|----|----|----|
| T | 2 | 9 | 16 | 23 | 30 |
| W | 3 | 10 | 17 | 24 | 31 |
| T | 4 | 11 | 18 | 25 |    |
| F | 5 | 12 | 19 | 26 |    |
| S | 6 | 13 | 20 | 27 |    |
| S | 7 | 14 | 21 | 28 |    |

**June**

| M |   | 5 | 12 | 19 | 26 |
|---|---|---|----|----|----|
| T |   | 6 | 13 | 20 | 27 |
| W |   | 7 | 14 | 21 | 28 |
| T | 1 | 8 | 15 | 22 | 29 |
| F | 2 | 9 | 16 | 23 | 30 |
| S | 3 | 10 | 17 | 24 |    |
| S | 4 | 11 | 18 | 25 |    |

**July**

| M | 31 | 3 | 10 | 17 | 24 |
|---|----|---|----|----|----|
| T |    | 4 | 11 | 18 | 25 |
| W |    | 5 | 12 | 19 | 26 |
| T |    | 6 | 13 | 20 | 27 |
| F |    | 7 | 14 | 21 | 28 |
| S | 1  | 8 | 15 | 22 | 29 |
| S | 2  | 9 | 16 | 23 | 30 |

**August**

| M |   | 7 | 14 | 21 | 28 |
|---|---|---|----|----|----|
| T | 1 | 8 | 15 | 22 | 29 |
| W | 2 | 9 | 16 | 23 | 30 |
| T | 3 | 10 | 17 | 24 | 31 |
| F | 4 | 11 | 18 | 25 |    |
| S | 5 | 12 | 19 | 26 |    |
| S | 6 | 13 | 20 | 27 |    |

**September**

| M |   | 4 | 11 | 18 | 25 |
|---|---|---|----|----|----|
| T |   | 5 | 12 | 19 | 26 |
| W |   | 6 | 13 | 20 | 27 |
| T |   | 7 | 14 | 21 | 28 |
| F | 1 | 8 | 15 | 22 | 29 |
| S | 2 | 9 | 16 | 23 | 30 |
| S | 3 | 10 | 17 | 24 |    |

**October**

| M | 30 | 2 | 9 | 16 | 23 |
|---|----|---|---|----|----|
| T | 31 | 3 | 10 | 17 | 24 |
| W |    | 4 | 11 | 18 | 25 |
| T |    | 5 | 12 | 19 | 26 |
| F |    | 6 | 13 | 20 | 27 |
| S |    | 7 | 14 | 21 | 28 |
| S | 1  | 8 | 15 | 22 | 29 |

**November**

| M |   | 6 | 13 | 20 | 27 |
|---|---|---|----|----|----|
| T |   | 7 | 14 | 21 | 28 |
| W | 1 | 8 | 15 | 22 | 29 |
| T | 2 | 9 | 16 | 23 | 30 |
| F | 3 | 10 | 17 | 24 |    |
| S | 4 | 11 | 18 | 25 |    |
| S | 5 | 12 | 19 | 26 |    |

**December**

| M |   | 4 | 11 | 18 | 25 |
|---|---|---|----|----|----|
| T |   | 5 | 12 | 19 | 26 |
| W |   | 6 | 13 | 20 | 27 |
| T |   | 7 | 14 | 21 | 28 |
| F | 1 | 8 | 15 | 22 | 29 |
| S | 2 | 9 | 16 | 23 | 30 |
| S | 3 | 10 | 17 | 24 | 31 |

11   School holiday dates
11   Departure dates for Mountain Biking Adventure Family Holiday
11   Bank holidays

Quantitatively, Caribbean destinations such as Jamaica experience a busier peak season during the northern hemisphere winter, fuelled by high flows of US tourists to what is for them a relatively close winter sun destination. In the late summer and autumn these flows slacken, partly as a response to the climate. The Caribbean hurricane season, which starts at this time, not only means a heightened risk of storms, but is also associated with rainier, cloudier weather. UK tourists, especially to 'off the beaten track' parts of the Caribbean islands, are often surprised by the relatively low numbers of other tourists holidaying there during the months of the British summer.

Calendar events can also play a part. For instance, the varying date of Easter has an influence on tourism flows in the skiing market. When Easter is early (as it was in 2005, for example) there is more likely to be good snow for skiing in more ski resorts, leading to higher Easter flows than in the years when Easter is late (as it was in 2003). On the other hand, some potential customers have a perception that the period after Easter is too late to go skiing, so an early Easter may

**Figure 5.22** *Family holiday departures and school holiday dates*

reduce tourism flows across the whole season. Markets such as skiing tend to be based on short breaks. At Christmas and New Year, such breaks are popular with customers just before and after the bank holidays themselves. When Christmas Day and New Year's Day fall during the week, the weekends can be used for ski breaks with minimal extra time taken off work. However, if these bank holidays fall on a Saturday or Sunday, tourism flows can be reduced.

Economic factors also affect tourism flows over time. Interest rates (making it more or less expensive to pay for a holiday using a credit card) are one example of a variable economic factor. Another is currency exchange rates. When the relative values of sterling and the euro change this can increase or decrease tourism flows to eurozone destinations. Changes in exchange rates between the pound and other currencies (such as the US and Canadian dollars) also have a potentially fluctuating impact on tourism flow volumes.

Political and security considerations are important too. In the 1990s, war severely curtailed inbound tourism to parts of former Yugoslavia, which was then breaking up into separate smaller countries. In 2006, the World Travel and Tourism Council (made up of leading world travel industry executives) forecast that one of those countries (Montenegro) would be the most rapidly growing tourism economy in the world for the third year in succession. Table 5.4 shows the forecast growth in travel and tourism demand for the most rapidly growing tourist destinations, 2007–16, together with comments on the causes of the variations shown. As a country becomes more politically stable, foreigners feel safer travelling there and organisations feel greater security in doing business there.

### VFR

Visiting friends and relatives (VFR) is, along with leisure tourism (holidays) and business tourism, one of the three main purposes of tourism. The UK school holidays predictably correlate with periods of higher tourism flow to parts of the world, including the Caribbean and south and southeast Asia, where many British people have relatives and friends. This is an example of quantitative variation.

### Extending the season

Resorts that experience quantitative variation in tourism flow may try to broaden their appeal beyond the peak and high season. Staging special interest events and festivals is one means of doing this. The

**Table 5.4** *Forecast demand for travel and tourism, 2007–16*

| Rank | Country | Percentage growth |
|------|---------|-------------------|
| 1 | Montenegro[2] | 10.2 |
| 2 | China[4] | 8.7 |
| 3 | India[4] | 8.0 |
| 4 | Romania[1] | 7.9 |
| 5 | Croatia[2] | 7.6 |
| 6 | Vietnam[3] | 7.5 |
| 7 | Latvia[1] | 7.3 |
| 8 | Maldives[5] | 7.2 |
| 9 | Albania[1] | 7.0 |
| 10 | Cambodia[3] | 7.0 |

Notes:
[1] Former eastern European countries developing tourism after the end of communist rule.
[2] Former Yugoslav countries, now at peace after civil war in the 1990s.
[3] Southeast Asian countries, now at peace after wars in the twentieth century.
[4] Rapidly developing countries with a newly emerging middle class, generating domestic tourism.
[5] Other.

Cannes Film Festival is held annually; in 2006 the festival was from 17 to 28 May. The festival helps extend the main tourism season forwards from early summer into late spring. Table 5.5 gives the dates of other conferences held in Cannes in 2006.

**Table 5.5** *Major conferences in Cannes, 2006*

| Conference | Dates |
|------------|-------|
| Real estate conference | 14–17 March |
| World digital content market | 3–7 April |
| Film festival | 17–28 May |
| Lions advertising festival | 18–25 June |
| Boat show | September |
| World audiovisual content market | 9–13 October |
| World luxury travel market | 5–8 December |

## Trends over time

Chapter 5.5 examines recent and likely future trends in special interest tourism.

# Support your learning

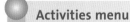

### Information sources

*TravelMole* (**www.travelmole.com**) is a news and resource centre for the travel industry that sends recipients a free daily newswire by e-mail. It is a useful way to keep up to date with developments in special interest tourism and with travel and tourism issues in general.

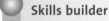

### Skills builder

Use the proportional flow map technique, as shown in Figure 5.20, to present and then comment on a pattern of tourism flow.

### Activities menu

1 Explain why the events shown in Table 5.5 are important to the tourism economy of Cannes.

2 *Vocational scenario*
   Imagine you are one of team of writers compiling an online travel guide to a resort other than Cannes for next year. You are asked to compile a report on calendar events that incoming tourists may be interested in attending.

3 Use a resource such as *TravelMole* to research and analyse a recent change in special interest tourism.

4 Evaluate the extent of the change you researched and analysed in Activity 3.

# 5.5

# Recent and future trends

Special interest and activity holiday markets are changing. Demand across both markets has been increasing in recent years. There has been a growth in the demand for more independent travel experiences and in the provision of challenge and adventure-based holidays, exploring more 'off the beaten track' destinations. However, the rate and direction of change has not always been constant and some destinations and types of experience have seen greater growth than others.

As well as the size of demand, special interest markets have seen change in:

- the destinations to which people travel — more long-haul, more 'off the beaten track'
- tour operators active in the market — more online, more small and specialist operators, as the market has grown
- customer types — greater diversity, for example more family groups
- patterns of tourism flow — more out-of-season, shorter breaks

## Case study: The snowsports market

Figure 5.23 shows recent changes in the size of the snowsports special interest market for UK tourists. **Trends** are general directions and rates of change, which may underlie occasional anomalous years or blips. In the case of the snowsports market, there has been a consistent direction of change, with increases in both the size of the market (as measured by the number of travellers), and in the proportion of passengers making independent arrangements rather than booking packages through tour operators.

Future trends can be predicted. The simplest way to do this is to extrapolate recent or current trends forwards. This can be reasonably safe if it is done over a short period of time to extend the pattern into the short-term future. Figure 5.23 shows data for a 5-year period — extrapolation forward for a longer period would be risky in terms of likely accuracy. Of course, up to date data can be accessed from new editions of source publications — in this case the annual Snowsports Analysis report of the Ski Club of Great Britain.

More sophisticated and longer-term predictions should take into account judgements about likely future impacts of the factors in such changes. These factors are explained below (see 'Factors in change').

Figure 5.24, which gives information about the types of accommodation used by snowsports tourists over four winter sports seasons, shows five interrelated trends. The percentage of snowsports tourists using catered chalets (where meals are provided) fell until 2004, while the proportion using hotels remained consistent at 33%. Increases were shown by the three other categories, although only the self-catering chalet accommodation option grew in popularity in the two most recent seasons shown.

Table 5.6 shows data relating to the size of the UK domestic ski market to Scotland as a whole and to individual destinations. Recent and future trends can be interpreted from this information.

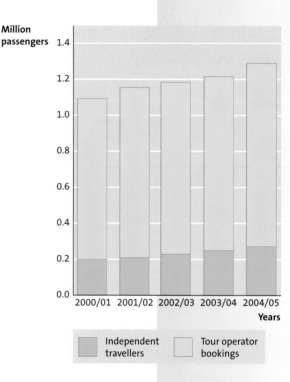

*Figure 5.23* Total UK snowsports market

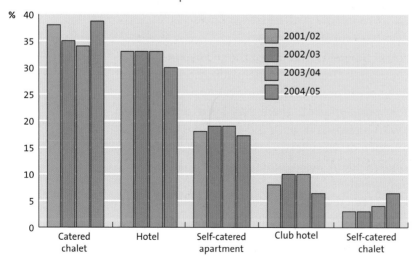

*Figure 5.24*
Accommodation type used by snowsport tourists

*Source*: Snowsports Analysis 2004 (**www.skiclub.co.uk**)

**Table 5.6** *Skier days spent in Scotland*

| Destination | 1998/99 | 1999/2000 | 2000/01 | 2001/02 | 2002/03 | 2003/04 | 2004/05 |
|---|---|---|---|---|---|---|---|
| Cairngorm | 110.0 | 98.6 | 110.0 | 81.4 | 44.8 | 58.5 | 55.5 |
| Nevis range | 37.7 | 42.8 | 35.9 | 19.8 | 10.8 | 20.9 | 18.3 |
| Glencoe | 30.2 | 29.3 | 37.1 | 18.4 | 7.6 | 7.0 | 12.0 |
| Glenshee | 89.3 | 54.6 | 118.0 | 55.4 | 34.8 | 27.5 | 36.5 |
| Lecht | 32.7 | 40.1 | 64.0 | 62.7 | 54.6 | 50.6 | 25.3 |
| All Scotland | 299.9 | 265.4 | 366.0 | 237.6 | 152.7 | 174.5 | 147.1 |

*Note*: Data are thousand skier days.

*Source*: Ski Club of Great Britain.

# Factors in change

Factors that have fuelled the growing popularity of special interest holidays have been:

- changing life–work balance
- accessibility of special interest destinations
- growing availability of facilities
- changing attitudes in society

## Life–work balance

**Life–work balance** refers to the emphasis individuals place on work on the one hand and family/home/leisure on the other. This is often expressed in the amount of time they allocate to each of these sides of life. More than 10 years ago there was a greater cultural pressure on people to place work high on their agenda. This was particularly true during the 1980s. UK workers still have a higher average number of working hours per week than the citizens of many other countries. Over the last 10 years there has been a degree of re-assessment, as people have put more emphasis on the family/home/leisure side of their lives.

A result of this is a greater emphasis on holidays and on travel as a life-enriching experience, leading in turn to a growth in the demand for special interest holidays. Cultural tourism, for example, is life-enriching while adventure tourism activities can be a bonding experience involving all the members of a family (Figure 5.21).

## Special interest destinations

There was rapid growth in mass tourism abroad during the 1950s and 1960s. This was followed by an expansion in leisure travel to long-haul destinations, initially to mass tourism destinations (Florida's resorts in the USA, for example), but building a desire among customers to venture further. In MEDCs, such as the USA, there was already a well-developed travel infrastructure in place, making it relatively easy for travel and tourism suppliers to offer UK tourist customers special interest trips. These included things like skiing in the Rockies, cultural tourism to Memphis (home of Elvis Presley) or itinerant go-as-you please driving and mobile home holidays to the western National Parks or California. As air travel opportunities have expanded, more 'off the beaten track' destinations in less-visited world regions such as

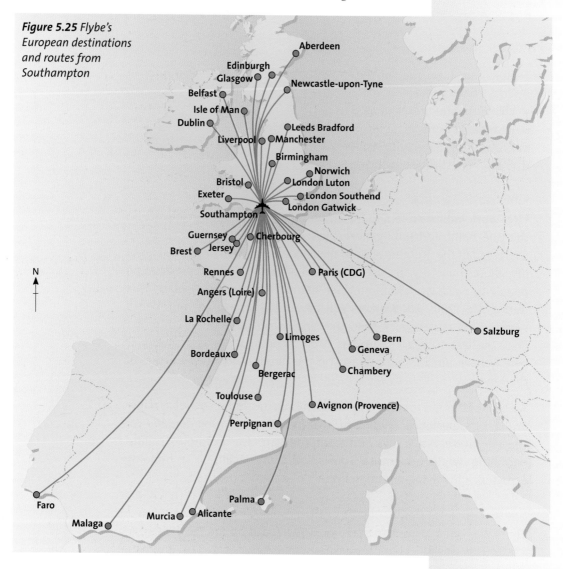

*Figure 5.25* Flybe's European destinations and routes from Southampton

South America have become accessible, opening up opportunities for tour operators and transport providers to market destinations such as Cartagena in Colombia (see Figure 5.4) and its literary and music festivals.

At the same time, the rise of budget or 'no-frills' airlines in the short-haul market has made less-visited (and potentially special interest) destinations much more accessible. In the skiing market, for example, airports such as Geneva are much better served by flights from the UK than was previously the case. This is also the case for the smaller regional airports both abroad (like Chambery in the French Alps) and in the UK. Figure 5.25 shows the Flybe airline routes from Southampton airport and the company's destinations in Europe (**www.flybe.com**).

## Special facilities

The growing availability of facilities geared to special interest tourists is well-illustrated by the 'weddings in paradise' special interest market. Figure 5.26 shows a wedding in Jamaica, one such location for UK tourists. All-inclusive hotels in popular wedding destinations, such as the Caribbean islands or Mauritius, have increasingly provided special facilities to appeal to wedding market customers. Beaches hotel at Negril in Jamaica has provided gazebos on the sand as focal points for ceremonies held on the beach itself.

*Figure 5.26* A wedding on the beach in Negril, Jamaica

Cris Haigh/Alamy

## Changing attitudes

Changing attitudes in society over the last 10 years have included the perceived relative importance of the work and family/home/leisure sides of life, as mentioned above. They have also included a heightened awareness of cultural, environmental and health issues among the travelling public and by the management of travel and tourism organisations. Environmental awareness and health consciousness have boosted the ecotourism and adventure tourism markets — overlapping as they are.

Increased interest in sport, adventure and education as leisure activities are closely related trends which have had similar effects. For example, growth in demand and supply of 'learning to cook better' holidays in destinations such as southern France and Tuscany in Italy has been encouraged by awareness of the health benefits of Mediterranean food and an attitude that cooking such food is life-enhancing and fun — an appropriate focus for a holiday.

Attitudes such as those discussed above are particularly noticeable among the growing 'grey market' of healthier and better off mature adults. This age group is growing, but changes in the life–work balance have also fed into the increased demand for special interest tourism from this group and those a little younger. The last decade or so has seen a rise in the number of 40-somethings 'down-sizing' their lives by making career choices that have led to reduced workloads and increased the amount of time available for family, home and leisure. The middle age market is therefore more numerous, more health-, environment- and culture-aware and more non-work focused than has been the case before. Travel and tourism organisations are aware of this and see the age groups concerned as a major target market.Laterlife.com (**www.laterlife.com**) is an internet company aimed specifically at the grey market (Figure 5.27).

*Figure 5.27*
*Laterlife.com website*

All the factors described above have contributed to an increasing demand for short-break holidays across the range of specialist interest markets. The factors do not operate separately, but are interlinked — as shown by Figure 5.28.

## Future trends

By considering the factors that have affected recent trends in markets, and judging how important these are likely to become, it is possible to evaluate likely future market developments.

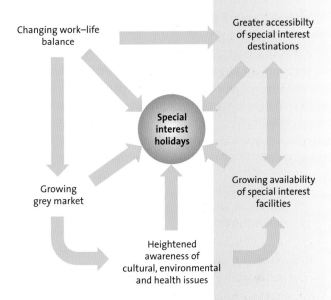

**Figure 5.28** *Factors in the growth of special interest holidays*

In the case of the skiing market, the Ski Club of Great Britain's annual Snowsports Analyses 2004 and 2005 led to the following predictions.

- Technological developments, such as faster internet access, interactive television and the greater flexibility of mobile, hand-held devices, are likely to continue. These developments will make it easier to research and book ski holidays, so the total market size (by this factor alone) seems likely to grow.
- The increased market share taken by independent travellers can be safely expected to grow further (by extrapolating current trends) but, on the other hand, the technological developments will make it easier to arrange tailor-made holidays. This may prove to be a lifeline to specialist tour operators whose market share may decline more slowly as a result.
- In the short term, there is likely to be an increasing range of destinations as the total market expands and tour operators and budget airlines seek new opportunities. The opening up of Serbia as a ski destination for UK tourists is one example of this. In the medium term the pool of more accessible ski destinations will become exhausted and this growth will slow.
- There will be a growth in the total long-haul skiing market and in the provision made for it by budget airlines — for example, the introduction of flights to Canada in 2002 by the no-frills carrier Zoom (**www.flyzoom.com**).

# Support your learning

## Information sources

1 Independent travel agencies and tour operators form a significant part of the specialist tourism market. Local offices can be a useful primary source.

2 The Association of Independent Tour Operators (**www.aito.co.uk**) represents many smaller, niche operators.

3 The Passenger Shipping Association is a useful cruising market information source (**www.the-psa.co.uk**).

## Skills builder

Use data sets, such as those given here for the skiing market, to analyse recent trends in special interest markets and make justified predictions for the future.

## Activities menu

1 Use Table 5.6 to describe, and suggest reasons for, trends in the number of skier days spent in Scotland.

   *Vocational scenario*
   Imagine that the UK governing body of a sport has commissioned a report into recent and current trends in the provision of special interest holidays involving participation in the sport. Choose one sport and prepare an executive summary (brief outline of the main points) of the report.

2 You need to interpret a graphical presentation of recent changes.

3 You need to analyse the causes of trends you identify.

4 You need to evaluate the likelihood of these trends changing in the future.

# Adventure tourism

Adventure tourism holidays are built around one or more **adventure tourism activities** (ATAs) — leisure pursuits that are marketed by tour operators as exciting experiences and which involve a degree of physical challenge.

- Diving, trekking and overlanding holidays are examples of single-focus adventure tourism holidays. Overlanding is travelling long distances by minibus or truck (see Figure 5.29).

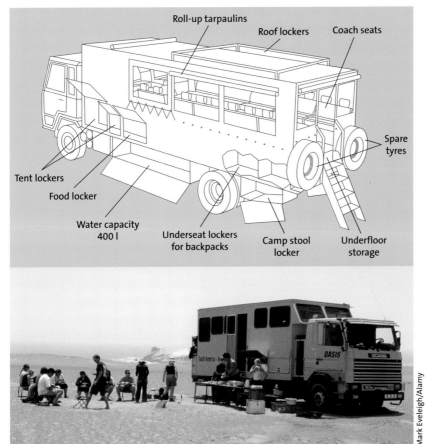

*Figure 5.29*
*Overlanding by truck*

Mark Eveleigh/Alamy

- Skiing is another ATA — see the case study in Chapter 5.5.
- Abseiling, parasailing and white-water rafting are examples of ATAs sold to tourists as components of a multi-focus adventure holiday or which they may purchase as part of a more general holiday, either abroad or in the UK.

Factors in the development of ATAs are
- environmental
- historical
- accessibility

## Environmental factors

The natural environment (landscape and climate) of some destinations encourages adventure tourism activities. Many mountain destinations, such as the Scottish Highlands, Snowdonia, the Alps, Pyrenees, Rockies and Andes, have fostered the growth of adventure tourism. In some places the ATAs available vary seasonally. In the Alps, for example, winter snowsports give way to other activities in the summer months, including climbing and mountain walking.

## Historical factors

In the UK, the establishment of National Parks and Areas of Outstanding Natural Beauty encouraged the growth of domestic tourism from urban areas, focused in part on ATAs such as sailing, canoeing, mountain walking and climbing. Figure 4.12 in Chapter 4.2 shows Britain's National Parks. Hill walking and long-distance walking were boosted by the development of long-distance footpaths such as the Pennine Way, which officially opened in 1965.

Some destinations have a history of expeditions and exploration that has encouraged the development of adventure tourism. Examples include the Alps (skiing and climbing), the Himalayas (trekking) and the Red Sea (diving). Potential customers perceive these as 'classic' destinations to experience in their pursuit of adventure and tour operators are able to market holidays to these destinations in that light.

## Accessibility

Where ease of access to areas used for ATAs has improved there is a greater incentive for tour operators to provide adventure tourism packages. The advent of budget airlines has been important here, particularly in Europe. Access to skiing destinations, for example, has been considerably enhanced in recent years

The costs involved in reaching and experiencing destinations for ATAs have fallen in real terms. This is not just because of the growth of no-frills budget airlines — many adventure tourism destinations involve long-haul travel to South America, Africa, Asia and Australasia. The costs of holidays such as diving around the Maldives or of adventure tourism in far flung destinations like Patagonia in Argentina have lowered in comparison to the rising disposable incomes of Western tourists. Although demand has risen, so has supply — of travel, accommodation, specialist operators, instructors and support services (including online support). The net result has been a fall in price (removing inflation from the calculation).

### Other factors

Social factors that have contributed to the growth of ATAs are shown in Figure 5.30. Other factors have been the increased use of ATAs as a means of personal and group development for employees and students. The rising demand for more active holidays has also been stimulated by increased environmental awareness. Ecotourism ATAs seek to have minimal effect on the natural environment and to bring positive social benefits to local communities. Figure 5.31 shows a poster used to promote an ecotourism trek in Tanzania.

**Discussion point** ⬤

How have supply and demand changes affected travel and tourism pricing?

*Figure 5.31*
*An ecotourism trek*

African Iniatives

*Figure 5.30* Social factors in the growth of ATAs

Increased car ownership

More leisure time

Higher disposable incomes

*Growth of ATAs*

Longer holiday entitlements

Greater popularity of health and fitness

Table 5.7 shows organisations involved in providing and promoting ATAs. These organisations play a major role in the development of adventure tourism which is illustrated by the case study below. The values and attitudes of such organisations differ. Private sector organisations are motivated by the need to make profits, but specialist providers such as these are often small to medium in size and may well have been founded by an enthusiast. Thus, the profit motive, while still present, is often tempered by a valuing of the activity for its own sake. The company may believe that running a business in this field is about sharing the experience as well as about making money.

**Table 5.7** *Organisations providing and promoting ATAs*

| Sector | Organisations |
|---|---|
| Private | • Activity providers — often small or medium-size enterprises that organise the actual activity (e.g. canoeing or sailing), including equipment and instruction<br>• Adventure travel companies — specialist tour operators in the ATA market, for example The Adventure Company<br>• Equipment and clothing manufacturers that cater specifically for the needs of ATA customers and whose goods are often for sale in shops and on internet sites that specialise in outdoor and travel supplies<br>• The media — television travel programmes feature ATAs periodically which builds interest in the market. Travel supplements of newspapers and articles in general interest magazines perform the same function. Specialist ATA tour operators place classified advertisements in the media<br>• Specialist websites such as **www.adventureshow.co.uk** — the site for the Adventure Travel and Sports Show |
| Public | • National tourist offices of destination countries<br>• Local authorities which may run outdoor education ATA facilities or regulate ATAs organised by schools and colleges (see Chapter 5.3)<br>• National Park authorities and the Forestry Commission — the regulatory bodies of parts of the countryside used for ATAs<br>• National governing bodies of sports (see Chapter 5.3) |
| Voluntary | • Youth groups, clubs and charities which organise ATAs<br>• National Trust — the host body for ATAs organised on its properties<br>• Youth Hostels Association (YHA) — a major ATA provider |

All organisations involved with ATAs share the priority of health and safety for participants, staff and members of the public. Health and safety is specifically considered in Chapter 5.3.

The National Trust is a charity which owns many stately homes, their grounds and large tracts of land (including much of the coast of the UK). Care for its property is the prime function of the National Trust, and in hosting an ATA the National Trust will place great value on conservation and protection of the environment.

The development of adventure tourism in any destination (in the UK or overseas) may be due to a single (or dominant) ATA, for example surfing in the case of Newquay in Cornwall, or it may be the result of travel and tourism organisations providing a variety of ATAs. This is often the case in destinations that attract significant numbers of countryside recreation tourists, such as the UK's National Parks.

## Case study: The 7stanes of Scotland

The 7stanes are seven mountain biking centres in southern Scotland that are managed by the Forestry Commission Scotland. 'Stanes' is Scottish for 'stones'. Figure 5.32 shows the locations of the centres in relation to nearby airports and ferry ports. In 2004 the 7stanes attracted over 400,000 adventure tourists, both domestic and inbound, creating a positive economic impact for Scotland worth an estimated £3.56 million.

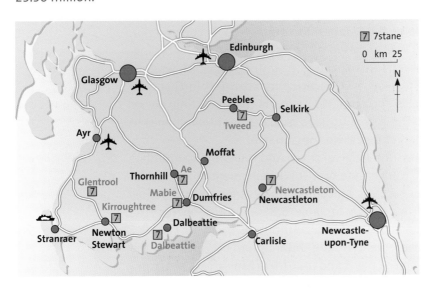

*Figure 5.32*
*The 7stanes*

The Forestry Commission Scotland (which manages the national forest estate in Scotland on behalf of the government) developed the 7stanes project in collaboration with a series of public sector partners that included:

- the Dumfries and Galloway and Scottish Borders tourist boards and the local authorities of those regions
- Scottish National Heritage
- Scottish Enterprise
- the European Union

**Figure 5.33** *Mountain biking at Ae*

Forestry Commission

Figure 5.33 shows the Ae-line trail in Ae Forest. Glentrool, in Dumfries and Galloway, is one of the 7stanes. In summer 2006, construction began on an 8.5 km trail targeted at entry-level and family cycling. Before this there was only a 61 km cross-crountry trail, which was not suitable for beginners. Now, ATA participants attracted to Glentrool range from first-timers to committed experts. By attracting novice riders the Forestry Commission Scotland management team hopes to build the size of its target repeat business market.

Table 5.7 summarises the range of travel and tourism organisations that can be involved in adventure tourism development.

- As far as the public sector is concerned, the partners in the 7stanes project are much as shown in Table 5.7 — tourist boards, the Forestry Commission itself and local authorities.
- Private sector involvement in the 7stanes project includes the provision by commercial travel and tourism organisations of accommodation in the area, transport to the centres and tour packages involving mountain biking at the centres.
- One link between the voluntary sector and the 7stanes project is the use of the centres for sponsored rides for charity. The International Mountain Biking Association (IMBA) is a global voluntary organisation involved in the running of the sport (a governing body). The IMBA awarded Scotland its 2005 Global Superstar award because of the growth in mountain biking centres there, exemplified by the 7stanes.

## Case study: ATAs in an overseas destination

Adventure tourism knows no bounds — that is the nature of adventure. As a result, ATA examples can be found across the world. Overseas destinations particularly associated with ATAs include:

- mountain ranges, such as the Himalayas, Andes, Rockies and Alps
- the Caribbean (its islands and the Caribbean Sea itself)
- the Amazon Basin

Identifying these places as adventure tourism destinations is a broad-brush approach. It provides a summary of major regions within which adventure tourism attractions are located. Destinations such as the Caribbean are large and varied regions in themselves and too complex to form a viable basis for meaningful study. For research purposes, it is necessary to narrow the destination focus to more specific places. Examples would be the Inca Trail in Peru, the Everest National Park in Nepal and the Blue Mountains in Jamaica.

## Managing the impacts of adventure tourism

Overseas adventure tourism destinations are often in fragile environments and bring tourists into contact with people who have different cultures and traditions. The Blue Mountains in Jamaica are an example (Figure 5.34). As the adventure tourism market continues to grow, pressure grows on the natural environment and the likelihood of significant social impact on local communities increases.

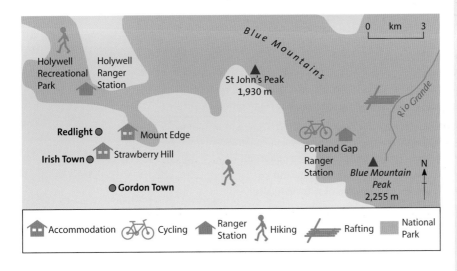

**Figure 5.34**
*ATAs in Jamaica's Blue Mountains*

Tourism impacts can be positive. Some local people from villages in the Blue Mountains, such as Irish Town and Redlight, have found employment in hotels such as Strawberry Hill or as tour guides (Figure 5.35). For them, such work means an increased income and often a welcome change of lifestyle from subsistence farming and labour in the construction industry. The money earned by individuals is spent in businesses locally and so benefits the region. However inequalities can grow within rural village communities, especially in LEDCs such as Jamaica, where local cash businesses may be thin on the ground. In such places the traditional pattern of life can be affected negatively.

Chapter 4.3 explains the impacts tourism can have, using Jamaica as an example. Table 5.8 summarises the main positive and negative impacts of adventure tourism.

*Figure 5.35* A local guide with tourists on a walk in the Blue Mountains

Stephen Rickerby

*Table 5.8* The impacts of adventure tourism

| Economic impacts | • Increased income<br>• Jobs<br>• Economic development<br>• Infrastructure improvements such as water and electricity supply, roads, airports, sanitation systems<br>• Over-dependency on tourism<br>• Economic leakage — profits leak away to companies based away from the destination |
| --- | --- |
| Sociocultural impacts | • Loss of privacy for local people to lead their own lives in a traditional way<br>• Visitor congestion<br>• The 'copy cat' effect, causing a diminution of cultural diversity<br>• Greater understanding between people of different cultures |
| Environmental impacts | • Erosion and clearance of the natural landscape, including vegetation and soil<br>• Aesthetic, atmospheric and noise pollution<br>• Trespass damage to agricultural land<br>• Disturbance to and loss of wildlife habitats<br>• Litter<br>• Water contamination and marine pollution<br>• Assistance to wildlife conservation |

### Minimising negative impacts

Sustainable tourism management seeks the long-term protection of the environment of a destination and of its local people. This includes maximising the positive benefits of tourism and channelling them towards environmental conservation and to aid local communities. Examples are explored in Chapter 4.4.

Careful management of ATAs that is sensitive to potential environmental impacts and to the needs of the host community is needed for the long-term sustainability of adventure tourism itself, as well as of the destination. Sustainable management of adventure tourism developments includes:

- maximising the revenue taken locally and ensuring that as much of it as possible stays in the locality
- providing staff training and professional development that builds environmental awareness and cultural sensitivity
- involving the local community in tourism so that tourists and locals are not alien to each other
- identifying the likely sustainable carrying capacity of a destination and not allowing short-term profit to tempt providers to exceed this
- pricing tourism products and services so that appropriately channelled revenue is maximised while not setting low prices to attract excessive numbers of visitors
- educating tourist customers to be aware of their responsibilities to the environment and to the people of destinations they visit

Further details about sustainable tourism management can be found in Chapter 4.4.

## Participant benefits of ATAs

Adventure tourism activities benefit participant customers, who may be:

- individuals
- groups
- families
- businesses — corporate team-building events for example

These types of customer may be further sub-divided into serious competitors and recreational participants. Providers of ATAs need to be conscious of the needs of customers, who may range from novices and people having some fun on holiday to expert hard-core enthusiasts.

Awareness of skill levels not only ensures customer satisfaction, but is important for reasons of health and safety. For example, ski instruction is often available to customers according to their level of ability and ski runs are categorised by colour designations (up to black) to flag their level of difficulty.

The benefits people derive from participating in ATAs vary from person to person, but include:

- the enjoyment they derive from taking part in the activity — this may be simple physical exhilaration or a deeper spiritual satisfaction
- social interaction with other people — these may be fellow participants or local people (especially in a culturally different setting, for example the Blue Mountains of Jamaica for UK tourists). Some snowsports participants see après-ski socialising as equally important to them in pleasure terms as the skiing or snowboarding itself
- building a team ethos with work colleagues in shared ATAs and developing personal leadership skills
- helping to build or maintain health and fitness
- acquiring qualifications and awards through the ATA, such as the Duke of Edinburgh's Award scheme for young people or PADI (Professional Association of Diving Instructors) certificates for scuba diving in the UK

Participants' values and attitudes can change while participating in an ATA. This is especially likely if the activity is overseas and brings the tourist in contact with a fragile environment or with people of a different culture. The tourist may emerge from the ATA more environmentally or socially aware.

## Support your learning

### Information sources

1 Brochures and websites of adventure tour operators and the Adventure Show are gateways to the range of adventure tourism activities and destinations.

2 Adventure tourism includes outdoor pursuits centres; brochures sent to schools and colleges by the organisations that run these centres are further resources available to you.

### Skills builder

Develop your empathy skills by imagining you live in an LEDC and considering the benefits (and drawbacks) to you and your community of being an adventure tour guide in a rural area of your home country.

**Activities menu**

1 Use Table 5.7 as a checklist to help you make a chart of the organisation types involved in the development of one ATA in one destination.

2 *Vocational scenario*
Imagine you are working as an ATA provider. Make a piece of promotional material, such as a web page or a brochure page, that explains the benefits participants can expect to gain from your activity.

3 Research and analyse the development of ATA provision in your local area.

4 a Assess the economic, sociocultural and environmental impacts of ATAs in one chosen destination. Consider both positive and negative impacts.
 b Evaluate management strategies being used in the destination to try to maximise the positive impacts and minimise the negative.

# 5.7

# Cultural tourism

## Culture and tourism

The culture of the people who live in a destination includes their:

- way of life — including food and drink
- heritage — including buildings and artefacts
- artistic expression in forms such as music, art and dance

Tourists who choose to visit a destination because of the local culture are engaged in **cultural tourism**. The travel and tourism industry provides opportunities for cultural tourism, including selling holiday packages to destinations that are marketed in terms of their cultural appeal. Some cultural events such as the UK's Edinburgh Festival and the Rio de Janeiro carnival in Brazil (Figure 5.36) stimulate demand at particular times of year (i.e. August/September and February, respectively). Travel and tourism organisations such as transport and accommodation providers seek to satisfy this demand.

*Figure 5.36*
*Carnival in Rio*

### Cultural tourism and special interest markets

Aspects of culture are the major appeal of some destinations for some tourists. A visit to Barcelona to appreciate its architecture or to the Caribbean island of St Lucia for a jazz festival are examples of cultural tourism linked to special interests on the part of tourists. While not all special interest holidays are cultural tourism (sport and adventure activities for instance), it can be said that all cultural tourism holidays are special interest. This is because the motivating factor of culture is a reason for travelling that is specific and more narrowly defined than general travel and tourism.

# Travel motivators

**Travel motivators** are the reasons why people travel. Figure 5.37 shows a hierarchy of key travel motivators. Individual tourists decide upon particular trips for a variety of different reasons.

The prime reasons for travel are to have a holiday, to go away on business or to visit friends and relatives. While all three are distinct motivations there is much overlap; tourists can combine one of these reasons with another — staying with relatives in New Zealand is an example of a motivator UK tourists may combine with going on holiday.

In cultural tourism, the tourists' desire to experience the culture of a destination is the major secondary level travel motivator.

| Prime reason | Secondary sub-divisions | Tertiary destination preferences | Externalities |
|---|---|---|---|
| Leisure | Holiday | Climate | Destination security |
| | Sport or cultural event | | |
| | Educational trip | | |
| | Pilgrimage | Attractions | |
| Business | Conference/ exhibition | Festivals and events | |
| | Individual meetings | | Exchange rate |
| Visiting friends and relatives (VFR) | Stay with family | Accommodation/ restaurants/ bars | |
| | Meet friends | Transport (to the destination and within it) | |

*Figure 5.37*
*Key travel motivators*

For example, a tourist's motivation to visit Rio de Janeiro in February may be to attend the carnival. A visit to Rome at Easter may be for religious pilgrimage. Customers may be motivated to travel to a destination initially for leisure, but may become interested in the destination's culture during the course of their visit. For example, the traditional appeal of sun, sea and sand may initially motivate tourists to visit a Greek island such as Crete. While on holiday there, they may enjoy Greek food or become interested in the artefacts of the lost Minoan civilisation that once thrived there. These new cultural tastes and interests may in turn motivate them to return to Crete on another occasion, or to travel elsewhere in Greece.

Cultural tourists, like special interest tourists from other markets, are motivated by their interest — art, dance, music or architecture, for instance. The pursuit of this interest leads to the type of holiday they prefer. Choosing a destination may then be influenced by personal preferences, such as what the climate is like and what other attractions are offered.

External factors play a part too. Security concerns (or a return to stability) affect destination choice and so does the exchange rate between a tourist's home currency and that of the destination — making it more or less expensive to stay there.

## Maslow's hierarchy of needs

Psychologist Abraham Maslow developed his hierarchy of human needs in 1943 (Figure 5.38). The reasons why people choose to travel or indulge in a tourism experience can be matched to different levels in Maslow's hierarchy.

- The lowest level in Maslow's hierarchy is that of physical survival. Although it is beyond simple survival, the basic need to have a holiday as a rest from work comes into this category.
- The need for the chosen destination to be safe and secure meets Maslow's level 2.
- The need for social belonging is a motivator at Maslow's third level. A late-teenage tourist travelling to the Balearic Islands with friends is motivated to a degree by a need for acceptance by the peer group to which they belong. Following a sports team on a tour abroad or taking a romantic break to a European city are further travel motivators matching this level.
- Moving up to the highest levels of Maslow's hierarchy, the need for self-esteem and for self-actualisation are motivators for the cultural tourist. The stimulation and understanding gained by experiencing and studying works of art are level 4 and 5 motivators.

**Discussion point**

What are key travel motivators among A2 Travel and Tourism students?

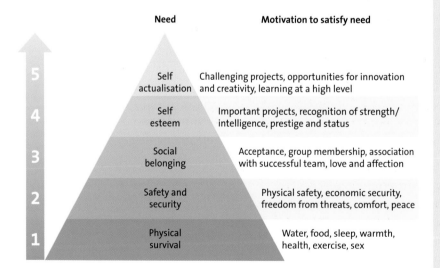

| Need | Motivation to satisfy need |
|---|---|
| 5 Self actualisation | Challenging projects, opportunities for innovation and creativity, learning at a high level |
| 4 Self esteem | Important projects, recognition of strength/intelligence, prestige and status |
| 3 Social belonging | Acceptance, group membership, association with successful team, love and affection |
| 2 Safety and security | Physical safety, economic security, freedom from threats, comfort, peace |
| 1 Physical survival | Water, food, sleep, warmth, health, exercise, sex |

*Figure 5.38 Maslow's hierarchy of needs*

## The movement of cultures

Cultural tourists travel to destinations for cultural reasons. Destinations have their own local cultures. For example, reggae music is indigenous to Jamaica. Appreciation of reggae and other Jamaican music is a motivator for cultural tourism to attractions such as the Bob Marley Museum in Kingston (Figure 5.15). Bob Marley was an internationally famous Jamaican reggae star who died in 1981.

However, it is not just tourists that travel. Cultures travel too. Disneyland Paris (Figure 5.39) is one example. American culture in this case has been moved across the Atlantic to France. Tourists from across Europe, and beyond, visit Disneyland Paris to see attractions like Main Street USA, where the shopping, food and drink is provided in a replica of a traditional American small-town main street. Accommodation such as the Santa Fe and Cheyenne hotels and the self-catering Davy Crockett Ranch further exemplify the American cultural base. Disney films are the theme park's inspiration, typified by Mickey Mouse.

*Figure 5.39*
*Disneyland Paris*

Pawel Libera/Corbis

The movement of cultures is a two-way street. Like many large cities, New York City has a Chinatown and a wide choice of restaurants including Italian, Japanese, Indian and French. Indonesian *rijsttafels* (rice tables) are a popular eating experience for international tourists visiting Amsterdam. Indonesia, as the Dutch East Indies, was part of the Dutch empire and parts of its culture seeped into the life of the Netherlands.

This movement of cultures allows tourists to sample a culture before visiting a destination where it is indigenous. UK tourists thinking of taking a holiday in Greece may try the food at a Greek restaurant in the UK before travelling to Greece itself. There is a good deal of cross-fertilisation here. A liking for the food may stimulate a desire to travel; similarly, returned tourists may like to relive their holiday by eating the food again in their home city.

In the same way, touring shows in the fields of theatre, music and opera, art, dance, and circus have spread different cultures from place to place. Figure 5.40 shows a piece of promotional material used to market the Chinese State Circus tour of the UK in 2006. Audience enjoyment of such events can spark an interest in the culture they are experiencing and create a market for cultural tourism, in this case to China.

Tourists can also take their culture with them. A good example of this is the anglicising of the central cores of some Mediterranean beach resorts.

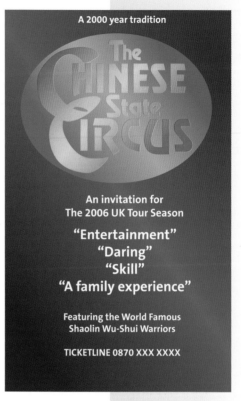

Here you can find British and Irish pubs and cafés, which may be owned by ex-patriots, providing British food such as fried breakfasts. Resorts like Alcudia in Mallorca and Ayia Napa are examples of this, at least in their busy commercial centres.

*Figure 5.40* The Chinese State Circus on tour

### Cultural characteristics

**Culture** is made up of all the experiences, behaviours and values which are learnt by living together with other people and the attitudes which people from the same background share.

Travel and tourism professionals deal with customers who have a variety of cultural characteristics. Understanding the cultural background of their customers gives travel and tourism professionals a better chance of achieving customer satisfaction when dealing with incoming tourists to their own country or accompanying a group of outbound tourists abroad. **Culture clash** occurs when people of different cultures fail to understand each other's attitudes and behaviour. A successful tour representative will anticipate and avoid potential culture clashes.

The cultural characteristics a tour representative needs to consider, about both customers and the host community, are:

- beliefs and values expressed by religion, tradition and customs — for example local customs on the day when worship takes place and during festivals such as Eid and Easter
- language — modes of verbal and non-verbal communication (including body language) that are considered polite and the register of language acceptable to people of a particular culture
- social customs — such as manners involved in greeting and bidding farewell and expected rituals and ceremonies
- food and drink — including types of food (for example, pork or beef) or drink (alcohol) that are not permitted by certain religions. There may be culturally acceptable times, places and ways to eat and drink
- dress — the degree of modesty in covering the body that is expected or dress codes at certain events or venues
- arts and crafts products may be seen to typify a culture and be sought after by tourists
- music and dance — when and where it is culturally acceptable to play music loudly

## Heritage appeal

Tourism to a destination because of its cultural heritage comes about because of its buildings and monuments, traditions of art and gastronomy or the festivals and events that are part of the lives of its people.

*Figure 5.41*
*The Acropolis, Athens*

Important attractions that draw tourists are often buildings and monuments. These are central to the cultural appeal of certain destinations. Their presence is a major travel motivator for the cultural tourist, and they feature prominently in promotional material. Examples include:

- the pyramids and temples of Egypt's Nile Valley
- the Acropolis in Athens (Figure 5.41)
- the Great Wall of China
- the Tower of London
- the Statue of Liberty in New York

Religious pilgrimages are a form of cultural heritage tourism and may focus on iconic structures. Examples of these include the Sikh Golden Temple at Amritsar and the Wailing Wall in Jerusalem. However, structures are not alone in defining the culture of a destination in the eyes of its potential tourist market. Literary and artistic festivals (such as those in Hay on Wye and Edinburgh) and cultural activities such as painting and cooking holidays in the French Loire Valley or the Tuscan Hills of Italy perform the same function. So do cultural events that attract tourists, such as the Changing of the Guard at London's Buckingham Palace, the St Patrick's Day Parade in New York and the Cannes Film Festival on the French Riviera.

The icons listed above may be a draw to a destination, but they then allow other cultural venues and events to become factors of secondary appeal to the cultural tourist. Thus the Ellis Island Museum in New York harbour benefits from Statue of Liberty tourists since it is the second stopping point on the ferry trip from Battery Park, Manhattan (Figure 5.42).

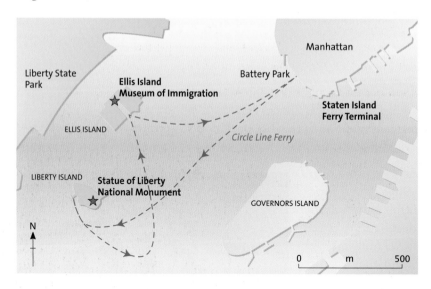

***Figure 5.42*** *Attractions in New York harbour*

Historic sites, such as the First World War battlefields in Flanders and even former concentration camps such as Auschwitz, exemplify 'dark tourism'. Past events involving death and/or destruction are of interest to modern cultural tourists and are a commercial focus for travel and tourism organisations.

Living museums do more than house artefacts and relics of the past, they re-enact some aspect of a place's cultural heritage. The Black

Country Living Museum in Dudley and the North of England Open Air Museum at Beamish in County Durham celebrate the industrial culture and heritage of their local regions. Tourists are attracted to learn about (and, in some cases, remember) the culture of another place and another time.

## Impacts of cultural tourism

Cultural tourism has an impact on the places visited, the local people, the travel and tourism industry providers involved and on cultural tourists themselves. Chapter 4.3 of this book deals in detail with the social and cultural impacts of tourism. The attractions and the culture that draw tourists are affected both positively and negatively by their presence. Positive impacts of cultural tourism include the preservation of local customs, a market for craft products, and mutual understanding between people from different backgrounds. On the negative side, there is a risk that local traditions and artefacts can become packaged for tourist consumption in ways that distort their meaning and tradition. Traditional dances, for example, may have deep spiritual meaning for local people and be traditional only on certain occasions. The cultural tourist, however, may only visit once and may be disappointed not to see them — and an inevitable tension results.

Tourism to ancient buildings such as Fountains Abbey in Yorkshire, which is a World Heritage site, brings in revenue that helps in its conservation. At the same time, the sheer passage of people through the monument has an impact on its fabric that needs sustainable management by the National Trust. Durham Cathedral (Figure 5.43) is another UNESCO-designated World Heritage site. It is a major cultural tourism attraction but also an active place of worship for members of the Church of England. Managing cultural tourism to churches so that it impacts as little as possible on current religious practices is a sustainable tourism issue for the regulatory bodies concerned. In the case of Durham Cathedral, this issue is dealt with by the Dean and Chapter of the cathedral. Sustainable tourism management is the subject of Chapter 4.4 of this book.

*Figure 5.43*
*Durham Cathedral*

TopFoto

# Support your learning

### Information sources

1 UNESCO's World Heritage website is a useful information gateway for world heritage attractions.

2 Cultural tourism attractions are well covered in travel guidebooks such as the Michelin Green Guides and the Rough Guides series.

### Skills builder

Help develop your communication key skills by making a study of tour operator and travel guide literature about cultural tourism to a chosen destination. Make your information into a short report.

### Activities menu

1 Compile a PowerPoint presentation about the cultural tourism appeal of one iconic heritage attraction.

2 *Vocational scenario*
   Imagine you are a trainer of prospective tour guides to the UK. Write a page for a training manual, explaining the cultural characteristics of British people the tour guides may need to take into account when hosting a visit by inbound tourists to a country market town.

3 Research and analyse heritage attractions and their appeal for cultural tourism in two contrasting destinations.

4 Assess the extent to which cultural tourism impacts on traditional ways of life in the two cultural destinations you chose for Activity 3.

# Appendix

## Analysis of major exam board A2 specifications

| Topic sections in this in this book | Awarding body (exam board) units | | |
| --- | --- | --- | --- |
| | AQA | Edexcel | OCR |
| 1 Current issues in travel and tourism | 10 Current issues in travel and tourism (m) | 8 Current issues in travel and tourism (m) | |
| 2 Managing people in travel and tourism | 9 Travel and tourism – people and quality (m) | | 16 Human resources in travel and tourism (m, d) |
| 3 Travel and tourism in practice | 8 Travel and tourism project (m) | | 10 Event management (m) *and* 11 The guided tour (o) |
| 4 Managing tourism developments and impacts | 11 Impacts of tourism (m, d) | 7 Responsible tourism (m) | 9 Tourism development (m) *and* 12 Ecotourism (o) |
| 5 Special interest tourism | 14 Special interest/ activity holidays (o) | 11 Special interest holidays (o) | 13 Adventure tourism (o) *and* 14 Cultural tourism (o) |

m = mandatory unit
o = optional unit (Edexcel and OCR candidates choose one from four for Single Award A2 Travel and Tourism and OCR candidates another two from four for the Double Award)
d = Double Award unit

### AQA

| | Single Award | | | Double Award | |
| --- | --- | --- | --- | --- | --- |
| A2 units | 8 | 9 | 10 | 11 | 14 |
| Topics in this book | 3 | 2 | 1 | 4 | 5 |

### Edexcel

| | Single Award — compulsory | | Single Award — optional Double Award — compulsory |
| --- | --- | --- | --- |
| A2 units | 7 | 8 | 11 |
| Topics in this book | 4 | 1 | 5 |

### OCR

| | Single Award — mandatory | | Double Award — mandatory | Optional | | | |
| --- | --- | --- | --- | --- | --- | --- | --- |
| A2 units | 9 | 10 | 16 | 11 | 12 | 13 | 14 |
| Topics in this book | 4 | 3 | 2 | 3 | 4 | 5 | 5 |

# Index